A Question of Time

Contemporary Psychoanalytic Studies
19

Contemporary Psychoanalytic Studies (*CPS*) is an international scholarly book series devoted to all aspects of psychoanalytic inquiry in theoretical, philosophical, applied, and clinical psychoanalysis. Its aims are broadly academic, interdisciplinary, and pluralistic, emphasizing secularism and tolerance across the psychoanalytic domain. CPS aims to promote open and inclusive dialogue among the humanities and the social-behavioral sciences including such disciplines as philosophy, anthropology, history, literature, religion, cultural studies, sociology, feminism, gender studies, political thought, moral psychology, art, drama, and film, biography, law, economics, biology, and cognitive-neuroscience.

A Question of Time

Freud in the Light of Heidegger's Temporality

Joel Pearl

Translated by Amir Atsmon and Joel Pearl

Rodopi

Amsterdam - New York, NY 2013

Based on the Hebrew edition of:
Joel Pearl
A Question of Time
Between Philosophy and Psychoanalysis
Which originally appeared in the Series **Interpretation and Culture**
(edited by Avi Sagi)
Published by Bar-Ilan University Press
Ramat Gan, Israel, 2011

Cover photo: Marina Habsburg Lothringen

Cover Design: Studio Pollmann

The paper on which this book is printed meets the requirements of "ISO 9706:1994, Information and documentation - Paper for documents - Requirements for permanence".

ISBN: 978-90-420-3642-0
E-Book ISBN: 978-94-012-0911-3

Printed in the Netherlands

This book is dedicated with 'Liefde'
To my Dutch family
Marina Habsburg Lothringen,
Muriel and Natacha d'Ansembourg

Contents

Acknowledgments

While concentrating on my wish to express my deepest gratitude to each and every one of you, without whom this book would not have come to light, I felt a particular urge to justify the mere act of writing. As many times before, when experiencing such strong feelings, I immediately found myself wandering amidst Søren Kierkegaard's philosophy. This time, I recalled a certain phrase from the preface of *Fear & Trembling*, in which Kierkegaard addresses his readers with what he perceives as a justification for his writing: "He writes because to him it is a luxury that is all the more pleasant and apparent the fewer there are who buy and read what he writes" (p.7).

At first glance, Kierkegard's justification seems rather odd: on the one hand, his saying addresses the reader who has already purchased the book; on the other hand, it is actually asking the said reader not to do what she had just done. Hence, he asks his readers to abolish the only possibility of the saying to be heard. Beyond the paradoxical nature of this saying, there can be no doubt about Kierkegaard's request that only few will leaf through the pages of his book. His ironic use of language is intended to allow his readers the possibility to acknowledge that their 'self' does not simply dwell in the public sphere of language, nor can it be found by retreating from it to a presumably private sphere, but rather that its existence takes place in the interface between them.

I do not think Kierkegaard cared much about whether or not his book would reach Copenhagen's 1843 bestseller list (if we want to adapt this insight to our own time we might think of Amazon.com) or alternately, if his book was read by just one person. I believe that what mattered to Kierkegaard was whether the reader of his book would be able to unveil his 'self', a self that he situated between the private and the public sphere, between the daily-day life and the transcendence of the Divine. Striving to accomplish such a goal is far from simple: the individual who takes upon himself the journey towards himself must overcome the concealing structure inherent in the very nature of language, the fact that language belongs fundamentally to the public sphere of meaning, our being subjected and constricted to a specific era, and the anxiety that accompanies the process of individuation.

Kierkegaard's irony lies in this facet of his writing which exposes the reader to the idea that even though the very act of writing takes place far from the eyes of the masses and in utmost discretion, that it is an act which is as close to the heart as possible - it cannot exist anywhere else but in the public sphere. Personally, I learned that despite the difficulties embodied in the act of writing, *Fear & Trembling* is an excellent example of a text which does succeed in disclosing the rare and elusive interval in which the possibility of the individual to be himself exists. From Kierkegaard's point of view, this possibility lies in receding from the mode of total identification with the public sphere and in discovering the existential mode situated in the interface between the public and private spheres.

In fact, the very act of writing, with all its difficulty (and this I believe is the crucial point), contains a possibility, even if it is for the most part unlikely, for a miracle: that the public sphere will expropriate from itself this elusive and rare place where the individual could come before himself.

With respect to this unlikely possibility implicit in Kierkegaard's writings, in what follows, I would like to share the sense of justification that accompanied me in the act of writing *A Question of Time*. A sense of justification that I could not explain to myself except as the rare privilege I had to encounter this elusive interval that the public sphere cared to expropriate from itself, just for me.

Such was the case when, as a young student, I chanced to participate in Professor Hagi Kennan's illuminating seminar on Heidegger. Up until this seminar, in which I heard Hagi talk about phenomenology, or if you will, talk phenomenology, I didn't know that it was possible to talk, listen, think and teach in such a way. In fact, the interpretative approach I employ toward Heidegger in this book springs from the fact that for me to read *Sein und Zeit* is always to read it via Hagi's approach to Heidegger.

Such was the case when I had the privilege to meet Nilly Szor, my dear psychoanalyst, who allowed me to feel the gentleness and endless complexity involved in the attempt to actually provide a space for the self and the other.

Such was the case that, when I chose to start my PhD in Holland, I had the privilege to meet my dearest friend Marina Habsburg Lothringen with whom I spent endless fascinating hours discussing the human experience and its peculiar mode of appearance in the therapeutic setting as we strolled along the beautiful grachten of Amsterdam.

Such was the case when Dr. Vered Lev-Kennan enlightened me with her superb insights into Greek Mythology and the story of Echo and Narcissus.

Such was the case, that in my attempt to rethink the phenomenological connection between psychoanalysis and Heidegger I came across *The Divided Self* by R. D. Laing who challenged the psychiatric doctrine and wrote an inspiring text that focuses on the interface between phenomenology and psychology.

Such was also the case when professor Beatriz Priel agreed to meet me in her office at Ben-Gurion university where her brilliant suggestions allowed me to find the right starting point for rethinking Freud from a phenomenological point of view.

If you allow me to broaden the horizon from which these rare and elusive intervals can appear, I can add the fact that fascinating thinkers with ideas considerably more radical than mine, such as Madrid Boss, Ludwig Binswanger, Erich Fromm, R. D. Laing and many more, took upon themselves the challenge of rethinking the therapeutic event through the phenomenological lens, but neglected the question of time. Or alternatively, the fact that many scholars inquired about the influences of philosophy on

Freud, but not about Franz Brentano's epistemology and its problematic notion of time.

What I am really trying to say is that the justification for writing this book lies in the fact that so many people have enabled me those rare intervals in which I could come before myself. Now that the time of writing has passed, and I was granted the honor of publishing my book under the Rodopi academic book press in the Contemporary Psychoanalysis Study series, I hope that it is time again for something of that unlikely possibility, in which the public sphere expropriates from itself a place for the sake of the individual to be present in *A Question of Time*.

Last and by all means not least, I would like to express my gratitude to Amir Atsmon, my translator, for his superb work and the many hours we spend working together. To my dear parents Dalia and Zeev Pearl, to my cool brothers Gil and Doron Pearl, to Edna Langenthal, Ronen Rashty, Nir Steiner, Yoram Ron, Irit Segoli and my beloved Clair.

Joel Pearl

Introduction

This book constitutes a philosophical attempt to rethink, from an existential-phenomenological perspective, the theoretical foundations of Freudian psychoanalysis. The following discussion will focus on the notion of time – both its significance in psychoanalytic theory and its function in the clinical encounter. The significance of time in Freudian theory will be grounded in Martin Heidegger's (1889-1976) notion of "Temporality" (zeitlichkeit).

As we examine the therapeutic method established by Freud, it seems that time plays a cardinal role in both the dynamics of the clinical encounter and its theoretical foundations. Psychodynamic therapy employs several aspects of time: through the recognition of past events which have molded the patient's private history; by observing the workings of the "transference", as a locus in which the present is read or perceived as a 'screen' upon which the patient's past experiences are projected; and by locating the unconscious fantasies and wishes which shape patient behavior presently and in the future. Nevertheless, as we survey the Freudian corpus, it is quite surprising to discover that Freud (1856-1939) had never established a comprehensive and methodical discussion of the concept of time. I would like to claim that this lacuna is by no means coincidental. However, it would be quite untrue to claim that Freudian theory is bereft of any notion of time whatsoever; its underlying notion of time is implicitly prominent throughout Freud's works. This notion, which might be described as scientific or objective, posits passage and change on an axis of linear time. In other words, psychoanalytic treatment indeed takes place upon temporal planes, but the manner in which these planes are addressed, both in the clinical encounter and in theory, presupposes an axis of linear time which precludes the event of temporality from being present as a distinct phenomenon. Temporal planes are addressed through a causally contextual matrix, which discovers any given moment upon an axis which includes events preceding and succeeding it. The metaphysical assumption that time is, in fact, a linear phenomenon and could be observed as a quantifiable sequence of intervals actually obscures a more basic locus of time, in which past, present and future are bound together into a single fabric. A complex notion of time such as this is offered by philosopher Martin Heidegger.

Unlike Freud, Heidegger does not consider linear time as resulting from a causal scheme of occurrence, but rather as derivative of existential time. This notion of time, which Heidegger refers to as "temporality", is unique in that it construes the field in which things occur in the world in light of a temporal fabric in which past, present and future are inseparable. According to this view, human experience should be understood not through scientific categories which posit a linear notion of time, but in light of an ontology based upon the temporal tapestry characteristic of human existence.

The study of human experience according to this temporal horizon of meaning will reveal the inherent layering of human existence as a modus of being-in-the-world. Therefore, in contrast with Freudian epistemology, which advocates a worldview in which time is a product of the psychic processes endemic to the locus of consciousness, Heideggerian thought, upon which my critique of Freud is founded, upholds a worldview in which the locus of consciousness is, in fact, a product of temporal structures. Throughout the final chapters of the book, I will employ Heidegger's notion of temporality as the platform upon which alternative theoretical foundations for psychoanalysis are laid down.

Unveiling the inherent problems in the theoretical foundations of psychoanalysis is of crucial importance to the way in which the clinical situation is construed; the motivation for writing this book stems, among other things, from my manner of reading and interpreting the significant crossroads contemporary psychoanalytic theory has now reached.

PSYCHOANALYSIS AT A CROSSROADS

The first steps taken by the psychoanalytic method upon the stage of history were based on a scientific methodology. The establishment of the psychoanalytic method upon the scientific value of truth set down the clinical and theoretical guidelines for the psychoanalytic corpus. Thus, for example, classical psychoanalysis depended upon an empirical worldview which pictured the psyche as a mechanism in charge of regulating the drives, be it consciously or unconsciously.

As the dazzling light of science fell upon the body of psychoanalytic knowledge, it cast its shadow on the clinical sphere, curtailing possible clinical dynamics. The notion of human experience which was at the root of scientific thought shaped the boundaries of appearance for both patient and analyst. The desire of classical psychoanalysis to keep the dynamics of therapy within the scope of scientific values destined the analyst to be a one-way mirror carrying out two cardinal roles: reflecting the world of the patient on the one hand and concealing the world of the analyst on the other. The dynamics of therapy were utterly dependant on the ability of the analyst to maintain clear inter-personal boundaries which would allow her to preserve the one-sidedness of the reflecting mirror and prevent her from responding to the patient's infantile needs. Placing this one-way mirror at the very heart of the therapeutic process, alongside the patient's inability to experience infantile satisfaction, increased the presence of repressed material in the patient's psyche and furthered its hold on her life. At this crucial junction, attributed to the very dynamics of therapy, the analyst had to extract unconscious material, bringing it into consciousness by providing an objective interpretation of the patient's behavior, thereby nullifying its control over psychic life.

Today, this dynamic process is no longer considered the sole fashion in which therapy may be carried out. Moreover, the dynamics endemic to the therapeutic event in contemporary psychoanalysis are inclined to engender the kind of experiences in which no clear boundary could be discerned between the world of the patient and that of the analyst. D. W. Winnicott, for instance, accounts for this kind of experience as something which takes place within the "intermediary area" between subjective and objective space. H. Kohut, for that matter, sees them as resulting from a dynamics founded upon an "empathic immersion" in the world of the patient and the facilitation of the kind of transference stemming from "selfobject" relations. In a nutshell, one might describe these changes in psychoanalysis as a transition from a body of knowledge oriented toward a one-person (the patient) psychology, to one which is oriented toward a two-person (patient and analyst) psychology. This cursory inspection of the therapeutic dynamics characteristic of contemporary psychoanalysis – Object Relations, Relational, Inter-subjective, Constructivist, Narrative, Perspective, Self-psychology and Neo-Freudian theories – indicates that the shadow delineating the borders of the clinical encounter for classical psychoanalysis has largely receded, and that current research is occupied in what might be termed as a search for a new methodology, one which does not rely upon an empirical worldview in its account of the human psyche.

From a wider historical perspective, contemporary psychoanalysis' abandonment of the empirical scope as its basis for fathoming the human psyche could be construed as part and parcel of the attempt made by Western thought to disown the endeavors of the Enlightenment and the worldview which posited the rational, autonomous and detached Cartesian subject as the exclusive foundation for human knowledge. The philosophical efforts to dislodge the Cartesian worldview and the categorical distinction between subject and object were already taking place at the beginning of the 19th century, in the context of existential-phenomenological thought. However, the systematic theoretical discussion of this issue in psychoanalysis became widespread mostly due to the influence of post-modernist thinking, during the second half of the 20th century. This paradigm sought to undermine certain modernist assumptions regarding the universal, rational and a-historical basis of human society.

As post-modernist notions came to the fore, psychoanalytic research and practice were thrust into a crossroads. The notion of steadfast concepts and universal axioms, characteristic of Freud's thinking, was cast aside by contemporary research; key ideas such as objectivity, individualism, truth and rationality, which were deeply entrenched at the basis of western thought after the Enlightenment, were now being questioned. Due to the direct influence of post-modernist thinking upon the very building-blocks of modern thought, the notions of the unified subject, of the possibility of objective knowledge of the world and of language as a truthful, logically-patterned instrument were done away with. Instead of discussing language as representing truth, the post-modernist deals with linguistic meaning, which she sees as an unstable occurrence, open to countless interpretations. Instead of discussing the ego, which was considered a necessary precondition for any act of judgment and the foundation of one's personality, the post-modernist deals with self-expressions and their varying capacity to produce a sense of self. Finally, instead of emphasizing objectivity, post-modern thinkers indicate social construction, which enables varying forms of reality discourse.

The notion of the human being endemic to post-modern thinking and therapy sees people as beings which are utterly immersed in social, linguistic and historical contexts, thereby subjugating anything indicating a personal dimension to the organizing structures beyond one's conscious self-perception and control. From a topographical perspective, one might say that the post-modern view suited the needs of the patient as it allowed her to hang on to the notion that the motivation for her actions is beyond her self-perception and it is this 'beyond' which was responsible for any personality disorders, much like the concept of the unconscious was in classical psychoanalysis. Nevertheless, this notion of the human being eradicated concepts such as freedom and choice, without which the notion of human experience could not contain any personal meaning. Following what post-modern speech coined as "the death of the subject" - the establishment of Jacques Derrida's Deconstruction, the formulations of Michel Foucault and Roland Barthes' declaration of "the death of the author" as the death of the subject – the notion of human subjectivity was stripped of any inherent aspect, trait or attribute and the personal dimension of human existence was reduced to a mere series of moments in which social, linguistic and historical vectors intersect within a matrix which is completely immersed in unlimited contextuality.

The crossroads facing contemporary psychotherapy and psychoanalysis is comprised of two paths, each resulting from the incorporation of the post-modern zeitgeist into their theoretical foundations. One path represents the benefits psychoanalysis has come by through its adherence to post-modernist thinking. The manner in which post-modernism illuminated the human being's immersion in society and cultural constructions facilitated the liberation of therapy from its one-person-psychology model and from the authoritative structure characteristic of classical psychoanalysis. This way of thinking brought about an awareness of otherness and of the more ambivalent and idiosyncratic layers of the clinical encounter.

The other path represents the fact that the comprehensive assimilation of the post-modern frame of mind into the theoretical foundations of psychoanalysis has rendered its object a mere fiction. The self, as it strives and experiences life, as it endeavors to integrate its diverse and distinct experiences, is nothing more than a casual expression of several intersecting vectors within a contextual matrix, lacking any personal attributes or character. The death of the subject is, in this sense, also the death of human experience. Therefore, this death strikes the person well before she could choose to need therapy as part of her horizon of self-possibilities. From this perspective, which considers psychoanalysis as a method dedicated to the study of human beings through an effort to assuage psychic suffering, this post-modern subject, once fully admitted, is a subject which already exists post-mortem. The crossroads which presents itself before contemporary clinical theories is a kind of dead-end, exposing the aporia now manifest for any theorizing about the clinical setting and the subject's field of appearance within it, whether as patient or analyst.

This book is not intended to be a critique of post-modern thinking. Instead, I would like to be as attentive as possible to the manner in which contemporary clinical theories have been constricted by this crossroads, offering an alternative path, through which contemporary research could dismiss the theoretical elements characteristic of classical psychoanalysis without paying the dear price of doing away with the experiencing subject or the personal aspect of experience, which is part and parcel of human existence. The attempt to construe the clinical setting as an interpersonal event and the transition to a two-person psychology are far from being the exclusive outcome of the spread of post-modern ideas throughout psychoanalytic circles. Instead, it is derived from the unique work of a group of thinkers (psychotherapists, analysts and philosophers) who operated between the 1920's and the 1960's, including Ludwig Binswanger, Erich Fromm, Frieda Fromm-Reichmann, Medard Boss and R. D. Laing. These thinkers set out against the empirical and mechanistic view of the human psyche prevalent in their time, their psychoanalytic thought deeply influenced by existential-phenomenological philosophy. Their work provided the background to the post-modern turn in western thinking. Alongside their rejection of the Cartesian subject, established upon the categorical distinction between subject and object, they put forward an alternative explanation of the personal, as it is expressed through what they termed "the living world". This explanation is sustained by drawing out the perspectives implicit within the pre-reflective and pre-thematic conduct inherent in everyday existence in the world.

Phenomenology, the fertile conceptual soil underpinning the work of these thinkers, deals with the structures of meaning prerequisite for experience. It describes the manner in which phenomena appear and studies the specific meanings of different modalities of experience. According to Husserl, the founding father of this method, the transcendental ego, the very basis of consciousness, provides meaning for both objects and people in the world around it. Setting the transcendental ego at the very foundation of the phenomenological method reproduced the categorical distinction endemic to Cartesian thought, leaving Husserlian thinking imprisoned by the same metaphysical dichotomy of subject/object. The existentially oriented phenomenologists who followed Husserl repudiated the existence of a transcendental ego and devoted their key efforts to the attempt to find a theoretical approach which studies human experience from the perspective of "the living world" – as it is experienced by the subject, without giving in to a conception of inside and outside, without becoming entrapped by juxtaposing the internal and external world (much like classical psychoanalysis had, by grounding itself in intra-psychic structures and their power-relations).

Existential-phenomenological thought had its own critique of modern thinking and insisted on the profound revision its key notions required – a revision which would take into account the immersion of the human in social, historical and linguistic structures. Nevertheless, it is still distinguished from post-modern thought through its view of individuality, autonomy, freedom and responsibility as essential conceptions, cardinal to the understanding of human experience. Heidegger manifested the notion of "the living world" through his depiction of human experience as a "being-there" which is always involved in the world it inhabits – a "being-in-the-world". Sartre retained the experiential link between the subject and the world through the concept of pre-reflective consciousness. From Buber's account of the self we learn that it is incomprehensible without the existence of a "thou" – the other, and that the process through which the individual understands herself always entails a mutual dialogue with a "thou". Each of these thinkers was able to maintain the primary connection between subject and world and provide room for personal existence without recourse to the Cartesian subject. For Heidegger, this was accomplished through the potential of the "being-there" to lead an authentic life. For Sartre, it was the manner in which the individual chooses to relate to the freedom which conditions her existence. For Buber, it was linking the I's intimacy with itself exclusively to the I-Thou relationship.

Between the essentialist assumptions endemic to modern thought and the desire to deconstruct characteristic of post-modern thought, there is, therefore, another option: the existential-phenomenological one, by which the psychological subject is construed as having a personal aspect as well as partaking in unique linguistic, historical and social contexts.

THE QUESTION OF TIME: BETWEEN FREUD AND HEIDEGGER

Prevalent among the various attempts at presenting a therapeutic technique which is founded upon existential-phenomenological tenets are those of Binswanger, Boss and Laing which tried to interweave psychoanalysis with Heidegger's ontological philosophy. Laing emphasized the patient's sense (or lack thereof) of ontological security, as a consequence of her inability to move within the ontological structures endemic to human existence according to Heidegger. Binswanger stressed that the patient's act of denial could be better understood in relation to the existential structure of ontological forgetfulness. Boss saw the notion of "falling prey to the world", by which Heidegger described the fall of the Dasein into the world, as constituting a renewed understanding of his patients' loss of freedom and self-control. Even though these studies are groundbreaking and provide considerable background for my own argument, I believe they all share a methodological fallacy. Throughout their endeavor to present psychoanalysis from an ontological perspective, not one of these scholars and analysts sought to link psychoanalytic concepts to the very heart of the ontological project – the temporal structure, which is the prerequisite for the ontological relationship between the Dasein and its world. According to Heidegger, the phenomenon of time is the horizon from which being emerges into the world and any scientific, social, historical or linguistic characterization always presupposes a temporal fabric. In order to be properly protected against any critique of the psychoanalytic endeavor on account of its metaphysical assumptions, one must examine its underlying notion of time. This examination would enable, in my opinion, an understanding of psychoanalytic foundations from an ontological-phenomenological perspective.

Alongside the philosophical claim which singles out Freud's problematic notion of time and highlights the need to base the psychoanalytic method upon theoretical foundations which are more temporally inclined, I wish to uncover a historical account encapsulating the seeds of the alternative path for contemporary analytic theory. Generally, when conceptual and historical psychoanalytic scholarship discusses the influence of philosophy on the work of Freud, it centers on thinkers such as Mill, Kant, Schopenhauer and Nietzsche. Their work indeed had much to do with the shaping of Freudian thought, but, as I see it, it is none other than Franz Brentano's philosophical work, or, to be more accurate, his ontology and its underlying notion of time, which carried the most significance for the formation of the psychoanalytic method.

When Freud was a student at the University of Vienna, he studied for three years under Brentano. Brentano, who considered himself a successor of Kant and Aristotle, tried to provide a phenomenological account of the soul. This account was based on empirical data and Brentano discussed it thoroughly in several lectures and seminars which Freud attended. In 1874, one year after Freud began his academic studies, Brentano's book, "Psychology from an Empirical Standpoint", was published. This book is devoted almost entirely to the conceptual endeavor to found an empirical psychology on an epistemological approach. One might say that the young Freud, who attended Brentano's lectures and even, on several occasions, met with him personally to discuss these issues, was fortunate enough to get acquainted with one of the most innovative and revolutionary approaches of his time, regarding the existence of an empirically based epistemology. By taking in Brentano's philosophy, a window was opened for Freud, through which he had the good sense to examine the same clinical findings available to his colleagues and posit them within an integrated and novel epistemology. However, the incorporation of Brentano's epistemology into Freud's thought founded the psychoanalytic endeavor on the metaphysical assumption of linear temporality inherent to Brentano's work.

Alongside the work of Freud, another line of thinking was being developed from Brentano's philosophy. In contrast to the underlying motivation of the Freudian project (studying the mechanism of the human psyche vis-à-vis its symptoms), this strain of thought endeavored to develop Brentano's theory of intentionality into a comprehensive phenomenological doctrine. Edmund Husserl, attending courses similar to Freud's, noticed the crucial implications of linear temporality on Brentano's epistemology in its entirety. Husserl elected to devise an alternative to Brentano's notion of time, one which is delineated in his 1905 lectures. Martin Heidegger, his student, elaborated this alternative into the creation of a new way of understanding the unique character of human existence in the world. He emphasized that human existence should be construed, first and foremost, in light of the temporal horizon of meaning.

As I see it, Freud's assimilation of Brentano's epistemology and its particular notion of time provided, in fact, the future path of the entire psychoanalytic method, containing a microcosm of its current crossroads. The manner in which Husserl read Brentanian epistemology and his understanding of the problems inherent in his master's notion of time enabled him to formulate a different path for development, one taken up by his student, Heidegger.

This book offers both a critique of the theoretical tenets underlying Freudian psychoanalysis and a reformulation of these tenets based on a theoretical infrastructure more attentive to temporality. These two tasks comprise an interpretation which moves backwards in time, returning to the historical moment in which the psychoanalytic method was conceived and seeking to clear a path which yet remains untrodden – one leading from Brentano to Husserl to Heidegger, which presents an alternative both to Freud's choice to found psychoanalysis upon scientific principles and to the post-modern matrix which provides the conceptual framework for contemporary psychoanalysis.

THE STRUCTURE OF THIS BOOK AND THE PRESENTATION OF FREUD AND HEIDEGGER

The attempt to encompass the thought of Freud and Heidegger in this short essay presents an insurmountable challenge. They are both counted among the most influential thinkers of the 20th century and the channels of thought which they have unlocked before the western subject continue to outline contemporary culture's quotidian and reflective progression. It is superfluous to state the number of books and papers written about each of them – I will make use of those most cardinal and relevant to the matter at hand.

Psychoanalytic theory saw many scholarly turns: seduction theory (1897) was abandoned in favor of infantile sexuality; the topographic conception of the mind was replaced by the structural one (1923); the distinction between sexual and self-preservative drives was outdated by the one between life and death drives (1919); the origin of anxiety, once postulated as unvented sexual energy, was later seen as stemming from a traumatic encounter between the individual and the world (1925); finally, scientific models were forsaken in favor of speculative models based on clinical observation. This plethora of modifications brought about several alternative depictions of the psychic mechanism at the root of human nature, making it impossible to present a comprehensive and unified notion of psychoanalysis. During its early days, psychoanalysis proclaimed itself as "discovering a new continent", heralding the importance of revealing the unconscious facets of the human mind; today, it seems to be discovering a multitude of islands, rather than a single continent. Therefore, I shall refrain from presenting the psychoanalytic method as a single, coherent doctrine, upon which my theoretical critique is implemented. Instead, I shall utilize the issue of the ontological status of time both as a means of describing psychoanalysis throughout its various stages of development, and as the basis for applying my critique.

The presentation of Freudian thought requires one to face a myriad of texts from several distinct periods. In contrast, Heidegger's thought is encapsulated in a very small number of texts, which are either explicitly relevant to the issue of temporality or dealing openly with Freud's work. Nevertheless, the problem in presenting Heideggerian thought stems from the fact that his notion of the phenomenon of temporality as underlying the human existential structure seems to contradict our basic intuition about the way our lives are led. We are accustomed to seeing the world as appearing through a linear matrix of time. When entering a café, for instance, we never find ourselves in a situation where we are first of all served the bill and only afterwards asked what it is we would like. Everything always reveals itself to us as a set occurrence within a consistent chain of circumstances. When we desire something, we, as it were, advance toward it through time, in a manner from which we gather that even though we are yet to obtain our desired object, we are quite close, then, indeed, it is right within our reach, and finally, that we have obtained or failed to obtain it. This everyday scheme seems so familiar, so sensible, that it blinds us, making any other mode of understanding the everyday appearance of things in the world fundamentally absurd. It is for this reason that the first part of the book – Heidegger and the Question of Time – deals with the possibility of providing an alternative in-depth description of the phenomenon of time, while focusing on one of the most fascinating models the 20th century has offered for the understanding of temporality. This part begins by stating the problems involved in the relationship between the structure of the subject and the notion of time in Descartes and Kant and introducing the Heideggerian alternative. I will refer mostly to "Being and Time" and to the final chapters of "The Basic Problems of Phenomenology", which provide a detailed and methodical discussion of Heidegger's formulations. These will enable me to uncover Freud's implicit assumptions about the nature of time and indicate their inherent problems. This critique will then serve as the infrastructure for a reformulation of the fundamental psychoanalytic structure from the perspective of temporality.

The second part of the book – Freud, A Temporal Lacuna – will open with a comprehensive analysis of the status of time in Freud's 1895 "Project for a Scientific Psychology". The "project" is an early, scientifically oriented, essay, which puts forth a mechanical model of the psyche. However, the methodological demand to provide an empirical explanation of the human psyche and the depiction of perception as a mechanical process leave the temporal presence of the object in consciousness unexplained. The conclusion drawn from an analysis of the "project" is that the phenomenon of time has been flattened out into the sequence of events itself. The problem with this approach lies, as I will demonstrate in the first part of the book, in the fact that the sequence of events itself (or, in Freud's case, the sequence of stimuli) cannot account for duration. Later on, I will methodically show how Freudian thought assimilated the linear notion of time which is at the root of Brentano's thinking. After exposing the problems inherent to Freud's notion of time I will demonstrate how this actually affects the course of clinical therapy, as manifest in the case history of "Dora", and proceed to show that this notion of time remains unchanged throughout Freud's work.

Having paved the way, through Heidegger, to understanding temporality as dwelling at the very heart of human existence and having exposed the manner in which the Freudian method is dependent upon the metaphysical assumption that time is a homogenous and linear sequence of events, the third part of the book – Psycho-ontology – will open up an alternative conception of the therapeutic method. This is done by comparing the way in which Winnicott, Kohut, Lacan and Leowald account for the narcissistic phase, the point where, I believe, one must begin reflecting Freud's psychoanalytic notions through the mirror of Heidegger's temporality. In conclusion, I will draw some general lines along which one could begin to implement the psycho-ontological approach upon both the theoretical foundations of psychoanalysis and contemporary psychoanalytic ideas.

Indeed, bringing Heidegger and Freud together both uncovers the problems inherent in the theoretical foundation of Freudian psychoanalysis and provides an alternative. However, this does not imply that the Freudian project is obsolete. Rather, by reading it in light of the phenomenon of temporality, I aim to show its continuing relevance to our time. Therefore, this book presents an invitation to consider temporality as the source of human being-in-the-world and to look upon these pages as a psycho-ontological attempt to rephrase that which always escapes articulation - in Freud's words, "the human psyche", in mine, the self's being-in-time.

Part One

Heidegger and the Status of Time

Introduction

This section deals with the special status which Heidegger grants the phenomenon of time in his thinking. The discussion will focus on his monumental work, *Being and Time* (Heidegger, 1996), and will also draw on certain chapters from his book, *The Basic Problems of Phenomenology* (Heidegger, 1982), which highlights his formulation of the temporal aspect of being. My main emphasis here is on the manner in which Heidegger describes Temporality as the fundamental horizon of meaning in human life and as the most appropriate perspective for the investigation of the human world. This perspective will provide an alternative to the psychoanalytic one which is fundamentally incapable, as I intend to show, of taking live temporality into account. In this context, discussing temporality is part and parcel of discussing the very nature of the subject.

In the early 20th century, the philosophical tradition provided us with two kinds of subjects – two distinct ways of construing subjectivity. According to one (Descartes and Kant), the subject is seen as having a transcendental nature, which is subsequently joined by physical and mental properties. This subject goes hand in hand with an abstract consciousness, seemingly detached from any cultural, historical or temporal context. The second approach, which is cardinal to our discussion (Heidegger), sees the subject as a being which is actively involved in the world and whose qualities and attributes are not added to its existence through the work of cognitive processes but are already manifest in its existence as a being whose very existence is rooted in its ability to interpret and constitute itself in time.

As we observe the psychological subject, which suffers depression, obsession and anxiety, it seems quite impossible to imagine a being which is more involved in the world. At first glance, one may get the impression that the entire psychoanalytic endeavor takes place in the domain of what we have called 'an involved subject'. This first impression is augmented by our tendency to understand Freudian theory as describing a struggle between drives over human behavior, a struggle which grows more and more intense through the contradictory desires diagnosed as part of infantile sexual development. According to this model of mental development, the growth of the individual is a constant struggle over sexual identity and human life altogether is lived out in some internal world where the pleasure principle demands discharge and the necessary encounter with the reality principle generates the internal drama which shapes psychic life. Freud's theoretical model presents itself as a description of the various processes which constitute the subject's very existence. In other words, the rhetoric it employs to account for the existence of psychic symptoms and the manner in which it offers the tormented psyche soothe, reveals the psychoanalytic project as a theory dealing with conditions and processes preceding the subject's existence.

Nevertheless, a more detailed investigation of Freudian theory would disclose that the Freudian subject is only seems to be an entity constructed through an array of physical and psychological processes which are immersed in the world. In fact, the psychological subject is posited a-priori as a being which transcends the world and is located outside time. Therefore, Heidegger's notions regarding the human mode of being in the world could provide an alternative: our encounter with these notions would endow us with a theoretical background through which we could rethink the structure of the psychological subject without succumbing to post-modern notions of subjectivity.

Throughout the first chapter, I will provide the background against which one could locate the Heideggerian notion of the subject in relation to the notion of subjectivity characteristic of traditional western thought and explain the starting point of Heidegger's ontological inquiry – Dasein (being-there). The following chapters will illustrate the Heideggerian subject's being in the world and present a detailed analysis of Heidegger's notion of human temporality. I will present the relevant background for understanding human existence according to Heidegger by focusing on two central models of subjectivity. Descartes and Kant will serve as prototypes for modes of thinking about subjectivity, as they have formulated the very models which Heidegger criticizes in order to leave behind the rupture and detachment western philosophy has engendered between the subject and the world it inhabits. This critique centers on the ways in which Descartes and Kant have positioned the subject in relation to time. The presentation of these models is cardinal to the understanding of both Heidegger's thought and the Freudian model. As I will demonstrate further on, the Freudian model of the human psyche, with its complex mechanisms – repression, transference and the unconscious – replicates the manner in which Descartes and Kant posit the subject in relation to time.

One

The Subject and Time

From Cogito to Dasein

THE CARTESIAN SUBJECT

Descartes was the first to utilize the concept of a subject whose essence is the thinking self. Descartes describes the subject as detached from the world. A good example for this could be found in the formulation of his philosophical motivation for the application of methodological skepticism, or, as it were, for the discovery of the singular fact to which it does not apply – the Cogito.

> I now know that even bodies are not really perceived by the senses or the imaginative faculty, but only by intellect; that they are perceived, not by being touched or seen, but by being understood; I thus clearly recognize that nothing is more easily or manifestly perceptible to me than my own mind (Descartes, 1970, p. 75).

The Cartesian project developed from a view which discovers human existence in the world as utterly immersed in the realm of thought.[1] Doubt, which is at the root of Cartesian philosophy, appears in this context as the aspiration for the knowledge belonging to the realm of thought, which could be valid in all possible circumstances. In order for Descartes to be able to doubt, he must already be in some kind of significant relationship with the world, one which enables him to acknowledge what he refers to as "bodies". For the human subject, being in a complex and significant relationship with the world always precedes the possibility of doubting. The assumption that the objects we encounter, or even the truths which guide our lives, are formulated exclusively within the realm of thought, conceals and reduces an essential field which involves the human mode of being in the world. Descartes views human existence solely through the prism of thought. In Michael Zimmerman's (1982) words, Descartes converted the beings we encounter in the world into representations, turning the subject-object division into the standard theoretical basis for any form of understanding:

---

[1] In this context, Gaukroger (1989) indicates that the identification of the human being with the realm of thought is a derivative of a one of Descartes' more fundamental beliefs, which relates the existence of God with eternal truth and thus enables human cognition to move beyond merely contingent knowledge of things (pp. 60-71).

> Descartes reduced beings to ideas or representations, whose validity is determined according to the standards imposed by the ego-subject. The self-validating subject, which is permanently present because it accompanies all its representations, now becomes the ground and standard for everything (p. 209).

Descartes pays no heed to this kind of argument not because his claims are in any way incoherent, but because has confined himself to a worldview which separates mind and body, thought and world, perceiver (subject) and perceived (object).[2] According to Heidegger, Descartes' point of departure is not derived from the human mode of being in the world but rather from a metaphysical worldview which partakes in the way he – as a human being - is relating to the world. Descartes the human being and, therefore, Descartes the philosopher, is oblivious to his mode of being in the world.

By introducing methodological skepticism into philosophy, Descartes compelled modern philosophy to exchange the search for truth (as expressing the connection between human beings and the world) for the search for inner certainty. The Cogito became the sole, unquestionable foundation for determining the reality and validity of objects.[3] Indeed, Cartesian thought grants one the autonomy of knowledge, but, in doing so, it cuts one off from the world. Descartes' thinking reduced the encounter with beings to an encounter with representations, whose validity is dictated by their unifying factor: the subject, the Ego. From this point on, only that which appears before the subject as an object, only that which the subject presents before itself –that is, represents – is real. In this manner, Charles Taylor (1987), commenting on the Cartesian insistence on certainty, shows that, according to Descartes, internal representations have, in fact, no need of the external world and have themselves become the source of all knowledge:

> This connection was central to Descartes' philosophy. It was one of his leading ideas that science, or real knowledge, does not just consist of congruence between ideas in the mind and reality outside. If the object of my musing happens to coincide with real events in the world, this doesn't give me *Knowledge* of them. This congruence has to come about through a reliable method, generating well-found confidence (pp. 467-468).

As a moment in history, the Cartesian subject marks the onset of epistemological thought as a reflective activity directed toward internal

---

[2] Baker (1996) provides further analysis of this division. He demonstrates that at the root of Cartesian dualism lies the distinction between introspection and observation (pp. 11-12).

[3] In her discussion of the manner in which Descartes employs methodological skepticism as a sheerly mental activity, Broughton (2002) indicates that the very employment of doubt renders the doubter anonymous and human singularity a mere ideal (pp. 21-37).

representations. The rupture thus made manifest between subject and object transposes the search for certainty into the internal world. The representations available to the subject's observation are there, as the subject itself is their unifying metaphysical factor. That is, the subject functions as an immutable given; were it mutable, the Cartesian worldview would dissipate altogether. Actually, its very existence relies on the presumed existence of a very particular relation between the subject and its representations, one which pushes the subject outside the world and worse yet – outside of time.

> For the whole duration of life is divisible into countless parts, all mutually independent; so from my having existed a little while ago it does not follow that I need exist now, unless some cause creates me anew at this very moment, in other words, preserves me. For it is clear, when one considers the nature of time, that just the same power and agency is needed to preserve any object at the various moments of its duration, as would be needed to create it anew if it did not yet exist (Descartes, 1970, p. 88).

The Cartesian subject's access to time enables access to a single given moment. Each new state of affairs, having been epistemologically perceived, always provides a specific representation of reality and thereby requires a new act of cognition. Each given moment in time is recognized by the subject as a homogenous moment, unrelated to any other, sealed off in itself. In this context, Descartes claims that time is infinitely divisible and that its parts might have been separate altogether, unless their sequence was maintained by divine intervention. In fact, one could state that Descartes needs God not only in order to carry the subject into the world he had lost to methodological skepticism, but also to restore it into time. Thus, from Heidegger's (1982) point of view, Descartes is a key example of the manner in which the philosophical tradition excludes time from serving an integral part of the subject, by relying on the categorical distinction between Cogitans (thinking) and Res extensa (bodies) (p. 154).

KANT AND THE TRANSCENDENTAL SUBJECT

Kant's philosophy established the eminence of the question of time in western thinking. It singled time out as the factor which affects our understanding of consciousness and which generates the image of the world reflected in it. Kant believed that notions of time contemporary to his (those of Newton and Leibnitz) were problematical as they considered time a quality pertaining to things in themselves. In order to clarify Kant's reversal of this contemporary worldview and his choice of time over space and the manner in which objects are presented to consciousness, in order to better understand the role of the subject in the process of perception, I will hereby provide a general outline of the Kantian structure of consciousness.

The Structure of Consciousness

Even though Kant maintained, like the empiricists, that knowledge of objects is always related to sensory experience, he believed, unlike them, that this knowledge is only possible once several preconditions have been met. Kant refers to the preconditions for the very possibility of experiencing objects as "transcendental conditions", which are both a-priori and universal. In this context, Di Givanni (1992) distinguishes between Kant's description of objects and the way in which these were understood by classical metaphysics. The object of transcendental inquiry is neither the manner in which objects appear in consciousness nor things as they are in themselves:

> The new assumption is that the thing in itself is indeed present to the mind in experience - not however as it is 'in itself', but only in the form of 'appearances' [...] Knowledge proper is achieved in the subsequent conscious active reproduction by the mind of these states, through a variety of representations that connect them together in forms of particular determinations of objects whose only reality consists precisely in *appearing* in these determinations (A 50-2/ B 74-6). Such objects are 'things' only with reference to us - things of appearance, in other words, rather than things in themselves (p. 418).

How things in themselves exist is a matter of indifference: our experience and knowledge of empirical objects are always already adapted to our perception of them, that is, to our own epistemological structure:[4]

> For experience is itself a way of cognizing for which I need understanding. But understanding has its rule, a rule that I must presuppose within me even before objects are given to me, and hence must presuppose a priori; and that rule is expressed in a priori concepts. Hence all objects of experience must necessarily conform to these concepts and agree with them (Kant, 1996, p. 22).

In this sense, Kant's transcendental idealism sees the preconditions for experiencing the possibilities of objects as identical to those required for experiencing the object as it is perceived (as a phenomenon). Kant uses the term intuition for all possible manners in which consciousness directly

---

[4] Kant's insistence on renouncing the study of the actual object and limiting philosophical inquiry to the preconditions of experiencing object possibilities is interpreted by Srzednicki (1983) as an insistence to create a story about the world which has two central attributes: one the one hand, it must be internally coherent; on the other, it could never provide a complete account of the world. In this sense, Srzednicki sees the relationship between the transcendental inquiry and the world as identical to that between dream phenomena and the world. Dream phenomena, which always involve the world in which one lives, could never be compatible with the dreamer's empirical knowledge of the world (p. 58).

perceives the object (whether it is external or internal). Consciousness judges intuitive data by observing it through the prism of its a priori concepts. By abstracting the sensory aspects of each object-related experience and removing the contents of perception, Kant claims that he has been able to attain the pure a priori structure of intuition (which is free of any empirical content whatsoever). In other words, what remains after we have removed everything related to the senses and cogitation is, in fact, pure intuition. The sheer form of phenomena is pure intuition and the sheer form of pure intuition is time.

Kant determines that since time is not an empirical concept, it is a necessary image, fundamental to all intuition. Each of our object experiences already contains a priori the concept of time. Time, therefore, does not exist in itself, nor is it an objective attribute of things; it is, rather, "the formal a priori condition of all appearances generally" (Ibid, p. 88). As pure form, time is not derived from experience but is one of its preconditions. The continuity and contiguity of things in time presupposes time a priori as a form fundamental to all possible sensory experiences – as a form of intuition.

> Time is a necessary presentation that underlies all intuitions. As regards appearances in general, we cannot annul time itself, though we can quite readily remove appearances from time. Hence time is given a priori. All actuality of appearance is possible only in time (Kant, p. 86).

Seeing that the temporal aspect of experiences cannot be dismissed, time is thus the universal precondition for any possible intuition or perception of appearances. Nevertheless, given that time is an a priori condition for the very appearance of objects, it cannot be considered inherent in the objects it conditions – it is, then, nothing more than a mode of intuition.

What exactly does Kant mean by his claim that time is a pure form of intuition? Kemp-Smith (1962) argues that Kant handles the notion of time using two separate approaches:

> There are two tendencies in Kant's treatment of time, each of which carries with it its own set of connected consequences. There is the view that consciousness of time *as a whole* preconditions consciousness of any part of it [...]. On the other hand, there is the counter-view that consciousness is only possible though the successive combination of its parts (p. 124).

In fact, one might claim that time operates on two levels in Kant's thinking: on one, it is granted transcendental and ideal status, on the other it is perceived as empirically evident. In principle, Kant states that the contents of sensory data are available to us through empirical intuition. We can also acknowledge time a priori as pure intuition, even though we are unable of knowing things in themselves. Kant indeed distinguished appearances from things in themselves, but he had no intention of claiming that appearances are illusory or of revoking their status as real. When we experience objects we are indeed experiencing things external to us and not subjectively perceived.[5] Our judgments are, indeed, objective but does this mean that time is an element of the external world? In order to answer this question we must consider the possibility that time is an objective event, meaning, that it is part and parcel of objects in themselves. In our everyday dealings with objects, when we take their existence into account, time, as a mode of observation, is already present in the manner in which objects appear. Therefore, acts of judgment regarding time are objective, meaning that time operates as if it possessed actual empirical status. However, when we investigate the status of time in relation to things in themselves, that is, things as external to the conditions of object possibilities, it seems that time is nothing other than a precondition for their perceptibility – that it has a transcendental and ideal status.

> I am saying, then, that the intuition of external objects and the self-intuition of the mind both present these objects and the mind, in space and time, as they affect our senses, i.e., as they appear. But I do not mean by this that these objects are a mere *illusion.* For when we deal with appearance, the objects, and indeed even the properties that we ascribe to them, are always regarded as something actually given – except that insofar as the object's character depends only on the subject's way of intuiting this given object in its relation to him, we do also distinguish this object as *appearance* from the same object as object *in itself.* Thus when I posit both bodies and my soul as being in accordance with the quality of space and time, as condition of their existence, I do indeed assert that this quality lies in my way of intuiting and not in those objects in themselves (Kant, p. 101).

Were time indeed a thing in itself, consciousness would have been unable to distinguish objective from subjective phenomena. Only due to the fact that time is a form of intuition (pure perception) which conditions the appearance of the object, is consciousness able to grasp appearances in a schematic and categorical manner, which a priori arranges them according to the intuitive modes of perception. Alternately, we could state that if time were an independent entity, independent of our preconditions for object experience, we would have been utterly incapable of grasping time as we indeed do in everyday life.

As far as cognition is concerned, empirical intuition (sensory data) provides the contents of perception, while time provides its form. Time, as a pure form, engenders a coherent ordering, according to sequence and contiguity, of appearances and establishes their internal relationships. In this

[5] One finds a comprehensive discussion of this issue in Findlay's (1981) introduction to his hermeneutical study, *Kant and the Transcendental Object*, in which he states that there isn't, nor could there be, any form of self-consciousness or object-consciousness without our susceptibility to the effects things in themselves have on us (pp. 1-28).

sense, time enables phenomena to change, without being itself a changeable phenomenon.[6]

The Role of Time

From the epistemological point of view, the role of time is to organize phenomena in a single, sequential order. In order to enable object-experience, the process of perception presupposes a unifying factor which could bind the multitude of phenomena together. Even though time, as pure form, is absolute and unified, in our dealings with phenomena we encounter different parts of it. In principle, time could be divided into infinite parts, which are seen as derived from absolute time: "to say that time is infinite means nothing more than that any determinate magnitude of time is possible only through limitations [put] on a single underlying time" (Kant, 1996, p. 86). A particular instance of time, a day, for example, is always already limited, always already a segment within infinite unified time. No concept can contain infinite parts, even though the role of concepts is essentially to relate to several possibilities at once. Our perception of unified phenomena as a specific coherent sequence requires intuition, as only intuition could contain an infinite number of parts (those of time). However, as we have already seen, if any knowledge of objects is to be possible, intuition alone is not enough, as knowledge requires us to combine intuition with concepts. Only when intuitions are represented by concepts, is our knowledge of objects made possible.

In the world available to human experience, concepts (the categories) are already a priori suited to object possibilities, even though one might ask how the a priori concepts consciousness has about objects become bound to the sensory intuition of any particular object. Kant replies that the connection between a priori concepts and sensory intuition is attained through the representation of an "I think". Unless all cognitive representations (both external and internal) were united to form a single cognition in the form of an "I think", our image of the world would have been divided among different 'I's, each responsible for different representations. The formal unity of consciousness (a precondition of our knowledge of objects) is attained since an "I think" accompanies each and every representation:

> The *I think* must be *capable* of accompanying all my presentations. For otherwise, something would be presented to me that could not be thought at all – which is equivalent to saying that the presentation either would be impossible, or at least would be nothing to me (Kant, p. 177).

---

[6] Kemp-Smith (1962) criticizes the notion of time as a form of pure intuition, that is, as having a transcendental and ideal status, by indicating that we are incapable of perceiving time without phenomena. He asserts that if objects were not perceived by consciousness, time itself would disappear: "We cannot retain time in the absence of all appearances of outer and inner sense. With removal of the given manifold, time itself must vanish" (p. 124).

But that which, according to Kant, already accompanies each presentation is the form of intuition (time and space), as we have learned from his discussion of the conditions of possibilities (transcendental deduction). Indeed, Kant goes on to state the following: "[…] presentation that can be given prior to all thought is called *intuition*. Hence everything manifold in intuition has a necessary reference to the *I think* in the same subject in whom this manifold is found" (Ibid, Ibid).

In the section "On the Original Synthetic Unity of Apperception", Kant adds to the epistemological structure of consciousness a factor which unifies and relates all object representations: transcendental self-consciousness. Guyer (1992), in his discussion of this section of the *Critique*, explains:

> Conditions for this unity of self-consciousness are thus also necessary conditions for knowledge of objects; and Kant maintains that there are '*a priori* rules' (A I08) for the transcendental unity of apperception that are therefore *a priori* rules for cognition of objects as well (p. 137).

From a different angle, one might argue further, that Kant had to posit transcendental self-consciousness not only because without it consciousness would have become a multitude of consciousnesses, but also because the object, as a phenomenon, would have evaporated into a myriad of indistinguishable phenomena. Transcendental unity, as an expression of transcendental self-consciousness, provides consciousness with the pure unity it requires in order to bind a priori concepts to sensory intuition. Without transcendental unity, our experience would have been chaotic and meaningless.

The Status of the Subject in Relation to Time

As we have seen, time in Kantian theory operates on two levels – the ideal and the empirical. We have also seen that time enables phenomena to change, while remaining itself unchanging, meaning that it is not, in fact, manifest in objects. In our discussion of the unity of consciousness we found that, if an object is to be perceived, self-consciousness must accompany all of that object's representations. Actually, in order to avoid the problem of multiplicity (both of consciousnesses and of object representations) Kant locates self-consciousness ("I think") outside time - in the sense of empirical change - by positioning it within the epistemological structure, as a transcendental representation. Kant describes time both as a form of intuition and as having empirical essence in the world of phenomena, thus creating a split subject structure. On the one hand, the empirical I belongs to the locus of empirical time; on the other hand, just as time cannot be engaged with objects, neither could the I be engaged with their cognition. As Keller (1998) puts it, describing the relationship between Kant's empirical and transcendental I:

> Kant refers to self-consciousness of the 'I think' as a pure or original apperception, a notion he explicitly contrasts with empirical apperception. [...] The 'I think' is supposed to be 'one and the same in all consciousness' (B 132). It must therefore also be the same in the different states of consciousness that characterize different persons. This context-independence of the 'I think' reflects its independence from any particular facts about the causal history of particular agents (p. 71).

Regarding the subject's relation to time in Kant's thinking, we might say that this double subjectivity, as it is described by Keller, reflects Kant's notion of time. Since the pure a priori condition for the appearance of objects is time as a form of intuition, the consciousness of the pure I is therefore, accordingly, the a priori condition for the unity of consciousness. Thereby, it is also a precondition for the very appearance of consciousness as a consciousness of something in particular. Heidegger (1982) provides his own formulation of this conclusion, in his analysis of the ontological status of Kant's (pure) ego, in which he demonstrates that the latter functions as an ontological precondition for the appearance of beings altogether:

> The basic conditions of the being of being, or of the perceivedness of beings, are therefore the basic conditions of the being-known of things. However, the basic condition of knowing as knowing is the ego as "I – think". Hence Kant continually inculcates that the ego is not a representation, that it is not a represented object, not a being in the sense of an object, but rather the ground of the possibility of all representing, all perceiving, hence of all the perceivedness of beings and thus the ground of all being. As original synthetic unity of apperception, the ego is the fundamental ontological condition of all being. The basic determinations of the being of beings are the categories. The ego is not one among the categories of beings but the condition of the possibility of categories in general (p. 128).

Kantian thought sees the subject (the "I think") as an abstract being, uninvolved in the world and incapable either of change or of displaying any individual properties. For Kant, the consciousness of the self - that is, consciousness of the self's consciousness of itself - is completely unrelated to its self-experience; is it not a relation which the self could experience or encounter in any way through a process of self-discovery. In fact, Kant prohibits the pure I from any manner of change, decreeing it timeless. Much like Descartes, who pushes the subject outside the temporal aspect, Kant fixes the subject outside the world of phenomena. Thus, Kant's "I think" could serve, according to Heidegger, as the hub which binds together the myriad cognitions of both objects and self, itself being outside time, outside of the mode through which objects appear.

THE HEIDEGGERIAN ALTERNATIVE: DASEIN IN THE WORLD

According to Heidegger, the Kantian notion of the subject had not exceeded the limits set by Descartes. Rather, it elaborated and developed the categorical division through which the world is made manifest in human experience: that between subject and object. The subject, in both these systems of thought, is first and foremost a being without attributes, void of any personal characteristics, to which qualities could be appended only incidentally – qualities such as I think, I judge, I want, I write, etc. In the second chapter of *The Basic Problems of Phenomenology*, in section B13, which discusses Kant's separation of ego and world, Heidegger writes thus:

> Basically Kant here retains Descartes' conception. However essential Kant's own investigations have become and will always remain for the ontological interpretation of subjectivity, the I, the ego, is for him, as it was for Descartes, res cogitans, *res*, *something*, that thinks, namely, something that represents, perceives, judges, disagrees [...]. Descartes calls all these modes of behaviour cogitations. The ego is something that has these cogitations (Ibid, pp. 125-126).

In order to avoid, in his philosophical inquiry, the dead end endemic to all the philosophical views which herald the existence of a pure subject, Heidegger abstains from initiating his inquiry with a theory of being and opts to allow our everyday experiences with the being of beings to provide his ontological investigations with a point of origin. Instead of trying to base a theory of the world on conjectures, intuitions and categories, Heidegger asks that we allow ourselves to see how we are already involved in the very world we wish to investigate.

For example, when we wake up each morning, as we turn on the faucet and fill the electric kettle with water, as we take a glass from the cupboard and put it on the kitchen counter, as we put in a teaspoon of coffee, pour in the hot water, stir just a bit and then let the grains sink to the bottom, to make the coffee more delectable, we are utilizing the things around us, using them in a way which indicates our ability to understand their function and their nature. In this context, one might say that the demonstrated human ability to employ the beings around us suggests that human beings understand the meaning of an entity's being, or, in other words, that we possess an implicit understanding of the concept of being. In the introduction to his *Being and Time*, Heidegger (1996) claims that the question of the meaning of being has been forgotten, and that he wishes to pose this very question as the starting point for his philosophical project: "This question has today been forgotten-although our time considers itself progressive in again affirming 'metaphysics'" (p. 1).

This understanding of the concept of being, implicit in our dealings with beings, has not been given sufficient attention. The ardour of inquiry peculiar to western thought, fervently dismantling beings to their elements and dividing subject and object, has overlooked the question of the meaning of being, leaving it veiled within the expanse of our everyday life.

Philosophy must look into the unique manner in which the objects of interrogation reveal themselves in everyday life; it must uncover the conditions which enable beings to appear as they are manifest in everyday life and enable us to know them. Heidegger terms the conditions which allow beings to reveal themselves 'ontological (ontologisch) conditions' and knowledge about beings is termed 'ontic' (ontisch) knowledge.

> The question of being thus aims at an *a priori* condition of the possibility not only of the sciences which investigate beings of such and such a type–and are thereby already involved in an understanding of being; but it aims also at the condition of the possibility of the ontologies which precede the ontic sciences and found them. *all ontology, no matter how rich and knit a system of categories it has at its disposal, remains fundamentally blind and perverts its innermost intent if it has not previously clarified the meaning of being sufficiently and grasped this clarification as its fundamental task* (Ibid, p. 9).

Strictly speaking, philosophy is not a questioning of pure beings but a questioning of the way in which beings are already manifest before us. When we say, "this coffee is too sweet", when we claim that someone said this rather than that, when we use the past or future tense in relating a certain event, we are always already articulating our thoughts according to the horizon of the meaning of being. We do this, even though we lack a conceptual, formal understanding of being. The meaning of being remains unavailable to us despite the fact that it is present in every use of language and that we live our lives in accordance with it. This relation between our implicit understanding of being and our mode of being in the world could be construed as a one of transparency. On the one hand, we already possess an understanding of beings in light of their being; on the other hand, when asked to explain the meaning of this being, we are unable to give a clear answer. The fact that we are unable to fix our gaze on the meaning of being, even though it establishes our encounter with reality, discloses its transparent structure.

> As a seeking, questioning needs prior guidance from what it seeks. The meaning of being must therefore already be available to us in a certain way. We intimated that we are always already involved in an understanding of being. From this grows the explicit question of the meaning of being and the tendency toward its concept. We do not *know* what "being" means. But already when we ask, "what is being?" we stand in an understanding of the "is" without being able to determine conceptually what the "is" means (Ibid, p. 4).

How can we complete an investigation while the very subject under scrutiny is transparent and shrouded in darkness? Philosophy, which devotes its efforts to the investigation of being, must rise up to this kind of challenge. We are unable to provide a strict answer to the question of being, as we would to questions dealing with specific beings.[7] Therefore, philosophy has to find a way for us to comprehend the specific mode in which this concept is always already inherent in any understanding of a particular being.

Therefore, our inquiry should focus on the search for the unique manner in which beings appear, that is, already revealing themselves in the light of being. Now, we have only to find the particular, exemplary being, which already possesses this unique relation to being. In order to do so, our inquiry will take, as its point of departure, the implicit understanding embedded in our everyday experience of beings. According to Heidegger, philosophy finds this particular relation in a specific being, whose relation to being is embodied in its very existence - Dasein.[8]

The fact that Heidegger chose to initiate his inquiry in everyday human experience reveals the existence of this experience as a 'being-there', as a being uniquely characterized by its involvement in this 'there', in this world, in which we live. Being-there, a term composed of the two attributes which define it as an existing human being, allows us to notice not only the noun (reality, Dasein), but also the infinitive as a verbal form, that is to notice human existence as a state of dynamic vitality, essentially different from that of other beings. This dynamic nature is expressed in Heidegger's assertion that Dasein is an ontic-ontological being, whose very existence already contains both layers: that of beings and that of Being.

Another explanation for this terminological choice is that unlike other concepts which have served traditional philosophy as objects of interrogation or points of origin for discussion, Dasein has none of the conceptual connotations which might lead our understanding to construe it as 'subject', 'spirit' or 'consciousness'. As we have seen in our discussion of the problems inherent to the subject's relation to time, such connotations promote a dualistic understanding of human existence, thus alienating it from its surrounding world. Heidegger's introduction of the notion of 'Dasein' is the proper place from which one could understand being, as it clears the discussion of any affiliated meanings. Constructing his argument around Dasein, Heidegger is able to launch his philosophical inquiry without having to consider any theological or critical foundation as the proper foundation to be accounted for by his philosophical discussion.

---

[7] For a comprehensive explanation of how Heidegger's phrasing of the question of the meaning of being is derived from the manner in which Aristotle distinguishes between being and beings, see Kisiel, 1993, pp. 221-271.

[8] In German, 'Dasein' means everyday reality. It is composed of two parts: a locative predicate, 'Da', and the infinitive 'Sein'; 'Da' could imply several distinct meanings, according to the manner and context of its usage. It could mean there, here, over here and hither. 'Sein' also entails several varying meanings: to be, being, existence and reality. Dasein is commonly translated as 'Being-there', which will be used hitherto.

> Da-sein is a being that does not simply occur among other beings. Rather it is ontically distinguished by the fact that in its being this being is concerned about its very being (Heidegger, 1982, p. 10).

Dasein's very existence already carries a relation to its own being. This relation is already manifest on the ontic level, as Dasein's relation to its own being is a characteristic of its ontological structure. In other words, Dasein is an ontic-ontological being, even though its ontological structure is readily concealed in everyday life. Therefore, asking how and what to be is not a merely a supplement to our existence, nor is it a quality of any given personality; rather, it is an attribute of Dasein's fundamental relation to its own being,[9] of its always-already-being-there. Should I go to work? Should I live with or without a family? Should I have children? Should I devote my time to a certain hobby? Should I lead my life according to the codes of ethics, aesthetics, religion and so forth – our 'being-there' is already immersed in all these life possibilities. Human life is not dictated by any specific ideal, nor is it reducible to any categorical identity. Homo sapiens as a biological definition or any other particular political or social identity do not reveal the essence of any particular human being, but only capture one facet of its being. Our being is always open to the numerous possibilities inherent in our very existence. This openness embodies a deeper structure in which the ontic layer of existence is rooted.

Dasein's interest in itself manifests as a fundamental relation which constitutes its very being. It follows, therefore, that an implicit understanding of this relation always already belongs to its existence: "It is proper to this being that it be disclosed to itself with and through its being. Understanding of being is itself a determination of being of Da-sein" (Heidegger, 1996, p. 10). Knowing itself through being, the knowledge Dasein has of itself and its world is thus inherent to the structure of its own being. Self-understanding is actually one of Dasein's ontological characteristics, a necessary relation within a spectrum of possibilities which belongs to its very being.[10]

---

[9] One must distinguish between what Heidegger is referring to as "self-relation" and what we commonly refer to as self-consciousness. While Dasein's relation to itself is a necessary relation, without which it would be lacking its very existence, consciousness, which could either exist or not exist in relation to this or that being, is revealed, through the prism of ontological inquiry, as a contingency.

[10] A fascinating elaboration of Heidegger's notion of the double structure characteristic of the being-there's relation to itself could be found in the writing of French philosopher Paul Ricoeur (1992). According to him, there is no sense in discussing the 'self' or any substantial and constant 'I'. There is only 'selfhood'. This means that human nature is essentially dual, and at any given moment we must declare that our self is our selfhood. In other words, the structure of human existence or our available paths for self-understanding are not derived from objective observation but from a kind of creation or interpretation which essentially includes some aspect of imagination (fiction) (pp. 180-201). In relation to the subject of this book, it is interesting to note that Ricoeur (1970) also chose to reexamine Freud's theoretical basis.

> Da-sein always understands itself in terms of its existence, in terms of its possibility to be itself or not to be itself. Da-sein has chosen these possibilities itself, stumbled upon them, or in each instance already grown up in them. Existence is decided only by each Da-sein itself in the manner of seizing upon or neglecting such possibilities. We come to terms with the question of existence always only through existence itself. We shall call this kind of understanding of itself existentiell understanding (Heidegger, 1996, p. 11).

Science and all other theoretical methods of investigating the world are specific ways through which Dasein could relate toward beings other than itself. Even ontologies dealing with something other than Dasein still rely on its ontic structure. Dasein's ability to relate toward the beings of its world is described by Heidegger as belonging to a pre-ontological understanding of being. In order to create an ontology which could provide the foundation for all subsequent ontologies (whose subject is not Dasein), any inquiry must rely on an existential analytic of Dasein (an existential analysis).

Two

"Being in the World"
The Two-Fold Structure of Everyday Life

PHENOMENOLOGY AS THE SCIENCE OF BEING

By focusing his ontological inquiry on everyday human existence (Dasein) and by extrapolating both the implicit understanding of being and Dasein's ontological relation to being from Dasein's everyday fields of meaning, Heidegger has no intention of claiming that his conclusions are thus limited to everyday frameworks of meaning. On the contrary, Heidegger wishes to extract from Dasein's everyday existence the ontological structures which constitute it, thereby uncovering the general meaning of being. Indeed, the ontological inquiry stems from everyday life, but its goal, however, is to reveal the fundamental, ontological structures embedded in it.

Throughout the philosophical tradition, the common answer to the question, "what is the essence of something?", resorted to the difference between the manner in which an object is perceived and that in which it exists in actuality. Another way of understanding this attitude relates to the claim that the world is constantly changing. If the world of phenomena is in constant flow, how are we to determine the essential properties of things? The underlying assumption here is that truth is constant, unchanging and determined, while the visible world is decreed transitory, even outright false. By approaching the question of the essence of things from this angle, we disjoin object and thing. Another way of construing the tension between a thing's appearance and its essence is manifest in the problem of multiplicity, that is, the legitimacy of conferring a single name upon a multitude of phenomena. What is the singular element which, though not necessarily integral to a phenomenon, still allows us to refer to a group of phenomena as such? Clearly, this is another occasion in which the truth or essence of a given object is perceived as external to it or beyond it.

Heidegger is not after a specific content which could serve as the essence of this or that phenomenon. Rather, he aims to uncover the very structure which sustains phenomena in general. He approaches the question of essence by considering it as part and parcel of the thing's field of appearance, in no way disjoining the thing as it appears from what it really is.[11] In order to

[11] The exposure of an ontological structure never negates the everyday appearance of phenomena; for instance: the way in which the ontological structure of human existence

elucidate the merits of phenomenology as the appropriate method to disclose the ontological structure embedded in everyday life, Heidegger calls attention to the word's etymology (phenomenology being the logos of phenomena). The Greek 'logos' could be translated in several ways: logic, judgment, idea, definition etc. Heidegger (1996) retraces the Greek origins, through which the root of the word 'logos' carries the notion of language (Rede, in German) in the sense of speech or discourse: "*Logos* as speech really means *deloun* (δηλουν), to make manifest 'what is being talked about' in speech" (p. 28).

By this he means that the fundamental purpose of dialogue is to communicate the subject of conversation, the being of that which is said, the manner in which this subject actually *exists*. Alternately, this could be explained in contrast to the notion that truth is the correlation between our assumptions or judgments about an object and the object itself. Heidegger argues that those who side with this solution for elucidating the meaning of discourse fail to notice the simple (or everyday) fact that judgment could apply to a certain object, or fail to do so, only after that object has been revealed as a being by the person performing the act of judgment.

The other part of the word, 'phenomenon', finds its origin in the Greek phainomenon, which is derived from the verbal infinitive phainesthai, "to show itself": "Thus *phainomenon* means what shows itself, the self-showing, the manifest" (Ibid, p. 25). The phenomenon, as Heidegger describes it, is something revealed, and as such, must be construed as hitherto concealed. When we observe a particular phenomenon, we are necessarily taking part in a process through which it is revealed to us after having been hidden. The role of phenomenology is to enable that which is hidden to come to light, to fathom thematically that which appears unthematically:[12]

> [...] what is understood phenomenologically by the term phenomenon [...] can be illustrated when we say that what already shows itself in appearances, prior to and always accompanying what we commonly understand as phenomena (though unthematically), can be brought thematically to self-showing. What thus shows itself in itself ("the forms of intuition") are the phenomena of phenomenology (Heidegger, 1996, p. 27-28).

---

is disclosed as a being-there or the way in which the being-there is revealed to be different from any other being. Ontological knowledge could contradict theoretical knowledge about human existence – such as the notion that human beings are spirits or subjects – but it leaves phenomena (our everyday perception of human existence) unaltered.

[12] While Husserl believes that phenomenology should study only that which can be fully and clearly revealed, Heidegger maintains that it could also be used to reveal obscure phenomena which could never be fully elucidated. For a more comprehensive explanation of this difference, see Dreyfus' (1991) commentary on Heidegger (pp. 46-54).

Therefore, the heart of phenomenological inquiry is the very concealment evident in the object's field of appearance, which, in turn, enables its disclosure. It seems that the phenomenon interrogated by phenomenology is none other than our implicit understanding of being as it is concealed by beings:

> Phenomenology is the way of access to, and the demonstrative manner of determination of, what is to become the theme of ontology. *Ontology is possible only as phenomenology*. The phenomenological concept of phenomenon, as self-showing, means the being of being–its meaning, modifications, and derivatives (Ibid, p. 31).

Phenomenology, as a way of understanding phenomena as they show themselves in themselves, is thus the proper method for uncovering the meaning of being in its entirety. Any fundamental ontology, according to Heidegger, is only possible as a phenomenology.

So far we have followed the introduction to *Being and Time*. Heidegger's focus here is on laying the primary foundations upon which he will establish his ontological inquiry: Dasein as the key to understanding the meaning of being and the introduction of phenomenology as the appropriate method for investigating this meaning. We now turn to discuss the first part of *Being and Time*, in which Heidegger elaborates his existential analytic of Dasein, in order to demonstrate the existence of temporality in Dasein's world as a horizon of meaning through which being could be understood. His first argument provides an ontological analysis of the phenomenon of the world. This analysis is based on the ontological distinction Heidegger makes between Dasein's way of being in the world and that of other beings. This distinction reveals the world as having a layered structure, in contrast with the manner in which the world of phenomena is epistemologically perceived, that is, as an objective entity located outside the world of the subject.

BEING AND BEINGS: THE LAYERED STRUCTURE OF THE WORLD

This ontological distinction serves our discussion in a two-fold manner: first, it provides a point of origin for further ontological inquiry; second, it distinguishes between the various layers manifest in the way we encounter the world. On one layer we have the world in its average, everyday or ontic meaning, on another, the world through its existential characteristics, those which facilitate our encounter the world as an ontic phenomenon. While Heidegger's initial purpose was, until now, to guarantee the proper entry into the questioning of being, as this point has now been formulated, we are no longer facing traditional philosophy's standard object of interrogation. That is, we are no longer facing a world which manifests itself as an object to be investigated, as something external to the subject which requires ontological proof of its existence or calls for an epistemological account of the way we came to know it. In Palmer's (1969) discussion of the relationship between subject and world in Heidegger's thought, he emphasizes that the phenomenon of the world precedes any possible conceptual division, whether objective or subjective:

> To conceive of world as separate from the self would be totally antithetical to Heidegger's conception, for this would presuppose the very subject-object separation which itself arises within the relational context called world. World is prior to any separation of self and world in the objective sense. It is prior to all "objectivity", all conceptualizing; it is therefore also prior to subjectivity, since both objectivity and subjectivity are conceived within the subject-object schema (p. 132).

In Heideggerian philosophy, the world as an object of interrogation is not present as distinct and closed off from Dasein but as a layered entity which is disclosed in various ways. This layering precludes any possibility of isolating the human being as existing outside the world and thereby annuls the foundations of Descartes' thinking, which posit skepticism as the appropriate philosophical method for any cognition of things in themselves.

Heidegger portrays Dasein as a being whose ontic-ontological mode of being includes the world in its average everydayness, thereby opening the notion of 'world' (Welt) for renewed understanding. The ontological layer of being (Sein) encompasses the ontic layer, in which beings (Seienden) exist (in traditional philosophical terminology, these are known mostly as objects). According to Heidegger, this distinction reveals being as an ontological concept which includes things as well as their being and the horizon of their possibilities. In contrast, when encountering beings, we encounter isolated entities existing on the ontic layer.

Within the philosophical tradition, one could refer to the Heideggerian distinction which renounces the metaphysical-epistemological tradition which isolated human existence from the world. Heidegger claims that this tradition, in fact, isolated human beings, leaving them external to the world, while treating the concept of 'world' as an object. In this sense, one might consider the Heideggerian endeavor as an answer to the skeptical methods characteristic of philosophy from Descartes to the present day.[13]

In order to demonstrate that the concept of 'world' cannot exist as it is described by the epistemological tradition (unless it is presupposed), Heidegger distinguishes between the object as it is separate from the world of

---

[13] Sections 19-24 of *Being and Time* demonstrate how Descartes' method distances his philosophy from the possibility of understanding the world's worldliness, the existential realm and the manner in which things in the world appear to Dasein first and foremost as ready-to-hand.

Dasein, and the object as appearing within a world which belongs first of all to Dasein's ontological array, that is, through the existentiale[14] of "being-in-the-world". Heidegger makes this distinction by employing two concepts: Zuhanden, or 'ready-to-hand' and Vorhanden, or 'present-at-hand'. These refer to the distinction between what is 'present' and what is 'within reach' or 'handy'. Within this distinction, Heidegger favors readiness-to-hand in regard to the manner in which we encounter things in the world. Philosophy, in abiding by Cartesian and Kantian subject structure, drains the practical layer through which objects appear of its significance. Reflective observation thereby lacks this field of meaning in which objects obtain their particular significance. Things in everyday life are not manifest before us as physical objects external to the subject[15] but, rather, as ready-to-hand. Olafson (1995) discusses this essential change in our understanding of objects, by comprehending them in light of Heidegger's readiness-to-hand in lieu of seeing them as manifesting their presence in the subject's consciousness. He indicates that while the philosophical tradition conceived of the object as an unchanging entity, Heidegger sees it as an entity open to change and having various modalities of appearance.

> But if, instead, one thinks of these modalities as the modes in which such objects themselves are present to the perceiver, then the variations that are so intimately bound up with them take on new significance. In place of the old contrast between the changes going on in the perceiver and the unchanged object, one would have to think of several sense modalities in a different manner as the ways in which the presence of an object is realized (p. 59).

In interrogating the world according to the categorical distinction between subject and object, philosophy sees objects from a distance, ignoring their pre-critical readiness-to-hand in average everydayness. Heidegger terms this pre-critical mode in which beings show themselves in the world "care" (Sorge). Care is one of Dasein's existentiales, one which enables the encounter with things as ready-to-hand, a modality which ontologically precedes the existence of entities as present-at-hand (as objects).

> In order for knowing to be possible as determining by observation what is objectively present, there must first be a *deficiency* of having to do

---

[14] Heidegger distinguishes between the human mode of being in the world and that of beings through the concept of "Existenz" – while humans exist in the world, entities are simply in it. Heidegger discerns two distinct existential levels: the term 'existentiale' refers to the a priori ontological conditions characteristic of human existence, while the term 'existentiell' indicates particular acts, decisions and modes of behavior made possible through Dasein's existential structure.

[15] The philosophical tradition formulated this question thus: how is it possible for objects external to the subject to exist? Or, how could they be known as they are in themselves?

> with the world and taking care of it. In refraining from all production, manipulation, and so on, taking care of things places itself in the only mode of being-in which is left over, in the mode of simply lingering with [...] *On the basis of* this kind of being toward the world which lets us encounter beings within the world solely in their *mere outward appearance*, and as a *mode* of this kind of being, looking explicitly at something thus encountered is possible (Heidegger, 1996, p. 57).

If Dasein is existentially defined as a being which always relates itself to its own being, then the entities it encounters in the world always manifest themselves in relation to it. This relation, which exceeds mere cognition or epistemology, transforms entities from mere objects to objects characterized first and foremost as entities which Dasein takes care of. For instance, we could consider a telephone placed on a desk as present-at-hand, as an independent object possessing nothing but physical properties. However, in average everyday experience, while showing itself as ready-to-hand through care, the telephone appears not as an object – to which we can join the qualities of ringing, having a dial etc. – but as primarily intact or broken, as the expectation for its ring and so forth. Moreover, Heidegger considers our experience of things as present-at-hand as derived from a disruption of usefulness of things in the world and our practical engagement with them.

Heidegger's central claim is that treating both subject and object as present-at-hand leads the philosopher straight into the skeptical bind, which cannot be undone using the metaphysical scheme of subject and object.[16] In investigating the relation between human beings and the objects surrounding them, the traditional approach overlooks the phenomenon of the world. The question regarding the validity of the external world arises at the outset, through the very formulation of this problem – is there, and in what way, a correspondence between the idea (the mental representation) and the thing in itself (that which exists in the external world)? Heidegger's solution for this problem is that understanding is a mode of being-in-the-world (in-der-Welt-sein) which could be comprehended philosophically by studying how knowledge is manifest as something with which we are already engaged in our everyday life.

> In "mere" knowledge about the context of the being of beings, in "only" representing it, in "solely" "thinking about it", I am no less outside in the world together with beings than I am when I originally grasp them (Heidegger, 1996, p. 58).

Knowledge is not an assortment of linguistic claims projected onto an object, nor is it a means of bridging between the internal and external world, rather, it is, from the outset, a characteristic of "being-in-the-world". The object of Heidegger's interrogation, Dasein, contains this relation to the world and

---

[16] For instance, the way Descartes (1970) interrogates his piece of wax (p. 72).

therefore already appears and exists “in the world”. When we question Dasein’s modes of understanding, these modes are already part of its world. That is, the existentiale disclosed at this stage of the ontological inquiry is that of “being-in-the-world”. The decisive significance of “*within*-the-world” could be better comprehended by comparing the relation between Dasein and an object, to the relation between two objects. A desk could touch a computer in the sense that there is no distance between them, however, it could never encounter the computer as a computer. In other words, the table’s existence is a worldless existence. The matter is quite different for Dasein, since it is a being which relates itself to being, it could meet the computer in a way which acknowledges it and knows it for what it is. For Dasein, the encounter with objects always takes place ‘within-the-world’, since being-in-the-world is an ontological constituent of Dasein.

THE WORLDHOOD OF THE WORLD

We might conclude from the examples through which Heidegger clarifies Dasein’s existence in the world that the manner in which human beings comprehend their everyday environment is antithetical to that of Husserl and Kant. According to them, we require a mental or intentional synthesis in order to perceive the world around us as we do. This means that perception, as an event, is dependent upon the activities of consciousness. When Heidegger describes our knowledge of the things around us, his examples presuppose Dasein’s involvement in his environment. As far as Heidegger is concerned, our perception is not a bundle of perspectives from which synthesis creates a unified object, nor are we matching objects with the activities appropriate to their physical properties. Instead, objects obtain their significance through the field of practical implications, through our employment of them in a world structured in terms of goals, rooted in the existentiale ‘*Care*’.

> Thus, this phenomenological interpretation is not cognition of existent qualities of being; but rather, a determination of the structure of their being. But as an investigation of being it independently and explicitly brings about the understanding of being which always already belongs to Da-sein and is “alive” in every association with beings […] Everyday Da-sein always already *is* in this way; for example, in opening the door, I use the doorknob. Gaining phenomenological access to the beings thus encountered consists rather in rejecting the interpretational tendencies crowding and accompanying us which cover over the phenomenon of “taking care” of things in general, and thus even more so beings *as* they are encountered of their own accord *in* taking care (Ibid, p. 67).

In light of the traditional philosophical tendency to regard things in themselves as excluded from the everyday appearance of the world, we might claim that Heidegger has reversed our notion of the world. Treating objects as detached from the world is a reflective possibility derived from the fact that they are already manifest in average everydayness as both familiar and meaningful. In fact, according to Heidegger, reflection takes place when objects are removed from their practical contexts: when something is broken or missing, it becomes a subject for reflection.

Heidegger's mode of inquiry is rooted in the transition from the traditional worldview, which considers entities as particular things with a graspable, substantial essence, to the view which sees entities as belonging to a fabric of usability and handiness. In this manner, the object is disclosed as embedded in a web of practice, activity, culture and so forth. This kind of disclosure allows Heidegger to introduce his next concept, that of the worldhood of the world (die Weltlichkeit der Welt). In other words, the uncovering of the object as emerging from the fabric of usability and handiness, opens up the possibility to comprehend the manner in which it comes into being and is granted its concrete identity. Instead of being conceived as an isolated entity, the object is now seen an entity belonging to a layered structure. Thus opened, the object as an entity is restored into being, into the ontological array. This move allows us to acknowledge the worldhood of the world as the horizon of meaning for Dasein's encounters with objects in the world.

> The what-for of serviceability can in turn be relevant. For example, the thing at hand which we call a hammer has to do with hammering, the hammering has to do with fastening something, fastening something has to do with protection against bad weather. This protection "is" for the sake of providing shelter for Da-sein, that is, for the sake of a possibility of its being (Ibid, p. 78).

Comprehending the hammer in terms of handiness encompasses an entire set of characteristics which operate in the background, but are concealed from us when we comprehend the hammer solely as present-at-hand. In the above quote, Heidegger leads us away from the traditional understanding of the hammer as an isolated, closed off object, and into its discovery within the world of Dasein's possibilities for being, or of the worldhood (Weltlickeit) of the world. The Worldhood of the world is not to be understood as a mathematical set of coordinates which locate the object in space, rather, it is a being which reveals itself through handiness and disclosed through Dasein's already existing "within the world". Any disclosure occurring within it, takes place within the context of the worldhood of the world and not within the world as existing objectively. Each disclosure is first of all a disclosure of the relations which constitute it, those existing in a context of handiness, within "the worldhood of the world". In this context, Palmer (1969) stresses the distinction between experiencing the world as we inhabit it and as we perceive it scientifically:

> The term "world" in Heidegger does not mean environment, objectively considered, the universe as it appears to a scientific gaze. It is closer to

> what might be called our personal world. World is not the whole of all beings but the whole in which the human being always find himself already immersed, surrounded by its manifestness as revealed through an always pregrasping, encompassing understanding (p. 132).

Each useful thing (Zeug) we encounter in everyday practical activity always exists for-the-sake-of or in-order-to (das Um-zu). The pen manifests itself for us to write with and its handiness is comprehended through the manifold engagements or tasks which define its position within the domain of the activities it can perform. In this sense, every useful thing we engage practically already derives all its properties from a fabric of relations manifest in the work-world. Useful things are revealed as isolated from their practical environment only when something disturbs their handiness. Heidegger lists three possible disturbances: if a tool is damaged (the pen doesn't write) it becomes visible as unusable; when a tool is absent (we can't find the pen) it reveals itself as unready-to-hand; likewise, when something hinders our use of a tool (the pen fell under the cabinet and we can't get it out). These three examples demonstrate how a tool's everyday practicality is disturbed, leading us to treat it as unready-to-hand. In these instances, we seem to consider the tool only categorically, as a theoretically isolated entity. However, noticing our way of taking care of a tool, we see that any attempt to mend it requires us to consider its readiness-to-hand. Why do we use a pen? In order to write. Any attempt at repair discloses the tool as something we encounter through a fabric of relations. Therefore, the theoretical approach to the tool is derived from the practical and not the other way around.

THE SELF AND THE THEY

After uncovering the worldhood of the world as an ontological condition which enables Dasein to disclose things (beings) as they show themselves in average everydayness, Heidegger broadens the scope of his phenomenological inquiry and moves on to question the manner in which Dasein is disclosed to itself and the nature of its encounter with other Daseins.

The question Heidegger poses at the outset of this investigation is 'who is Dasein in its everydayness'. The answer is that Dasein is a being which is always myself, always 'I am' (Ich bin). Meaning that in each particular instance, Dasein is something which is mine. Thus formulated, the question of the self highlights the ontological structure which constitutes Dasein, while forsaking an important ontic aspect on which Heidegger wishes to affix his phenomenological gaze. Whenever Dasein is understood as an 'I am', this understanding includes an ontic aspect in which the self is comprehended through its differentiation from Others. Fixing our phenomenological gaze upon the ontic aspect discloses that the immediate characteristic of Dasein as that which is always mine, already belongs to a reflective approach, laden with metaphysical presuppositions about the substantial nature of the human being as a persisting subject, an entity interpreted in light of the horizon of meaning of an entity which is present-at-hand. In order to avoid such perils in our attempts to comprehend who Dasein is in its everydayness, we must try to comprehend it in light of its being-in-the-world.[17]

> The clarification of being-in-the-world showed that a mere subject without a world "is" not initially and is also never given. And, thus, an isolated I without the others is in the end just as far from being given initially (Heidegger, 1996, p. 109).

By understanding Dasein's selfhood in light of the horizon of meaning of being-in-the-world, we see that others are not manifest through a negation which engenders the self, but as others which always already belong to the way in which Dasein discloses itself to itself, comprehends itself and announces itself: "'The others' does not mean everybody else but me—those from whom the I distinguishes itself. They are, rather, those among whom one does *not* distinguish oneself, those among whom one is, too" (Ibid, p. 111).

Heidegger describes this ontological mode, in which one is not distinguished from the others as a being-with (Mitsein). This existentiale feature is not derived from the empirical fact that human beings live together, but from the fact that their existence is structured in advance as living with others in the world. Dasein encounters other Daseins as a being-with in the world (Mitdasein). The ontological relationship between Dasein and the others is manifest in a being-with (Mitdasein), which, on the one hand, enables Dasein to know others and thus to know his everyday self, while on the other hand, reducing his particular existence to the impersonal existence of the others, the 'they' (das 'Man').

> "The others" whom one designates as such in order to cover over one's essential belonging to them, are those who *are there* initially and for the most part in everyday being-with-one-another. The who is not this one and not that one, not oneself and not some and the sum of them all. The "who" is the neuter, the *they* (Ibid, p. 123).

For instance, the way mass media utilizes information in the public sphere (television, the printed press and the internet) reduces the notion of a given other into that of 'the others', in which each other is revealed as identical to the next. Being-with-one-another levels Dasein down from being-oneself to having a they-self. In this sense, there is no room whatsoever for the other's existence. The phenomena of the others or of the 'they' slowly dissolves and disappears from our gaze by growing to encompass any possibility for otherness. This disappearance of the phenomena of the others is the greatest peril to the Dasein's personal existence. "The Dictatorship of the they" is apt to take over

---

[17] Dasein's properties, uncovered by focusing the ontological inquiry on everyday existence, are part and parcel of its being, rather than characteristics subsequently joined to a primary theoretical structure.

its personal life: nameless by nature, it is an unknown variable in the equation of everydayness. We enjoy ourselves the same way that the 'they' do. We frequent cafés, we use the same expressions in order to speak our mind. We desire the very same things. The same institutions teach us how to live and think and what we should believe. Ontologically, the field in which Dasein finds its possibilities for being itself becomes a public sphere and Dasein thereby loses itself, loses the possibility of being-itself.

> Everyone is the other, and no one is himself. The *they*, which supplies the answer to the *who* of every Da-sein, is *nobody* to whom every Da-sein has always already surrendered itself, in its being-among-one-another (Ibid, p. 120).

The answer to who is Dasein in everydayness is that its self is the they-self. In contrast to this kind of self, Heidegger posits the authentic self (das selbst eigentlich) as a Dasein which, while being-among-one-another, develops a different relation to its own being. As Dasein knows itself through its they-self, it lives out it life according to the meaning provided by the 'they': in Heideggerian terms, Dasein acquires its pre-ontological understanding of the world from the average interpretation of the 'they'. The fall into the 'they' is manifest not only in the acceptance of popular notions and beliefs, not only through the imagery Dasein embraces, but perhaps, first and foremost, in the fact that the world exists as a world of objects. The existence of the world through the structures of objects and facts is already the outcome of absorption in the 'they'. Accepting the interpretation the 'they' provides amounts to an obfuscation of the world and of worldhood in average everydayness. It also entails the forgetting of the question of the meaning of being as it is understood in light of the horizon of being, in which existence is disclosed as a present-at-hand entity. One of the central topics Heidegger deals with here is the question of authenticity. I will refrain from elaborating about it now, as the next chapter (which discusses the notion of temporality), focuses on the temporal structure of authenticity.

Heidegger makes the transition from the first part of *Being and Time* (devoted to providing an existential analytic of Dasein), to its second part (which discloses the temporal structure embedded in the existential constitution of Dasein in terms of temporality) through a discussion of the unique modalities of Dasein's existential structure which transcend average everyday meaning (sections 34-42). So far, Heidegger described a world permeated with human significance, having depicted (harmoniously, perhaps) the human way of being in the world in a manner which presented the ontological realm, somewhat figuratively, as a kind of home for Dasein. Toward the conclusion of the first part of *Being and Time*, a new perspective announces itself, one which emphasizes the sense of uncanniness and alienation evoked by the ontological structure Dasein inhabits.

THE UNCANNINESS OF EVERYDAYNESS

In the sections relating the theme of the first part to that of the second part, Heidegger discusses the manner in which Dasein discovers the basic uncanniness of its being in the world. He does this using the two notions of thrownness (Gewofenheit) and falling prey (Verfallen). Dasein's thrownness into the world is an existentiale, while its falling prey to the world is an existentiell, meaning that falling prey is a mode of thrownness. Seeing that Dasein as being-with is fundamentally disclosed to itself through the they-self, it is lost in a world already uncovered by the 'they'. From its very first moments in the world, Dasein finds itself constrained to comprehend itself and its being through a world belonging to others.

> This term, which does not express any negative value judgment, means that Da-sein is initially and for the most part *together with* the "world" that it takes care of. This absorption in […] mostly has the character of being lost in the publicness of the they. As an authentic potentiality for being a self, Da-sein has initially always already fallen away from itself and fallen prey to the "world" (Ibid, p. 164).

As Dasein's being is first and foremost a structure of possibilities, the inauthentic disclosure of the world is manifest in the fact that the field of possibilities, through which Dasein encounters itself and its world, has already been dictated by its existential structure. Unwittingly, Dasein falls prey to those frameworks of meaning belonging to the world as it is uncovered by the 'they'. Even the most private of lives, led in solitude or in secret, is still lived out according to the meaning of life already proclaimed in the publicness controlled by the they. Average everydayness, in which Dasein spends most of its life, is completely permeated by the world as it is uncovered by the they. Dasein's falling away from itself in favor of the significance provided by the they is not some kind of repressed, unconscious experience: this fall is actually beyond the scope of Dasein's personal or collective history – the world as it is uncovered by the they is part and parcel of its own being.

> As factical being-in-the-world, Da-sein, falling has already fallen *away from itself*; and it has not fallen prey to some being which it first runs into in the course of its being, or perhaps does not, but it has fallen prey to the *world*, which itself belongs to its being (Ibid, Ibid).

Dasein is an entity which is dispersed in various modes of being in the world, or alternately, it is a being which achieves its unity through its capacity to immerse itself in a single way of being-in-the-world. I could be the only person on earth to ever read some book so many times. I could likewise detach myself from the everyday encounter with manifestations of publicness such as newspapers or even alienate myself from the close friend with whom I am engaged in an intimate relationship. But none of these actions could transgress the meanings proclaimed by the they, as these are all possibilities of being whose form was already dictated by the they. As Dasein, human existence discovers itself not through abstract reflection on its very nature, but by acquiring positions and roles within the social structures into which it was born. Human beings comprehend the meaning of being human from their very preoccupation with human activities, which always already contain a cultural mediation offering specific ways of self-understanding. The interpretation offered by cultural mediation is formally not my own. The general structure of the interpretation provided by the 'they' causes us to forget our limitations and the finitude of our existence. This general structure turns into a 'medium' in charge of producing more and more possibilities for all of us to choose from. As a result, the ego is presented as enduring in time, while the myriad possibilities flash before its eyes, providing it with a sense of boundlessness. Nevertheless, those who live out their lives through the schemes of subject-object and ego-world remain oblivious to their falling prey to the possibilities offered by the world.

Understanding the existence of Dasein as structured by its falling prey to the world uncovers Dasein as a being conditioned to lead an alienated life, seeing that each moment of its existence manifests a world which excludes its ownmost self. At first glance, it seems that Heidegger's description of falling prey to the world precludes Dasein's possibility for any manner of self-disclosure that is not already dictated by the 'they', rendering revealed everydayness as replete with inauthenticity. As we shall soon see, however, Heidegger conceives of one mode of being capable of enabling inauthentic everyday Dasein to acknowledge the authentic structure of being. This state of mind is anxiety (Angst).

As a mode of being, Anxiety reveals the unique relation between Dasein and the world. It discloses to Dasein its own existential structure. This relation is made possible seeing that in states of anxiety average everyday meaning is no longer capable of providing things with their specific significance, thereby revoking Dasein's ability to cling to the field of possibilities offered by the 'they'. In order to elucidate this unique property of anxiety, Heidegger distinguishes between this state and fear. While the affect of fear is always directed at something in the world, anxiety never occurs in response to any particular worldly object.

> How is what Angst is about phenomenally differentiated from what fear is afraid of? What Angst is about is not an innerworldly being. Thus it essentially cannot be relevant. The threat does not have the character of a definitive deterimentality which concerns what is threatened with a definite regard to a particular factical potentiality for being (Ibid, p. 174).

Nothing worldly is responsible for anxiety. It is not directed at some particular object as fear is; no object could provide the cause for its occurrence. Furthermore, when anxiety strikes things stop belonging to the world, they manifest themselves before Dasein as neither present-at-hand nor ready-to-hand. In times of anxiety things vanish, meaning that they can no longer provide any sense of ontological security and that the frameworks of meaning through which Dasein is used to encounter them collapse.[18]

> In Angst, the things at hand in the surrounding world sink away, and so do innerworldly beings in general. The "world" can offer nothing more, nor can the Mitda-sein of others. Thus Angst takes away from Da-sein the possibility of understanding itself, falling prey, in terms of the "world" and the public way of being interpreted (Heidegger, 1996, p. 175).

Anxiety is thus a mode of being which does not allow Dasein to maintain a self-understanding grounded in the world as uncovered by the 'they', seeing that the occurrence of anxiety precludes the possibility of understanding itself through its relation toward worldly things: "So if what Angst is about exposes nothing, that is, the world as such, this means that that about which Angst is anxious is being-in-the-world itself" (Ibid, Ibid). As anxiety tears down average everyday significance, the world which was hitherto Dasein's field of existential possibilities becomes alien, indefinite and threatening. In fact, that which is disclosed to Dasein after it had revealed the uncanniness of everydayness is the very structure of being-in-the-world and its primordiality. Uncovering this gap or this relation between Dasein and worldly things discloses to Dasein the fundamental difference between its structure as being-in-the-world and its immersion in everydayness. The difference between these two modes of being available to Dasein enables it to acknowledge its existential movement toward the world, whether authentic or inauthentic. Anxiety, therefore, opens the possibility for Dasein to acknowledge it own existential structure: "Da-sein (…) is ontically distinguished by the fact that in its being this being is concerned about its very being" (Ibid, p. 10).

Moreover, Dasein's uniqueness is also manifest ontologically, since, unlike other beings, its concern about its very being is an essential mode of its being. Following the discussion of anxiety as facilitating Dasein's liberation from the inauthentic world of the 'they', this concern with its own being could be formulated in terms of the care embedded in its existential structure, the care it has for its own mode of being in the world.

> Da-sein is a being which is concerned in its being about that being. The "is concerned about…" has become clearer in the constitution of being

[18] This collapse of the average everyday significance of things during anxiety could also be accounted for from a different angle – through the manner in which objects no longer manifest themselves as ready-to-hand. This claim is presented by Hall (1993), which compares the rupture of the object's contextual grounding to Dasein's inability to understand itself through its field of possibilities for being in times of anxiety (pp. 122-140).

> of understanding as self-projective being toward its ownmost potentiality-for-being. This potentiality is that for the sake of which any Da-sein is as it is (Ibid, p. 179).

If the analysis of the state of mind of anxiety revealed the ontological aspect of its being as existing between worldly things and being-in-the-world, it now becomes apparent that care is a characteristic of its being which relates Dasein and the world. In fact, Heidegger's notion of care is founded on Dasein's existential movement within the field of possibilities. This field is not a mere assortment of possibilities external to Dasein, but an integral part of its being. Dasein's worldly life, its understanding of itself and its surrounding environment are always derived from its self-projection within its field of possibilities-for-being, from its being-in-the-world toward its manner of living its individual life in the world, as this life is a constant manifestation of care.[19]

Analyzing care as Dasein's self-projection toward its potentiality for being itself, discloses another aspect of the structure of its being. Since Dasein's self-understanding is a movement toward the possibility of being-itself, its existential structure is revealed as self-transcending.

> But ontologically, being toward one's ownmost potentiality-for-being means that Da-sein is always *ahead* of itself in its being. Da-sein is always already "beyond itself", not as a way of behaving toward beings which it is *not*, but as being toward the potentiality-for-being which it itself is. This structure of being of the essential "being concerned about" we formulate as the being-ahead-of-itself of Da-sein (Ibid, p. 179).

This "beyond-itself" does not concern some isolated and closed off entity but the Dasein, being first and foremost a being-in-the-world. Therefore, its projectedness involves two other aspects related to its encounter with the world. Its being-ahead-of-itself occurs first, in light if its being-in-the-world and second, in light of its being-together-with worldly things.

> Da-sein means being-ahead-of-oneself-already in (the world) as being together-with (innerworldly beings encountered). This being fills in the significance of the term *care*, which is used in a purely ontological and existential way (Ibid, p. 180).

Care is disclosed as an existentiale of Dasein's being which unifies all other existentiales – being-beyond-itself already in-the-world; being-beyond-itself as a being-with with other Daseins; being-beyond-itself as being-among worldly objects - granting them structural unity. This unity is lacking if we comprehend these modes of being as produced exclusively by everyday structures of significance immersed in the public field of meaning originating

---

[19] Although I will not dwell on this issue, it is important to note that according to Heidegger, life, as a constant expression of care, always includes a certain feeling of dread.

in the 'they'. As being-in-the-world, Dasein is ontologically related to the way in which worldly things disclose themselves, and cannot help being involved through a relation of care toward its surrounding world and all worldly phenomena: "Care not only characterizes existentiality, abstracted from facticity and falling prey, but encompasses the unity of these determinations of being" (Ibid, p. 180).

Heidegger's notion of the fundamental relation between human beings and the world as one of care indicates how profoundly different the human entity is as traditional philosophy perceives it and as it is allowed to disclose itself through ontological investigation. The subject, deemed a mere representation accompanying internal qualities or providing a center around which representations of epistemological data could be consolidated, has been replaced by Dasein as a constant expression of care, maintained between Dasein's modes of being and its being-there. This is how Avi Sagi (2002) presents the essential difference between the traditional philosophical discourse regarding the subject and Heidegger's notion of it:

> Philosophical discourse does not account for the fact that the human being is not just a subject to which various qualities are appended. The human being is also a choosing, judging and considering being, one which designs its life through the goals it sets itself. The human being is not the subject of the qualities of consciousness. In Heidegger's terms, the I is a being concerned about its being, a being which shapes and reshapes its world and its life in accordance with the notions and values it embraces. Classical philosophical analysis failed to account for the fact that the I is a self-constituting and self-interpreting being. It treated it as if it was a static, rather than dynamic, being; it presupposed that the I's identity is a given or should have been such, ignoring the fact that it is constituted throughout the I's actual life (p. 19).

Heidegger's world is from the outset a historical and cultural world. What Heidegger refers to as 'environment' and 'being-in' are the modes through which Dasein always exists where meaning is already established. The field of possibilities derived from Dasein's being precludes the possibility of understanding human existence according to the structure of the pure subject. Dasein always manifests itself through action and through the manner in which it already exists in relation to its surrounding environment. Anxiety, which Heidegger links to the very nature of being-in-the-world, is a mode of being which enables Dasein to sense its separateness from the world. Indeed, this sense of separation is only temporary and Dasein must soon return to the world. Still, this self-transcending movement, beyond and back to itself, provides Dasein with its potential for being-itself. In this context, authenticity always manifests itself as a relation between the individual self and the world in its totality, though this does not mean that authenticity or individuation are expressions of subjectivity. Dasein operates within the world and transcend it but it is also, necessarily, Das 'Man'. This averaged person is not some external layer, nor is it one or many concrete beings to which the individual tries to resemble or which it endeavors to placate. Rather, Das 'Man' is an immanent constituent of Dasein's existential structure.

As for the manner in which traditional philosophy depicts the subject, we might say that Heidegger is thereby criticizing this kind of understanding of the human subject for obscuring the split between the they-self and the authentic self. That which enabled western ontology to conceal the dynamic and layered structure of the human being by depicting it as a self-contained monad, is the specific manner in which this tradition conceived the relation between the subject and time. This was demonstrated through Descartes and Kant who considered the subject an a-temporal being, removed from the course of time. In Heidegger's opinion, the very removal of the ego from the flow of time leads to an inauthentic comprehension of being and worse, advocates inauthentic ways to live. Zimmerman (1982), by relating inauthenticity and the notion of the self as persisting in time, agrees with this:

> For the most part, unfortunately, the self interpretation offered to us by Others is misguided. We understand ourselves all too often, not as openness, but as things— egos in need of gratification and security. This inauthentic self-understanding arises because we are unable to bear the truth about what it means to be human— that we are finite mortal Being-in-the-world. In the face of our mortality, we interpret ourselves as enduring substances (p. 30).

In the first part of *Being and Time*, Heidegger provides us, through his ontological investigation and the preliminary analytic of Dasein's being, with the proper terminology in order to comprehend the subject as involved in the world. In the second part of his book, he goes on to describe the essential relation manifest between the subject and time, or, more precisely, between Dasein and temporality. The subject we will focus on throughout the next chapter is the manner in which Heidegger furnishes us with an understanding of the structure of human being (both authentic and inauthentic), while relinquishing the possibility to describe it as a timeless structure. In other words, if by positing the human subject as external to time traditional philosophy was able to attribute human beings with a persisting identity in spite of its mutable qualities, we must now inquire into the essence of that element which unifies the manifold layers and phenomena characteristic of human existence. Heidegger answers the following: it is temporality and the particular mode in which Dasein operates and encounters itself within it.

Three

Being-There in Time

CARE AND TEMPORALITY

As we have seen, toward the end of the first part of *Being and Time*, Heidegger presents a twofold analysis of the notion of care. He claims that care is both one of Dasein's existentials and a mode of being which encompasses all other previously described modes of being (existentials). Heidegger's transition from the preliminary analysis of Dasein to an analysis grounded in the notion of 'time' could be understood in light of section 65, in which he explicitly states that the ontological structure of care is temporality. Heidegger's emphasis on the meaning of care within the existential structure of Dasein opens a new path for understanding the manner in which Dasein encounters worldly phenomena. According to Heidegger, in order for a particular phenomenon to have any meaning, it must be projected upon a primary horizon of possibility (Dasein's openness to the world), from which it will emerge as a specific possibility. In other words, the event of meaning always already includes the specific possibility emerging from the horizon of possibilities upon which it was projected. Therefore, care for the way things appear in the world is not a subjective affect but the very mode of being through which Dasein comports itself in the world: in everydayness, the meaning of things is always disclosed through their projectedness upon the horizon of possibilities.

> Meaning is that in which the intelligibility of something keep itself, without coming into view explicitly and thematically. Meaning signifies that upon which the primary project is projected, that in terms of which something can be conceived in its possibility as what it is (Heidegger, 1996, p. 298).

I find section 65 essential to Heidegger's philosophical argument (his ontological inquiry), seeing that the entire existential structure described so far is thereby suddenly transformed. What was hitherto formulated as the existential foundation for human existence is seen in a new light, from the perspective of time, and is revealed as a manifestation of even more primordial structures. This section embodies a change in the ordinary everyday manner (or, alternately, the average manner, belonging to field of meaning constituted by the 'they') in which we understand time. The common notion of time considers each moment to be a particular point along a linear axis, comprised of a series of moments, each of which is clearly delineated as preceding the not-yet and succeeding the already-has-been. This notion is abandoned in favor of one altogether different. We might say that, at first glance, this alternative notion of time contradicts our most basic intuitions regarding the nature of time.

In order to comprehend the decisive significance of this change in the notion of time, we ought to have another look at Heidegger's analysis of care and the way it uncovers Dasein's existential structure as a. being-beyond-itself; b. already-being-in-the-world as being-with other Daseins; c. being-alongside worldly beings. As we have seen, in order for something to have meaning at all, it is projected upon its horizon of possibilities for being itself. What is uncovered by relating the general structure of meaning to care is that Dasein's existence takes place through its projectedness upon and onto its horizon of possibilities (ahead of itself) toward being-together-with and alongside other Daseins and beings in-the-world. Understanding the being of Dasein in light of care as a projection which provides the framework of meaning by which its life is led, makes it possible to consider Dasein's very existence as a constant manifestation of a relationship between past, present and future.

"Ahead of itself" expresses Dasein's openness to the future. "Already in the world" indicates its openness to the past. The past discloses itself through the fabric of contexts in which present-at-hand beings attain their identity in light of their handiness, or, alternately, through the manner in which Dasein always already encounters itself in light of the being of others. The characteristic of "Being-together-with beings" suggests an openness to the present. Recognizing Dasein's openness to temporality enables Heidegger to acknowledge the human existential structure as containing all three modalities of time at once. This kind of understanding contradicts the naturalistic approach which considers time to be a linear succession of instances, sequentially interrelated in terms of before and after and intuitively arranged as past (the preceding moment), present (the current moment) and future (the following moment). Heidegger terms the phenomenon through which time is revealed as the unity of its three modalities 'Temporality' (Temporalität).

According to Heidegger, temporality is an articulated unity of the three forms of time within which no temporal mode exists in isolation; it is structured as a circle in which the past simultaneously maintains its hold on the present and future while the future has a hold on the present and the past. Nevertheless, Heidegger sees fit to grant precedence to the future dimension of the temporal phenomenon.

> Futurally coming back to itself, resoluteness brings itself to the situation in making it present. Having-been arises from the future in such a way that the future that has-been (or better, is in the process of having been) releases the present from itself. We call the unified phenomenon of the future that makes present in the process of having-been *temporality* (Ibid, p. 300).

In our attempts to understand how time is manifest in the human world in light of Heidegger's notion of temporality, we must comprehend the manner in which Dasein encounters each moment as a unity of the three modalities of time; we must expose the ontological structure of the moment by relating Dasein's projectedness onto its horizon of possibilities and onto its possibility for being-itself as well as for not being-itself. Whenever Dasein, a being projected onto the world in light of its horizon of possibilities, encounters worldly things or other people, this encounter with the world occurs after it has already been projected onto a horizon of possibilities. This means, from an ontological point of view, that beings in the world disclose themselves through Dasein's openness to the future.

As this future belongs to the very structure by which Dasein is open to the world's possibilities, we might say that the presence of the future ontologically precedes any particular encounter in the present. In other words, the future is inherently present in human existence, thus preceding any given present. In a certain sense, we might also say that when Dasein encounters things in the world, the future is exactly what has already been – a future having-been. Therefore, from a temporal perspective, each moment always contains the future as that which has already been and that which emerges from the past toward the present. Seeing that human existence is revealed as a projection onto the future which heads toward the past and emerges in the present, Heidegger construes the future as encompassing all three modalities of time, granting it ontological primacy. More accurately, the future is favored as, ontologically, the past and the present are disclosed to Dasein through the future (we will soon see that this refers to the future as an 'ecstasis' rather than as a moment which is yet to be).

After elucidating the notion of temporality in section 65, Heidegger demonstrates that the structure of care is, in fact, a temporal motion which brings the future that has been from the past, into the present. That is, the structure of care is temporality: "We call the unified phenomenon of the future that makes present in the process of having-been *temporality* [...] *Temporality reveals itself as the meaning of authentic care*" (Ibid, Ibid). Having described care, at the close of the first part of *Being and Time*, as a characteristic which unifies all the other existential characteristics of Dasein, the ontological structure in its totality is now uncovered as existing in the field of meaning provided by temporality. In other words, we now discover that Dasein's ability to relate to its own being and to the being of other entities is, in fact, derived from the relation between its existential structure and time – from its having a temporal structure.

THE ECSTATIC STRUCTURE OF TEMPORALITY

Temporality is not some framework of meaning, some medium through which Dasein encounters the world, nor is it a property or a category appended to Dasein, enabling it to observe the world: it is essentially identical to Dasein itself. It is not enough for Heidegger that we understand Dasein as living in time; we must see it as a being whose very existence is already a form of temporality. Human existence is essentially a temporal occurrence. Moreover, when we comprehend Dasein as a temporal occurrence, we must not think of temporality as a given entity comprised of three distinct logical components or metaphysical elements; it must be fathomed as a phenomenon in itself. The phenomenon of temporality is an inherent unification of the three forms of time. In fact, as temporality provides the a priori condition for Dasein's ability to relate to its own being (through care) and as this relation is essential to its being the kind of being that it is, we find that there is, in fact, no difference between Dasein and temporality. Being-there in the world is a constant manifestation of the phenomenon of temporality as it is formulated from the perspective of care: "The totality of being of Da-sein as care means: Ahead-of-itself-already-being-in (a world) as being-together-with (being encountered within the world)" (Ibid, Ibid).

The exceptional ability Dasein has to be simultaneously 'ahead', 'behind' and 'alongside' itself[20] constitutes its capacity for self-transcendence. This meaning is suggested by the word ex-ist, which Heidegger reads in light of the Greek εκσтατικον, which means 'standing beside itself'. Dasein's ontological structure (a being-together-with-alongside-beyond) is made possible seeing that it is itself a manifestation of ecstatic (ekstatisch) processes. The three modalities of time – past, present and future – are the ecstases which constitute the temporal array embedded at the root of the ontological structure.

> Future, having-been, and present show the phenomenal characteristics of "toward itself", "back to", "letting something be encountered". The phenomena of toward…, to…, together with… reveal temporality as the *ekstatikon par excellence. Temporality is the primordial "outside of itself" in and for itself.* Thus we call the phenomena of future, having-been, and present, the *ecstasies* of temporality (Ibid, p. 302).

How are these ecstases interrelated? What specific significance is granted to the fact that Dasein's self-transcendence dwells in the very heart of temporality? How are we to understand the manner in which temporality evades us when we think of time in an everyday sense? These are the questions Heidegger deals with in the fourth chapter of the second part of *Being and Time*, "Temporality and Everydayness" and the concluding chapter, "Temporality and Within-Timeness as the Origin of the Vulgar Concept of Time". Nevertheless, I wish to present his further thinking on the subject of temporality in light of the second part of his essay, *The Basic Problems of Phenomenology*, seeing that it provides a more detailed account of the structure of temporality. Here, Heidegger finds his point of departure for the discussion of temporality in an analysis of Aristotle's notion of time.

---

[20] This characteristic belongs *de facto* also to the manner in which Dasein encounters beings and other Daseins in the world.

HEIDEGGER READING ARISTOTLE: THE 'NOW' AND THE HORIZON OF TIME

Heidegger goes back to Aristotle as the source of the everyday notion of time, demonstrating that temporality is an essential precondition for the Aristotelian analysis of time.[21] I will now present a concise description of Heidegger's discussion of Aristotle in order to provide further grounds for understanding the manner in which temporality is involved in each moment and in which Heidegger's notion of everyday time is derived from it.[22]

According to Heidegger, Aristotle's analysis of the concept of time is rooted in the notion of 'the moment' as a 'now'. When we observe the change occurring in a process of motion, we are able to notice the number of passing moments through by our ability to say (express) 'now' every time we spot a change. Marking the moment of change as a 'now' creates a kind of fixed parameter by which the moments preceding and succeeding the 'now' emerge (Heidegger, 1982, pp. 242-245). The change observed is formally constructed as a continuous motion, a transition from one state or position to another. By expressing the moment as a changing 'now', we create a frame of reference for the preceding moment and an expectation for the succeeding one. Therefore, time is the counting of moments before and after each change. The very act of counting delineates the boundaries of the moment, enabling us to measure its duration. This stretching (from before to after) which structures the moment is the precondition for any possible change so that, in fact, the now unifies before and after, allowing us to consider time as a form of continuity throughout change. As the moment faces both backwards and forwards it cannot be reduced to a single instance but, instead, contains time as a duration occurring within it. This means that change takes place within the moment.

In light of this analysis and according to Heidegger's thinking, time cannot be an assortment of moments manifesting themselves as homogenous (identical) instances along a linear axis. This is because time is an occurrence taking place inside each moment, while each moment in itself constitutes a change in the flow of time. The temptation to consider the moment as nothing more than a demarcation in time or a setting of boundaries within the field of time (as Aristotle's analysis suggests), is a false inducement to exchange the field of time for that of space. Demarcation is only one of the aspects of the moment. The moment is, first and foremost, a duration in transition which remains open to the preceding and succeeding moments. While it does mark a certain limit or finitude in time, it is not itself such a limit, whether of time or within it. Heidegger's analysis is here implying that we must embrace a different understanding of the moment, one radically antithetical to any

---

[21] In this discussion, Heidegger is referring to Aristotle's (1941) "Physics", book 4, chapters 10-14.

[22] A detailed explanation of Heidegger's reading of Aristotle's concept of time is found in William Blattner's (1999) third chapter, which is devoted to the difference between world-time and time-reckoning in *Being and Time* (pp. 127-184).

approach which tries to construe the phenomenon of time as a specific worldly occurrence. The moment as a transition (change) stretching between the previous and the following moments includes something like a horizon (Horizont), in which - and only in relation to which – could any possible change disclose itself.

Looking back, we can say in summary that Aristotle sees time as that which we count throughout change. That is, the phenomenon of time is equated to counting the various instances of a motion which we can recognize as standard (patterned). Therefore, the specific quality which enables us to encounter the phenomenon of time lies in our ability to count the standard motions before and after each change. Furthermore, if time is indeed equivalent to the number of changes, then human existence in time is identical to the existence of the object counted within the count. While indeed acknowledging the unique status of the moment as containing the occurrence of change, the worldview provided by Aristotle still construes time in terms of empirical or observed change. Thereby, it standardizes the moment, reducing the phenomenon of time to a sequence of instances and uncovering this sequence as a collection of identical time-frames. According to Heidegger, being in time means, first and foremost, being disclosed in light of a horizon of temporality in which each moment already encompasses the three modalities of time. This means that the phenomenon of time is excluded from being an entity existing in time like a collection of instances which merge to form a linear axis. The phenomenon of time embraces all possibilities for change and is thereby uncovered as the a priori horizon for the possibility of beings to manifest themselves in sequential order or as having internal duration.

> Given that time embraces beings, it is required that it should somehow be *before* beings, *before* things moving and at rest, encompassing them. [...] It is an embracing horizon within which things given can be ordered with respect to their succession (Ibid, p. 252).

Heidegger agrees with Aristotle's claim that in order for time and change to disclose themselves we must be able to count the 'now'. But in his view, in order for the various instances of 'now' to be at all countable, change must already be contained in the moment as a phenomenon. Therefore, Heidegger argues that in order to be able to observe moments in transition, Aristotelian 'now' must already exist in light of the a priori horizon of temporality as that which enables moments to persist as before and after now.

TEMPORALITY: THE PRIMORDIAL STRUCTURE OF TIME

In what manner is our life led, from the outset, in relation to time? More precisely, in what manner is our life led in relation to time as the a priori horizon of the moment? First, we must say that time is not something to which Dasein relates as it relates itself to all other beings alongside it. Moreover, it is not some abstract entity we must take into account in planning our practical everyday living, nor our 'exceptional' living, for that matter. Time discloses itself as long as we take care to organize our activities and occupations in relation to the time they require. Dasein is related to time even if this relation is not explicitly or thematically indicated. Its very existence lies in 'taking time' for its being-itself and for its relationships with the surrounding world.

Implicitly, Dasein is always already saying 'now' as it engages with, takes care of and employs something present in its world. In putting the book down on the table, in looking over a well-written paragraph, in walking down the street, I am relating to the book I've read, to the contents which moved me and to Sirkin street as being (as existing). It is not entirely different for me to say, implicitly, 'not-yet-now', in stating that this paragraph is not well-phrased or, for instance, when the father of a small child says "you can't cross the street by yourself". When we express ourselves in this manner, we are actually directing ourselves to something in the future. In implicitly saying 'no-longer-now', while politely refusing dessert after a healthy meal, we are, in fact, directing ourselves toward something in the past. Heidegger terms these modes of activity enpresenting (gegenwärtigen), expecting (gewärtigen) and retaining (behalten) in relation to present, past and future, respectively.

> When I say "then" this means that in this form of discourse I am expecting a particular thing which will come or happen on its own or I am expecting something I myself intend to do. I can only say "then" when I am expecting something, only so far as the Dasein as existent is expectant. Such a being-expectant, an expecting, express itself by means of the then. It utters itself in such a way that it does not expressly mean itself but nevertheless displays its own self in this expression of the then. When I say "at the time" I am able to say it with understanding only in if I *retain* something bygone. It is not necessary that I should explicitly recollect it but only that I should somehow retain it as something bygone. The at-the-time is the self-expression of the *retention* of something former, something erstwhile. [...] And finally, whenever I say "now" I am comporting myself toward something extant or, more precisely, toward something present, this having-there of something present, a having which expresses itself in the now, we call the enpresenting of something (Ibid, p. 260).

Unlike *Being and Time*, in which Heidegger, despite the radical nature of his thinking, adheres to common time-related terminology, *The Basic Problems of Phenomenology* entails a search for terms which could express the novelty and complexity of the ecstatic structure. Therefore, the modalities of time manifest in the ecstatic structure of temporality are enpresentation, retention and expectation. Each of these modalities is ecstatically related to some being, occurrence or situation and enables the encounter with them. When we measure time with a clock, we measure it as a sequence of instances organized linearly. Countable time, time in the Aristotelian sense, is a derivative of temporality. As Heidegger puts it, relating to the manner in which we date time: "Time in the common sense, the now as seen via this dating relation, is only the index of original temporality" (Ibid, p. 269).

The sequence of instances as now-moments can be arranged linearly seeing that time, as a form of duration, is already ecstatically embedded in each moment, thus supporting the linear structure of time in the form of a horizon. Temporality enables the everyday structure of time because its own structure is fundamentally rooted in transcendence. In other words, in measuring time by quantifiable lengths, we are already doing so in light of the horizons of the past and the future.

> Within itself, original time is outside itself; that is the nature of its temporalizing. It is this outside-itself itself. That is to say, it is not something that might first be extant as a thing and thereafter outside itself, so that it would be leaving itself behind itself. Instead, within its own self, intrinsically, it is nothing but outside-itself pure and simple (Ibid, p. 267).

The notion of time manifest in the Aristotelian model is in fact the paradigm of everyday time, the basis upon which clock-time was created. According to Heidegger, the notion of time could be generally divided in two: primary (original) time, meaning temporality (Temporalität) and secondary time, meaning everyday time (Zeitlichkeit).[23]

The disclosure of the world in its average everyday meaning is a derivative of temporality, that is, of the original structure of time. Beings manifest themselves in-the-world because the ecstases (as a temporal unity rather than distinct modalities of time) are essentially open (through their self-transcendence) to the horizon in which beings disclose themselves. Manifesting the unity of enpresenting, expectation and retention, each moment already constitutes a duration in time that, in everyday meaning, could be pinned down to a specific date. The ecstatic horizon of temporality demarcates every entity Dasein might encounter, enabling all things to manifest themselves already as a duration in the horizon of time. Still, temporality is not another dimension or layer, distinct from our own world, nor is it an idea located in a world beyond. Temporality is the very form in which things manifest themselves – temporality temporalizes the very appearance of beings in the world.

It follows then that temporality is that by which Dasein already exists in-the-world. Dasein leads it life through taking care of its surrounding world, since temporality, as constant self-transcendence, opens it to the possibility of the world. More precisely, temporality – as Dasein's most fundamental structure– already contains the existentiale of being-in-the-world.

---

[23] Note that in contrast with *The Basic Problems of Phenomenology*, in *Being and Time* Heidegger uses the term Zeitlichkeit to denote primary time, that is, temporality.

PROJECTEDNESS, UNDERSTANDING AND MEANING

The disclosed world in which we live does not need to be mediated by an array of internal representations and judgments in order for us to be able to inhabit it. Our surrounding environment, the things we encounter and engage with, are not raw material to be processed by a system of transcendental categories. The world does not need to be conceptualized in order to manifest itself as a familiar, inhabitable place. Our various modes of dealing with beings, such as cognition, desire and action - the constitutive elements of science, psychology and ethics - already entail an understanding of the meaning of being.[24] This kind of knowledge enables Dasein to comport itself with beings. The claim that Dasein is a temporal being encompasses much more than the claim that Dasein lives within time. Temporality is the structure of Dasein as Dasein's own existence is ecstatic.

> If original time qua temporality makes possible the Dasein's ontological constitution, and this being, the Dasein, is in such a way that it temporalizes itself, then this being with the mode of being of existent Dasein must be called originally and fitly the *temporal entity simply as such* (Ibid, p. 271).

Dasein's understanding of itself and of the beings in its world is the result of its own projection upon its possibilities. These possibilities are not mere ideas Dasein possesses about its involvement with some particular entity or other, rather, they are part of the entity's field of appearance as it is uncovered through Dasein's specific engagement. Dasein is capable of understanding beings in general because they are projected onto their possibilities for being. Moreover, as Dasein's possibilities are part and parcel of its ecstatic being, Dasein is never present in the world as an absolute, objective fact. Dasein is a constant projectedness onto a world whose very existence presupposes the temporal structure. If it weren't for prejectedness, beings would have no meaning in Dasein's world. Alternately, Dasein would have no world for being-in. Ecstatic temporality brings Dasein's understanding of its own existence into being.

> To understand means, more precisely, *to project oneself upon a possibility*, in this *projection* to keep oneself at all times in a possibility. A can-be, a possibility, is *there* only in projection, in projecting oneself upon that can-be. If in contrast I merely reflect on some empty possibility into which I could enter, as it were, just gab about it, then this possibility is not there, precisely as possibility; instead for me it is, as we might say, actual (Ibid, p. 277).

---

[24] As Heidegger argues in the beginning of *Being and Time*, Dasein already possesses a prethematic understanding of being.

If this is so, why do we tend to understand ourselves in terms of cognition? Why are we so accustomed (in science, in theoretical study, in traditional philosophy and in our everyday reliance on our common sense) to consider understanding as the outcome of comprehensive reflection, through which the 'ego' as an entity emerges as an object of cognition? In this context, it is most interesting to inquire why is it that temporality, as the basis for human disclosedness in the world, evades us?

Heidegger addresses these issues by claiming that they are rooted in Dasein's tendency to understand its being in terms of beings, to comprehend itself in a manner which ignores the ontological uniqueness of its own being. Seeing that the world Dasein inhabits manifests itself through care and that things themselves are disclosed through its engagement with them, Dasein tends to forget itself in the things with which it is engaged. Alternately, seeing that the phenomenon of the world is disclosed to Dasein through the very temporality which enables its self-transcendence in its engagement with things in-the-world, that which evades it is none other than this very (its own) transcendence. Dasein understands its own being mostly through notions relating to the sphere of bodies (Res Extensa) because it has "fallen" into the world it inhabits, into the world as it is disclosed through its average everyday meaning (Heidegger, 1982, pp. 271-272; 1996, pp. 126-130). This fallenness originates in the fact that Dasein as being-togther-with is revealed to itself in-the-world mostly through the they-self: it is lost in a world already uncovered by the interpretation of the 'they'. The decisive matter in this context is that Dasein's life is led in the same manner as the life of the 'they'. Accepting the 'they''s interpretation of the world causes the worldhood of the world to disappear within the average everyday notion of the world. When average everydayness is the sole path leading Dasein to the world, its understanding of its own being is reduced to the terms of presence-at-hand (to the being of things).

> As the Dasein encounters time, time gets interpreted also as something as somehow extant, particularly if it reveals itself as a being in a certain connection precisely with extant nature. [...] The time that is known as the now and as a manifold and succession of nows is an *extant sequence*. The nows appear to be intratemporal. They come and go like beings; like extant entities they perish, becoming no longer extant (Heidegger, 1982, p. 272).

When we observe the various modes in which time is disclosed in the world of human beings, time, or, more accurately, the manner in which we live it, marks the gravity of our fallenness into the world. As the meaning of Dasein's world is fundamentally conditioned by the way it projects itself onto the horizon of possibilities, we might say that in understanding (living) its life as taking place within the framework of a collection of homogenous moments manifest in time, it had already lost the horizon of possibilities from which it could emerge (return) with its ownmost possibility for being-itself.

A METAPHYSICS OF PRESENCE

The phenomenon of the world is derived from the phenomenon of temporality, in which beings are projected onto the horizon of time – their horizon of possibilities for being in general. In the final chapter of *The Basic Problems of Phenomenology*, section 21, Heidegger elaborates on how beings, understood in light of Dasein's sphere of handiness as ready-to-hand (Vorhanden), are disclosed in the world through the temporal horizon.

Dasein's encounter with the world of beings is one which takes place as expectation, retention and enpresentation – beings are enpresented into the present and within it. This process transpires in light of the unity of the three modalities of time, a unity which functions in relation to beings as a horizon which both limits and enables their field of appearance. As we are dealing with present-at-hand entities, we must understand the particular way in which temporality enables the field of appearance in which entities are given their possibilities for being present in the world. According to Heidegger, the phenomenon of temporality includes the possibility of opening a unique temporal horizon through which entities emerge as present-at-hand. Temporality temporalizes the entities' field of appearance through a temporal horizon pertinent to the ecstasis of the present. Heidegger terms the temporal horizon which uncovers the possibilities of the present Praesens.[25]

> Each ecstasis as such has a horizon that is determined by it and that first of all completes that ectasis' own structure. Enpresenting, whether authentic in the sense of instant or inauthentic, projects that which it enpresents, that which can possibly confront us in and for a present, upon something like *praesens*. The ecstasis of the present is as such the condition of possibility of a specific "beyond itself", of transcendence, the projection upon praesens (Ibid, p. 306).

In fact, we would be more precise in saying that temporality temporalizes the disclosure of beings in a manner which provided the ecstasis of the present with a certain extent of control over the temporal structure in general and the event of disclosure in particular. The horizon in light of which entities are revealed as present-at-hand is indeed the temporal horizon, but it has undergone a certain modification. When beings are projected onto the horizon of their possibilities for being and emerge as present-at-hand, the ecstasis of the present condenses the general transcendence of the temporal structure into its own particular transcendence. The self-transcendence of the temporal structure is a positive characteristic of temporality. Consequently, any specific transcendence by a particular ecstasis occurs, in fact, within the temporal structure. In the case at

---

[25] In order to distinguish between the two forms of present Heidegger refers to in this chapter, he borrows the Latin 'Praesens' (meaning present). The significance of the difference between these two forms of present and its cardinal role in the temporal structure of existence is the subject of the following discussion.

hand, the ecstasis of the present establishes a certain hierarchy within the temporal structure. In its self-transcendence, the ecstasis of the present shapes the horizon of time in its own image and gains control over the other temporal structures (the ecstases of the past and the future), in relation to the field of appearance of beings. It discloses them as present-at-hand, as available for engagement in the everyday world of Dasein.

> This praesens is the horizonal schema of the ecstasis which determines primarily the temporalizing of temporality of all dealings with the handy. We did indeed show that the temporality of dealing with equipment is a retentive-expectant enpresenting. The ecstasis of the present is the controlling ecstasis in the temporality of commerce with the handy (Ibid, p. 308).

At this point I would like to indicate that the Praesens is different from the moment understood as now, seeing that the moment is a phenomenon in time. The moment as a temporal occurrence encountered in the world already presupposes the existence of a temporal horizon which enables the existence of duration within it. Furthermore, the Praesens should not be considered identical to an enpresenting (Gegenwärtigen) within time, as the Praesens in not ecstatic or self-transcendent. Rather, the Praesens is a particular horizon which complements the ecstatic structure of enpresenting and the modality of the present. Temporality as a dynamic, essentially self-transcendent structure is openness in its most primordial sense. When temporality enables Praesens to emerge from the ecstasis of the present, it undergoes a certain temporal convergence, which alone enables the enpresenting of beings in the present.[26]

The final sections of *The Basic Problems of Phenomenology* are devoted to elucidating the manner in which the temporal horizon enables the disclosure of beings in the world. These sections intend to open a possibility for understanding the everyday existence of the world from a temporal perspective. That is, they offer an alternative to the understanding that the world is advancing, moment by moment, along a linear axis of time. Heidegger's explanation teaches us that the manner in which temporality makes possible the existence of the everyday world is related to the manner in which it temporalizes itself toward the disclosure of things in the world. The world as we know it is always already temporalized, always already disclosed in light of a particular temporal horizon. This horizon is therefore a changeable, dynamic phenomenon and not merely a homogenous field. It is modified by the nature of the specific temporal situation in which it is opened. The particular horizon is thus the very temporalizing of temporality.

---

[26] For a discussion of the extent to which Heidegger adheres to temporality and its horizons as a source for the openness which enables beings to manifest themselves in the world, see Dastur, 1996, pp. 158-170.

> *Temporality is temporality with regard to the unity of the horizonal schemata belonging to it*, in our case the present with regard to praesens. In each instance, the inner Temporal interconnections of the horizonal schemata of time vary also according to the mode of temporalizing of temporality, which always temporalizes itself in the unity of ecstases in such a way that the precedence of one ecstasis always modifies the others along with it (Heidegger, 1982, p. 307).

Anything in the world possesses, by its very existence, its own temporal structure. Alternately, each phenomenon is first and foremost the expression of the temporal relations belonging to its existential field. The attempt to describe the world as a single unit and to explain the phenomenon of time exclusively in terms of worldly significance levels down the temporal-ontological layeredness embedded in every phenomenon. We might say that in Heidegger's view, by refusing to acknowledge the temporal occurrence in our reflective worldview, we are actually operating within a metaphysics of presence (whether in our understanding of our everyday activities and inter-personal relationships or in the fields of science and philosophy).

From a different angle, we might say that the worldview we have created is imprisoned within a metaphysics of presence. In this context, De Boer (2000), in her book, *Thinking in the Light of Time*, specifically emphasizes the kind of temporality employed by science in its objectification of beings in a process which veritably severs the ecstasis of the present from those of the past and the future:

> The embedment of Present in the other ecstasies disappears when the familiar involvement with beings at hand overturns into the objectifying beholding of present things. The specific dynamic of awaiting and retaining stops at the instant that we start to objectify beings: the hammer is then detached from the workshop and from its practical possibilities, only to appear again as a thing with quantifiable properties. Heidegger takes the temporal precondition of this overturning to lie in the movement in which the temporal ecstasis Present breaks away from its juncture with Future and Past to become independent and overshadows the other temporal moments. […] The meaningfulness that constitutes the structure of world makes way for a homogeneous space within which something has certain properties and obeys certain laws. This temporal modification grounds the positive science (pp. 52-53).

By grounding our research in a method whose object of interrogation is limited to the present field of appearance, we have, in fact, already given up on any possibility of gaining an intimate knowledge of the place in which we live and of an existential sphere which is not disclosed exclusively in terms of presence.

TEMPORALITY AND SELFNESS: AN INVERSION OF THE NOTION OF TIME

At the outset of *Being and Time*, right before departing on his phenomenological-ontological journey and immediately following the introduction, in which he explains the necessity of the philosophical inquiry into the meaning of being, Heidegger states that time always served as a criterion (albeit naively) for distinguishing various types of being. Thus, for instance:

> "Temporal" beings (natural processes and historical events) are separated from "atemporal" beings (spatial and numerical relationships). We are accustomed to distinguishing the "timeless" meaning of propositions from the "temporal" course of propositional statements. Further, a "gap" between "temporal" being and "supratemporal" eternal being is found, and the attempt is made to bridge the gap (Heidegger, 1996, p. 16).

Such disregard or insensitivity toward the temporal aspect of being (characteristic, according to Heidegger, of traditional philosophy) encapsulates the phenomenon of time in binary schemas like those mentioned above. The phenomenon of time is quickly assimilated into our array of concepts and representations in the form of criteria which enable the mapping, division and classification of reality. Another way of describing this important issue lies in the way various method of inquiry present the visible/tangible/perceptual aspect of the object as a kind of temporary mask in contrast with substantial depictions which capture its true nature.[27] In this case, the criteria for classifying reality are posited outside of time, as it were (that is, beyond the world of phenomena), and depicted as unchanging truths, while phenomena are described as contingent and secondary to the object as it really is. The consequence of such approaches is the creation of a rupture between the thing itself and its worldly manifestation, between phenomena and their essence. A different perspective for illuminating the unique attitude Heidegger developed toward the phenomenon of time will focus on our relation to language. As the reader may recall, in the beginning of *Being and Time*, Heidegger argued that the western interpretation of the Greek 'logos' cast off its original meaning as discourse (Rede). The tendency to explain linguistic meaning as derived from propositions engenders an a-temporal field through which being is uncovered in static terms, constrained by a metaphysics of presence. This presence conceals,

---

[27] According to Heidegger, the methods characteristic of western thinking such as Descartes' and Hume's skepticism, Kant's transcendental method, Husserl's logical and scientific positivism and, to a certain extent, intentionality, have failed to overcome the alienation between the phenomenon and the substantial formulation produced by reflective/scientific thought.

as we have seen, Dasein's self-projection onto the horizon of time as the origin of the phenomenon of meaning.[28]

The Heideggerian project endeavors to develop a unique sensitivity toward the temporal dimension by inquiring how it is already employed as a criterion for the classification of beings, by examining the way in which it is related to the constitution of worldly phenomena and finally, by demonstrating analytically that time could be discussed as a phenomenon in itself. According to Heidegger, unless these questions are answered, any possible ontology is bound to fail.

In discussing the philosophical tradition from Aristotle to Bergson and the assimilation of the phenomenon of time within a binary schematization of being, Heidegger writes the following:

> In contrast we must show, on the basis of the question of the meaning of being which shall have been worked out, *that-and in what way-the central range of problems of all ontology is rooted in the phenomenon of time correctly viewed and correctly explained* (Heidegger, 1996, p. 16).

The answer to the ontological question must be grounded in an elucidation of the phenomenon of time. As we have seen, Heidegger replies that this phenomenon is the constant ecstatic transcendence of the three temporal modalities which creates a particular horizon onto which beings are projected and from which they emerge as possessing concrete characteristics. Meaning, the phenomenon of temporality does not dwell in time. Time, in this sense, is initially the horizon through which things disclose themselves; a horizon which enables such projectedness onto possibilities of being. In short, time is the mode in which we encounter that which is being.

Dasein is an essentially temporal being and must not be construed as an already-existing being projected onto time. Rather, it is a being which, by the very nature of its being, is already simultaneously open to the future, the past and the present. This temporal openness is the precondition for the existence and the understanding of the phenomenon of the world. Human beings are not *in* the time by which they are measured – they are temporal in their very being. Dasein's relation to its own being is existential, and its possibilities for being itself (its relation to its own being) are none other than the way in which it lives time. At this point, we can return to the question of authenticity, interpreting it as derived from Dasein's mode of living time.

As stated, the world is not external to Dasein but a basic element of its structure (an existentiale). We are born into a world whose culture and history are an integral part of who we are and of the way we inhabit the world. This

---

[28] A fascinating discussion of the binarization of the temporal dimension in the philosophy of language, through reducing linguistic meaning to a field of predicates, is found in Hagi Kenaan's (2005) description of the disregard for the temporal dimension of language in both the analytic and the continental tradition (pp. 19-84).

mode of being, which Heidegger terms being-in has, in fact, a two-fold structure: on the one hand, we live in-the-world by understanding it; on the other, this "in-the-world" is always already defined in terms of a certain state of mind. We have seen that Heidegger's discussion of Dasein through the notion of care suggests a structure which would enable us to see how Dasein, in its totality, lives in-the-world. Seeing that the general structure of Dasein as care is temporality, what we have yet to discover is in what way authenticity and inauthenticity are related to time. More specifically, what we have yet to find out is which time-formation is characteristic of authentic being and which is related to average everydayness.

> Factically thrown Da-sein can "take" time and lose time for itself only because a "time" is allotted to it as temporality ecstatically stretched along with the disclosedness of the there grounded in that temporality (Ibid, p. 377).

"Dasein can take time and lose time": even before we elucidate the exact meaning of this sentence we can see that the relation between Dasein and time is an open one and that its expressions are not limited to factual formulations. Dasein's self-attunement to time opens its possibility for taking or losing time, as time is its own being. In this context, regarding Dasein's possibility for individuation, we may inquire how is it that Dasein is able to actualize itself in light of temporality in a way which is not subjugated to 'the dictatorship of the they'.[29]

One way of understanding Dasein's relation to time is understanding time as a sequence of instances taking place alongside Dasein. Dasein could either concern itself with this sequence or ignore it. Time, therefore, manifests itself in a manner which might be termed impersonal, seeing that its moments are uniformly measurable and that their succession is detached from the course of Dasein's life. Alternately, we can allow time to manifest itself as belonging to Dasein's existence. Time would thereby gain its particular meaning as a stretching (duration) between a moment which is meaningful for me (for in it I began a certain action), to another meaningful moment (in which I concluded that action). From this perspective, the occurrence that took place in my world from the minute I began my action and up until its conclusion is no different from the time it took me to carry it out. These two different ways of relating to

---

[29] A discussion of whether Heidegger's formulation of the difference between authentic and inauthentic human existence could serve as an alternative to the ethical formulations characteristic of western thinking (Kant, Hegel etc.) or whether his radical position leads to nihilism is found in Kellner's "Authenticity and Heidegger's Challenge to Ethical Theory". It is interesting to note that even though Kellner (1992) states that the essential difference between notions of categorical ethics and Heideggerian authenticity lies in the manner in which Heidegger formulates the structure of the self, he nevertheless ignores the way in which the relation between the self and time opens or closes Dasein's possibility for authenticity (pp. 198-213).

time, either impersonally or by maintaining the relation between time and my being, are at the root of Heidegger's understanding of the possibility for individuation and selfhood.

In order to explain the essence of this relation, we must find out exactly how future, past and present are disclosed in Dasein's world.[30] If we distinguish the subject lost in everydayness from the one whose relation to everyday is expressed through a process of individuation, we could distinguish, respectively, two distinct forms of connecting the three elements of time:

A. The impersonal perspective regarding time sees Dasein's future as emerging before it and becoming its present. In this case, the only thing left for Dasein to do is to wait about for the possibilities supposedly residing in the future to become present. Indeed, Heidegger refers to this attitude toward the future as awaiting (Gewärtigen). From the perspective of temporality, we might say that Dasein is literally projected onto each of the possibilities coming from the future into the present and the past, as if each possibility for being-itself was its very self. This depiction uncovers the phenomenon of the future as detached from the existential structure of Dasein, as one which can only be encountered in the present, which also soon slips by. In this light, the phenomenon of the future is always left out – the future tense is lost. Now we ought to seek out Dasein's particular relation to the present. Portraying the future from Dasein's point of view as an awaiting for the moment the future becomes present presupposes a present, in an average everyday sense, in which Dasein positions itself as awaiting. In other words, Dasein allows the present to be the repository in which the future is collected, by accepting it exactly as it has already been uncovered by the 'they'. The present, in which Dasein positioned itself as awaiting the future to become present, is the world in which things, norms and even our most intimate feelings are granted their particular significance by everyday frameworks of meaning. Such positioning in the present manifests a forgetful relation to the past, not in the sense that Dasein is unaware of past occurrences, but that it forgets that what it has been is still an integral part of who it is. Meaning, it forgets that even though the past has-been, it never leaves entirely. The past is still present in its world as that which shapes its present and limits its future field of possibility to those frameworks of meaning opened by the 'they'. In short, Dasein's relation to time as a linear

---

[30] In Heidegger, the distinction between the individual and the one immersed in the 'they', between authentic and inauthentic, is not articulated hierarchically. In fact, the possibility for authentic living is a modification of the inauthentic condition and, as Overenget (1998) indicates, the authentic condition reveals the full meaning of inauthenticity in relation to Dasein's being:

> "Authenticity is a modification of inauthenticity. Authenticity is not an ideal state of being from which Dasein falls or is driven at a certain point in life. Authenticity has a measure of primacy over inauthenticity in that it reveals the full meaning of the latter, but for this very reason it is not a kind of understanding that appears prior to and independently of our dealing with the world" (p. 259).

sequence of instances traveling from the future to the present and the past represses or conceals temporality as the ontological foundation for the existence of the phenomenon of time. An existence void of self-individuation is manifest in the phenomenon of temporality as an awaiting which forgets and makes present.

B. In contrast with the concealment of temporality characteristic of average everyday time, self-individuating existence manifests and expresses the structure of temporality. The future is Dasein's expectation (Erwarten) to actualize its possibility for being itself. That is, the future is part of the formation – rather than the contents – of Dasein's personal existence. It is an expectation through which Dasein, as a being whose being is defined by self-transcendence, transcends toward its horizon of possibilities in order to return with the actual possibility of being itself. Much like the form of time characteristic of everydayness, self-individuated existence relates to the future in a manner which presupposes the existence of present and past. But now, in order for Dasein to be open to its future possibilities in the present, its relation to the present does not limit the objects it is concerned about to the interpretation of the 'they'. Rather, it allows the present to become a singular and unique moment (Augenblick), which integrates both future and past into its field of appearance.[31] Heidegger construes the authentic relation to the past as a repetition (Wiedertholen), seeing that what-has-been and is still visible in the present moment does, in fact, repeat itself. Hence, Dasein's authentic relation to time is the expectation and repetition manifest in the moment.

A Self-individuated Dasein maintains a different relation to time than that of a Dasein immersed in average everydayness. These modes of relating to time are in fact two distinct modes of being in the world. In the life of the Dasein immersed in everydayness, the past and the future accompany a continuous present in which the subject dwells, a continuous present which passes through the future and becomes the past. In contrast, the life of the self-individuated Dasein consists of a temporal movement arising from a future which has-been and which emerges again and again into the present. The subject who does not live in light of temporality sees time as an axis of instances which unfold themselves from the moment its life is begun to the moment it ends. In contrast, the subject who does live in light of temporality beholds time as a dynamic occurrence, maintaining that its own existence can never be reduced to a sequence of instances. The Dasein immersed in everydayness sees time as a linear succession because its worldview is

---

[31] De Boer (2000) discusses the temporal form of Dasein's existence in the world through the prism of the singular moment, emphasizing its modification of the ecstatic structure:

> "When Dasein has modified its primordial openness into a resolute and anticipatory one, it is no longer exclusively absorbed in making present, but explicitly accomplishes the movement of the 'toward-itself' (future) and the 'back-to' (past), in order to be present at something in an authentic way" (p. 58).

constrained by the interpretative frameworks of the 'they'. The self-individuated Dasein regards time as a movement which cannot be represented along a linear timeline, seeing that the perspective from which it observes time is itself a dynamic position, from which the temporal occurrence is only visible as a constant movement between the paths of time. The possibility of seeing the future aspect in the past (or any other non-linear relation) is grounded in Dasein's self-individuation, as part of its existential structure.

Dasein's relation to death provides another angle for considering the relation between modalities of temporality and modes of being (immersion in everydayness or self-individuation). It is interesting to note that, as a rule, the commentary on the subject's process of individuation in *Being and Time* tends to describe this process by tracing the transition made in Heidegger's text from the phenomenon of anxiety to the phenomenon of death and to that of conscience and resoluteness. As a result, the boundaries of the discussion of Dasein's possibilities for individuation are often restricted to the terms of the relationship between the self and the 'they'. What we leave behind by this kind of explanation is the possibility for understanding the change in Dasein's mode of being in the world as initially manifest through its position in respect to time, as its presence in any situation is always the expression of a unique temporal formation. Thus, for example, Olafson (1995) uncovers the essential difference between absence and non-being, in his discussion of the necessary connection between the phenomenon of death and the process of individuation:

> What is thus raised into visibility is the fact of presence in its first-personal, individuation form, which ends without leaving any trace of itself when I die and obtains during my life the kind of transparent implicitness that amounts to invisibility. But if presence ends in death of human being and if human beings die one by one, then presence is temporally bounded by what might best be called "nothingness". This is not "absence" [...] that is the form of non-being that applies to entities that are or have been or might be present within the world. Absence so conceived is an entity that is at the locus of presence and thus of absence as well, and death is the end of that entity. What ends in death is thus presence itself, and so one may say that in death nothing *is* anything anymore (p. 145).

Gelven (1970) expressed this differently in summarizing the two central conclusions arising from Heidegger's analysis of the phenomenon of death:

> What is it that we learn from Heidegger's analysis of death? Two claims strike me as being most important characteristics of one's awareness of death. The first is that death focuses *specifically* on the question of what it means to be–i.e., the so-called Being question (*Seinsfrage*). [...] The second [...] the awareness of death points out one of the most persistent doctrines of Heidegger's philosophy: that possibility means more than merely a future actuality. As a human being I live in the realm of

> possibilities —and it is in the realm of possibilities that authentic existence is realized (p. 157).

Even though his second conclusion involves the ontological precedence of the future field of possibility over that of the actual future, Gelven does not fully develop this insight into a methodic understanding of the way individuation is manifest in relation to temporality.

The absence of an interpretation providing a direct link between the phenomenon of death and Dasein's ability to acknowledge the temporal structures embedded in its own being is also felt in Macann's (1992) commentary, which demonstrates how the process of individuation described in *Being and Time* might prove a suitable grounding for the establishment of an ethics based on Heidegger's notion of authenticity. For instance, in summarizing the three characteristics of the existential understanding of the phenomenon of death, he argues:

> Thus the three characteristics seem to represent three steps along the way to authentic being-toward-death, first, a wrenching away from the 'They', second, a return to self, and third, a release from self for authentic being-with (p. 236).

Unlike such approaches, I propose to examine the way in which the phenomenon of death enables individuation as a primarily temporal event. First, let us see how the phenomenon of death is revealed when Dasein is considered as living along a linear timeline. Dasein is thus incapable of understanding death as it would the other possibilities it encounters. Death appears as a different kind of possibility. From the perspective which sees time as a succession of moments, death distinguishes itself from other possibilities by virtue of being the very last in line. Death is thereby grounded in spatial terms – it is further away than any other possibility. Death, as a remote phenomenon, becomes a possibility which can be repressed in average everydayness. The 'they' can provide refuge through sayings such as 'everybody dies', which relate death to people in general rather than the individual. This kind of saying conceals the private sphere in which Dasein's death appears differently, as a suspended possibility. In this sense, the phenomenon of death is formulated negatively. Based on what it is not – death, as the last possibility in line, is, at any given moment, that which is yet to happen.

From the perspective which considers the phenomenon of time an integral part of Dasein's structure, the possibility of death is granted a positive description as the possibility of impossibility.

> Its death is the possibility of no-longer-being-able-to-be-there. When Da-sein is imminent to itself as this possibility, it is *completely* thrown back upon its ownmost potentiality-of-being. [...] death is the

> possibility of the absolute impossibility of Da-sein (Heidegger, 1996, p. 232).

The possibility of death differs from other possibilities not because it is last in line, but because it is one for which Dasein cannot present any alternative. When Dasein has gained such an understanding of death, death manifests itself in its world as the most extreme possibility for individuation. Death is an imminent possibility for Dasein's being. Therefore, the phenomenon of death becomes the principle foundation of Dasein's possibility for individuation.[32] Facing a possibility that is revealed to be an imminent part of its being unlike any other (as any other possibility may remain unactualized), Dasein is unable to repress the existence of its own death.

From being the last in a chain of events, death becomes a constitutive occurrence in Dasein's life. Seeing death as part of Dasein's structure at each and every moment of its existence provides Dasein with the possibility of maintaining its self-individuation, a temporal movement from future to past and present, as a finite continuity. This temporal movement, by acknowledging its own finitude, enables Dasein to create an alternative life-story, one which differs from that imposed upon it by the 'they', a story of itself written in time.[33] This alternative story is intimately related to the inversion of time Heidegger introduces. The very capacity for telling such an alternative story is rooted in our possibility to liberate ourselves from a notion of time dominated by the now as a homogenous succession and to exchange it for an ecstatically structured being – a structure open to its own possibilities for being. At the heart of Dasein's possibility to live authentically is the ability inherent to its structure – the ability to move within time.

Throughout this chapter we have seen the tendency, common both to everyday meaning and to philosophical reflections about everydayness, to apply to time the binary categories subjugated to what Heidegger terms 'the dictatorship of the they' on the one hand, and to a worldview and a notion of time based on the Praesens on the other. Furthermore, we have traced Heidegger's critique of the reduction of temporality to a sequence of now-moments, emphasizing the manner in which an understanding of the ecstatic unity of temporality grounds Dasein's possibility to live either an authentic life or one whose particular significance is determined by the 'they'.

Heidegger's attempt to develop a keener sensitivity for the temporal dimension of existence uncovers the structure of temporality as the a priori condition for Dasein's being as a being-in-the-world alongside-beings and together-with other Daseins. Every moment of Dasein's life manifests the

---

[32] For a discussion of how this process of individuation, as a motion of projectedness onto the possibility of death and back into life, is a precondition of Dasein's being, see Hoffman, 1993, pp. 195-214.

[33] For a philosophical treatment of the relation between thought and narrativity, seen first and foremost as a temporal relation according to Heidegger's interpretation of the phenomenon of time, see Ricoeur, 1988.

temporal relations that are neither representative of the subject nor represented within it, but are themselves the subject. The Heideggerian effort to avoid the metaphysics of presence as it is expressed in the phenomenon of temporality and its modifiable horizons opens the possibility for us to understand Dasein's being as a constant expression of the phenomenon of time. Therefore, temporality, as the phenomenon underlining human existence, could prove an alternative theoretical foundation for disciplines in which human existence is perceived according to a notion of linear time, while maintaining the existence of the experiencing subject. In the following chapter I will argue that a. the psychological field of occurrence is in fact an expression of ontological and temporal relations; b. in light of Heidegger's findings, we may attempt to examine an alternative formulation of the tenets of psychoanalysis, by understanding them in light of temporality.

Part Two

Freud: A Temporal Lacuna

Introduction

In this part of the book, I will attempt to trace a phenomenon symptomatic to the psychoanalytic method: a blind spot which overlooks temporality. The attempt to show Freud's blindness to the question of time is far from simple. While Freudian theory contains several explicit references to time, implicitly, it harbors a comprehensive notion of time. I will seek to demonstrate that the conceptual framework underlying Freud's thinking about time is restricted to a linear notion of time, antithetical to Heidegger's Temporality as discussed throughout the first part of the book. As a first step in analyzing Freud's notion of time I will focus on one of his early works, the "Project for a Scientific Psychology" [1895]. The next step will show how his incorporation of Brentano's philosophy opened for Freud a window through which he could observe the same clinical findings known to his contemporaries and reposition them within the epistemological framework outlined in the "project". In addition, I will demonstrate that the incorporation of Brentano's epistemology into Freud's thinking meant grounding the psychoanalytic project in the metaphysical assumption of linear time characteristic of the views of his teacher. All this is found in chapter four. In the fifth chapter, I will show, through my analysis of the case of Ida Bauer, how the linear notion of time, dwelling at the core of psychoanalytic theory, limits the technique of interpretation put forward by Freud, stressing the need for a method of interpretation based on the phenomenon of temporality. Finally, in the sixth chapter, I will show that the temporal lacuna, made evident in my analysis of the "Project" and of Ida's case study, is prevalent throughout Freud's writings.

I have chosen to begin with an analysis of the "Project" as, in my opinion, it possesses a significant and extraordinary status within the Freudian corpus. This has three cardinal reasons: (1) While preceding *The Interpretation of Dreams* [1900], considered the first essentially psychoanalytic text, it is a microcosm of many of the tenets of psychoanalytic thought, such as the principle of constancy, which anticipates the Nirvana principle; a memory system located between consciousness and the external world, anticipating the topographical structure of consciousness; the notion that pathways of energy-flow on a cellular level create flow patterns, which is reiterated more fully in Freud's description of infantile sexuality and the evolutionary development involved in the flow of libido in erotogenic zones; the notion of primary and secondary processes, which came to mark the difference between the unconscious and conscious layers of the mind; the distinction between pleasure and un-pleasure, anticipating the pleasure principle; finally, the unique depiction of the role of the ego, which will become a central pivot throughout Freud's writings. (2) Seeing that the "Project" is located, in terms of the development of the psychoanalytic method, between its inception and its implementation as a therapeutic method, it encapsulates the conceptual structure of psychoanalysis in its most basic form. This allows us to gaze directly at the theoretical framework of psychoanalysis. (3) Being Freud's first attempt at providing a comprehensive account of the human psyche, its grants us the privilege of directing our gaze at its sources of influence. The latter is essential to my argument, seeing that in my view, the notion of time underlying the theoretical framework of the "Project" stems from the decisive influence of Brentano's philosophy on Freud's thinking.

Four

The Role of Time in the Psychic Mechanism

Freud's "Project" and its origins in Brentano

The "Project for a Scientific Psychology"[34] is a daring attempt to create a scientific psychological depiction of the human psyche. The method coursing through its veins is based on mechanistic metaphors and quantitative data and its goal is to construct an atomistic model which could facilitate the formulation of the general laws of action relating the primary elements of the system to human experience and the operations of the mind. I will endeavor to show how the above theoretical model is grounded in an elimination of the temporal constituent, i.e., human temporality. For this purpose, I shall begin by describing the model provided for the psychic mechanism per se.

THE PSYCHIC MECHANISM IN THE PROJECT

The Principle of Constancy

Already at the outset of his essay, Freud declares that the goal of his "Project" is to provide the scientific foundation for psychology. That is, to give an account of the existence of psychological phenomena which is founded on anatomy and physiology.

> The intention is to furnish a psychology that shall be a natural science: that is, to represent psychical processes as quantitatively determinate states of specifiable material particles, thus making those processes perspicuous and free from contradiction (Freud, 1966, p. 295).

What makes Freud's account so fascinating is the fact that the theoretical model he puts forth in order to explain the mechanisms of the psyche also works the other way, that is, it leaves room for the effect of psychological phenomena on anatomical-physiological processes. But let's not get ahead of ourselves; first, let's observe the manner in which Freud constructs the theoretical model of psychic mechanisms.

---

[34] This text remained unpublished during Freud's lifetime and therefore never received an official title. The title chosen for its first English translation (1950) was "Project for a Scientific Psychology" or, in short, the "Project" (as it is henceforth referred to). All quotes from Freud are taken from the James Strachey translation (Freud, 1966).

At the very root of this account is a material element which Freud refers to as "Neurones". These neurones function as a single, vast, bifurcating network. Between neurones, flows a quantity of energy termed Q. The flow of energy between neurones is not random – it obeys certain laws of motion. The most fundamental principle governing this model and regulating the flow of energy is the 'principle of constancy'. According to this principle, the psychic mechanism aims at stabilizing the amount of energy flowing through the system. The accumulation of energy in the system is tantamount to a state of tension and the mechanism is thereby constantly compelled to regulate and release that energy.[35] Unlike the representation of energy in general (Q), the particular amount of energy passing through the neurone network is termed Q'n.

The source of the energy flowing through the body is twofold: it is derived both from stimuli originating in the external world (the five senses) and from internal stimuli such as appetite and instincts. As far as external stimuli are concerned, the principle of constancy operates or is maintained in its simple form. The neurones are filled with energy due to an external stimulus, discharging that energy in order to release the tension they have accumulated. However, when it comes to internal stimuli, the principle of constancy undergoes a certain modification. As internal excitations cannot always be addressed, the process of discharging energy through the activity of the neurones must be suspended. That is, the mechanism must learn to identify, at any given moment, whether or not neurones are to release the tension that has accumulated in the system (even though this stimulus creates internal tension).

Memory and Energy Accumulation

At times of hunger, the internal stimulus (originating in the cells) is expressed as tension. If this need cannot presently be met, the mechanism cannot allow the principle of constancy to operate immediately. Recognizing various states of tension, relating them to the specific source of stimulus and adjusting the extent to which tension is discharged or suspended presuppose two patterns of activity in the psychic mechanism: the first is the capacity for memory, the second, the capacity to endure and sustain a state of tension in order to enable the psychic system to perform the required action in the external world, thus satisfying the internal need. Understanding these patterns of activity requires a more detailed explanation of the neurone network.

---

[35] This depiction of the principle of constancy will provide Freud (1955) with the grounds for the nirvana principle some twenty five years later, in "Beyond the Pleasure Principle", in which he describes the aspiration to reduce bodily tension to zero, as a tendency inherent to the existence of living organisms (pp. 55-56).

> There are two classes of neurones: [1] those which allow Q'n to pass through as though they had no contact-barriers and which, accordingly, after each passage of excitation are in the same state as before, and [2] those whose contact-barriers make themselves felt, so that they only allow Q'n to pass through with difficulty or partially. The latter class may, after each excitation, be in a different state from before and they thus afford a *possibility of representing memory* (Freud, 1966, p. 299).

Neurones are thereby divided into two groups: those utterly permeable to energy, that is, those which exhibit no resistance to the energy passing through them – these are neurones of perception, which Freud calls Φ - and those who do not allow energy to pass unhindered, resisting its passage to a certain degree – these are energy accumulating neurones, referred to as Ψ.[36] The existence of these two groups of neurones enables the mechanism to remember the different paths of Q'n flow, as these become fixed in the system by the Ψ group.

This description of the manner in which energy is channeled by the Ψ group does not invalidate the principle of constancy but rather modifies it to a certain extent. Henceforth, the mechanism is not intended to discharge internal tensions but to keep them at a level that is sufficient for performing the necessary actions in the world.[37] In fact, Freud perceives the functioning of the psychic mechanism in light of this change in the principle of constancy as exhibiting its "secondary functions". In contrast, its "primary functions" are seen as a state in which the psyche follows the principle of constancy without modification.[38] The neuro-physiological account Freud puts forward describes the relationship between the neurone network and the world in the following manner: the Φ group receives external stimuli, which cathect (charge) neurones without any resistance, and passes Q'n toward the Ψ group, in which

---

[36] The common characteristic of this group of neurones, according to Freud, is that each neurone contains a barrier which regulates the amount of energy it can be charged with. Not only does each Ψ neurone maintain a certain level of resistance to the passage of energy, it also manifests different types of connections with other neurones. This attribute increases the number of available variations for energy flow.

[37] This process of learning is a complicated biological process, as the mechanism must keep track of each need and its respective means for satisfaction, as these are expressed in the various pathways of energy flow in the neurone network. Meaning that the mechanism learns to channel energy according to the traces (memory) left in the network by the object required for discharge and the memory of the satisfaction derived from finding this object. This idea is presented, fully formed, in "Three Essays on the Theory of Sexuality" [1905], in which the relationship between object and instinct becomes a central pivot, characteristic of the evolutionary development of psychic life in infants and adults as well as of pathological cases.

[38] From the seventh chapter of *The Interpretation of Dreams* [1900] and up until his very last writings, this notion, depicted in the "Project" in economical-dynamical terms, is granted a cardinal position in Freud's method, described from the topographical perspective in which primary processes are part of the unconscious and secondary ones comprise part of the preconscious and conscious.

energy flow is modified and channeled. When Ψ group neurones become cathected, their interrelations become problematic. Once Q'n flow has reached the Ψ group, it encounters resistance on the part of its charged neurones. The steady flow of Q'n is dependent upon the capacity of available neurones to form a consecutive chain for transferring energy between them. Whenever energy flow recurs along a certain pathway, this indicates that the neurones comprising this passage are available for transfer and that tension is discharged in the most rapid and convenient manner. Through this process, the psychic mechanism establishes an array of internal memory which contains pathways for discharge modified to suit external stimuli.[39] Once the modification of the principle of constancy is elucidated, we might argue that the psychic mechanism stabilizes the system not only through the discharge of energy but also through its retention.

Pain and the Problem of Quality

The model through which Freud accounts for the stabilization of the psychic system enables him to explain the phenomenon of pain. If the general tendency of the mechanism is to discharge energy through a gradual process of motion between the two groups of neurones, the sensation of pain is therefore an irruption of energy into both groups at once, abolishing any gradation. All neurones are cathected, the barriers within the Ψ group are breached and the system is overflowed with energy. Seeing that energy, according to Freud's model, means tension, the overflow of energy is tantamount to unbearable tension: "Pain is thus characterized as an irruption of excessively large Qs into Φ and Ψ: that is of Qs which are of a still higher order than the Φ stimuli" (Freud, 1966, p. 307).

Right after discussing the phenomenon of pain, Freud moves on to a new section, entitled "The Problem of Quality". The question he is preoccupied with at this stage of the "Project" is how a system operating on the basis of quantitative relations allows for the existence of qualities. Or, from another angle, relating to the previous section in which he treated pain, how could this quantitative model account for a statement such as 'I am in pain'. In order to answer this question, Freud postulates the existence of a third system of neurones, that of consciousness, which he terms ω.

> Thus we summon up courage to assume that there is a third system of neurones—ω perhaps [we might call it]— which is excited along with perception, but not along with reproduction, and whose states of excitation give rise to the various qualities—are, that is to say, *conscious sensations* (Ibid, p. 309).

---

[39] Describing memory as a primary system located between consciousness and the external world is the basis of the notion of memory in the topographical structure, in which uncathected memories do not reach consciousness, i. e., become unconscious.

In Freud's view, the very existence of the sensation of consciousness is rooted in the ability to perceive qualities. But in what way does the quantitative aspect, described in detail through neurone systems Φ and Ψ, manifest itself in the form of quality in the third group? At this point, Freud regroups, as it were, returning to his previous assumptions and adding a new element. Thus far, we have seen that energy undergoes a gradual process which reduces its motility as it passes from the external world to Φ group, from there to Ψ group and finally to ω. Freud now augments this description by claiming that the quantitative passage of energy carries with it additional information: the period of energy flow, which Freud sees as a kind of generalization, entailing the qualitative aspect of things.

> So far I have regarded it only as the transference of Q'n from one neurone to another. But it must have still another characteristic, of a temporal nature; for the mechanics of the physicists have allowed this temporal characteristic to the other motions of masses in the external world as well. I speak of this as *period* for short. Thus I shall assume that all resistance of contact-barriers applies only to the transference of Q, but that the *period* of the neuronal motion is transmitted without inhibition in all directions, as though it were a process of induction (Ibid, p. 310).

Consciousness does not absorb the quantitative aspect of energy as do the other neurone systems.[40] Consciousness, being the last link in the neurone chain, is in charge of perceiving the qualitative aspect of the energy reaching it as a form of duration: a period. This period passes through the Φ and Ψ groups, but is not perceived by them as a quality, seeing that these groups operate in terms of quantity. In contrast, consciousness operates qualitatively, having been appropriated to the reception of periods / durations.

Pleasure and Unpleasure

The goal of the "Project" is to show how the psychic mechanism could be understood in neuro-physiological terms. However, as I previously stated, Freud's account is fascinating because his model works both ways. In essence, it also explains how psychological phenomena influence the neuro-physiological layer. At the heart of this possibility of influencing neuro-physiology are the sensations of pleasure and unpleasure.[41] "Besides the series

---

[40] In the following page of his text, Freud rectifies this claim, adding that a small amount of energy must still reach consciousness in order to allow its reception of qualities. Nevertheless, this energy dissolves without leaving any trace (Ibid, p. 311).

[41] In the psychoanalytic method, the pleasure principle is seen as opposed to the reality principle. This notion, finding its seeds in the "Project", is developed in several key texts, such as *The Interpretation of Dreams* [1900], chapter seven, and "Instincts and their Vicissitudes" [1915], undergoing a transformation, which I will later on discuss, in

of sensory qualities, it exhibits another series very different from that—the series of sensations of *pleasure and unpleasure*, which now calls for interpretation" (Freud, 1966, p. 312). The fact that Freud binds together consciousness and quality is of great importance. It is precisely this binding which allows him to posit pleasure and unpleasure as fundamental principles in the system of consciousness. Consciousness receives its data from the Ψ group, recognizing its qualitative aspect. Only thus is it capable of identifying the accumulation of energy in the system not only as tension but as unpleasure, and the release of energy not only as discharge but as pleasure.

> Since we have certain knowledge of a trend in psychical life towards *avoiding unpleasure*, we are tempted to identify that trend with the primary trend toward inertia. In that case *unpleasure* would have to be regarded as coinciding with a raising of level of Q'n or an increasing quantitative pressure: it would be the ω sensation when there is an increase of Q'n in ψ. Pleasure would be the sensation discharge. Since ω is assumed to be filled from ψ, the hypothesis would follow that when the level in ψ rises the cathexis in ω increases, and when, on the other hand, that level falls the cathexis diminishes. Pleasure and unpleasure would be the sensations in ω of its own cathexis, of its own level; and here ω and ψ would, as it were, represent intercommunicating vessels. In this manner the quantitative process in ψ would reach consciousness, once more as qualities (Ibid, p. 312).

Unless the period was transferred from the Ψ system to consciousness, the latter would have been unable to identify the energy it receives as possessing any qualities. The contents of consciousness are always already representations of quality. That which distinguishes pleasure and unpleasure from the other contents of consciousness is their function as the boundaries which shape the very process of thinking. As we have seen, consciousness, being part of the psychic mechanism, aspires to allow the discharge of the tension it harbors. Consequently, it aims at achieving pleasure and avoiding unpleasure.

Wishing, Avoiding and Ego

On the spectrum of experiences enabled by the psychic mechanism in relation to our modes of perceiving objects in the external world, we find, at one end, avoidance of the object and at the other, the desire to encounter it. Whenever we encounter an object, the process of our perception of it is regulated by the flow in the various neurone systems. When such an encounter brings satisfaction (pleasure), the system tends to keep on discharging tension via the pathway thereby established. This tendency is transcribed, in psychic life, as the wish to repeat the satisfying experience. When such encounters cause

---

texts such as "Beyond the Pleasure Principle" [1920] and "The Economic Problem of Masochism" [1924].

dissatisfaction, i.e. unpleasure, the psychic system strives to avoid any possible contact with such an object. These experiences are joined by several other psychic activities: whenever the encounter with the unsatisfying object is unavoidable, mechanisms of defense, such as repression, come into action; whenever there is a wish to encounter an object, the system must maintain internally the object's mnemic-image, which provides a temporary substitute for its actual perception. In order to exist, these two varieties of experience require a source of energy which is not dependant on the external world and is therefore always available. Such a source presupposes a higher level of organization regarding secondary functions: the storing of energy alongside its discharge. Freud refers to this kind of energy organization as Ego. The Ego is a group of neurones which is permanently cathected. Hence, it can only be located within the Ψ group, whose intra-cellular barriers are capable of sustaining its existence. The Ego neurone group is a collection of nuclear neurones, characterized by a high capacity for energy accumulation. Whenever the system requires energy to activate defense-mechanisms or preserve mnemic-images of wished for or avoided objects, this energy is released from the Ego, which thereby becomes a constitutive factor within the neuro-physiological array of the psychic mechanism.[42]

> For these two processes indicate that an organization has been formed in ψ whose presence interferes with passages [of quantity] which on the first occasion occurred in a particular way [i.e. accompanied by satisfaction or pain]. This organization is called the *'ego'*. It can easily be depicted if we consider that the regularly repeated reception of endogenous Q'n in certain neurones (of the nucleus) and the facilitating effect proceeding thence will produce a group of neurones which is constantly cathected and thus corresponds to the vehicle of the store required by the secondary function (Freud, 1966, p. 322-323).

Freud's depiction of the Ego as a collection of nuclear neurones providing secondary processes with energy indeed accounts for the problem of energy suspension and elucidates the source from which the aforementioned secondary activities receive their energy. However, a new problem arises. Since the encounter with the object leaves an internal trace, in the form of a pathway for the flow of energy which serves the system as a memory, we must inquire what keeps the system from considering an image possessed of great amounts of energy as a real object? In other words, what grants the system the ability to distinguish between the real object and an image powerfully cathected by the wish to encounter it? Or, from a different perspective, how

[42] In many ways, this description of the Ego as a repository of energy which enables the activation of various mental processes provided the theoretical background for the formulation of the goal of therapy: the release of the Ego from the hold of primary processes (irrational / pleasure principle) and facilitating the sound operation of secondary processes (rational / reality principle). See "Formulations on the Two Principles of Mental Functioning" [1911], (Freud, 1953).

does the psychic system tell truth from illusion? Articulating this problem leads Freud to the conclusion that pathological psychic activity indeed entails a failure, on the part of the mechanism, to make a proper distinction between the representation of the wished-for or avoided object and the object itself.

Freud is able to solve this problem through a process in which the mechanism performs a reality check using an internal test, which provides an indication of the representation's ontological status, that is, an indication of quality. When an object representation is present in consciousness and the urge for discharge increases, the Ego first suspends the discharge process, subsequently allowing, by means of additional cathexis, to see whether the object representation includes quality as well as quantity. We have seen that the perception of external objects involves information regarding the period of perceptual data in the form of quality. Consequently, should a representation be found, following inspection, lacking a qualitative aspect, the mechanism will know that it is facing a representation originating in the internal neurone system (Ψ) and that any attempt to discharge tension will lead to unpleasure.

> But if the wishful cathexis takes place subject to *inhibition*, as becomes possible when there is a cathected ego, a quantitative instance can be imagined in which the wishful cathexis, not being intense enough, produces no *indication of quality*, whereas the external perception would produce one. [...] It is accordingly *inhibition by the ego which makes possible a criterion for distinguishing between perception and memory* (Ibid, p. 326).

THE STATUS OF TIME IN THE "PROJECT"

Generally speaking, we might say that the change to which the psychic mechanism must adapt is the transition from primary to secondary functioning. If this transition is successful, the Ego becomes a constitutive factor in the psychic system, without which, or whenever its function is deficient, the difference between reality and illusion blurs or even disappears altogether. In general, the Ego's ability to function properly is dependent upon its being cathected with energy. That is, in order for the Ego to be able to tell reality from illusion, it must undergo a healthy developmental process, in which the notions of pleasure and unpleasure are prominent[43].

While it may seem, at first, that the "Project" is best understood as a strictly neurological description of the functional aspects of the brain and the nervous system, this is not the case. The "Project" exceeds such definitions as it contains a theoretical model of psychic processes. The physio-neurological facet indeed provides the grounds for explaining these processes, but the very

---

[43] Such a depiction of the Ego as an authority which underlines action and enables the distinction between reality and illusion is elaborated further in Freud's thinking as the formation of the Ego becomes a central aspect of his method and as the structural model finds its place at the fore of psychoanalytic theory [1923].

depiction of consciousness as capable of distinguishing reality from illusion and pleasure from unpleasure as well as the constitutive role of the Ego in relation to the perception of reality suggest that the "Project" is better construed as an epistemological essay relying on neuro-physiological foundations. Therefore, in this section, I would like to propose an epistemological reading of the "Project", one which would seek out that part of the psychic mechanism which allows Freud to connect human experience with the external world and uncover the specific notion of time in which this connection is grounded.

According to Freud, the relationship between human beings and the world is embedded in the relationship between the nervous system and external stimuli, which pass through the pathways of neurone networks subjected to the principle of constancy and its modifications and under the Ego's control. Hence, we are facing a system of energy flow, or, alternately, a system of data flow which manifests itself as a psychic system. This system protects itself from states of unbearable energetic tension by learning the patterns of energy flow, channeling it according to its own needs, establishing a source of energy to fuel activities in the external world and examining the ontological status of the representations of consciousness. The link Freud describes between human beings and the world is in fact a neurological-cognitive link. From an epistemological point of view, this link is constituted through the psychic contents present in consciousness in the following manner: neurone system Φ represents sensory data (meaning, the way neurones are cathected in relation to external stimuli); neurone system Ψ creates representations of the array of neurones cathected by external stimuli (thereby it comprises the mental contents of consciousness); finally, system ω is the system which is conscious of these contents.

The system of consciousness, as we have seen, is no ordinary neurone system. The processes taking place inside it, as the result of encountering Ψ system neurones, arouse an altogether different kind of stimulus than those pertaining to the Φ and Ψ systems. In these systems, stimuli are a response to the quantity of energy passing through; in consciousness, however, stimuli evoke a sense of quality. That is, as far as the psychic mechanism is concerned, the quantitative and qualitative aspects of energy are utterly distinct. Why was Freud in need of such a distinction? In explaining the aforementioned process, Freud approaches it by addressing what he termed "the problem of quality". In other words, the theoretical model he established was unable to account for conscious phenomena solely in terms of quantity.

> Consciousness gives us what are called *qualities*— sensations which are *different* in a great multiplicity of ways and whose *difference* is distinguished according to its relations with the external world. Within this difference there are series, similarities and so on, but there are in fact no quantities in it (Freud, 1966, p. 308).

Since quantitative data fall short of representing the world as we know it, and since the latter transgresses the boundaries of a quantitative account, Freud was obliged to add another element to his system. What is interesting about this element, as the above quote suggests, is that unlike the way in which quantitative data is moderately reduced, its energy channeled in order for the psychic system to be able to remember and recognize the object in front of it, qualities emerge into the psychic matrix exactly as they are in the external world. According to Freud, this new data is not processed by the system and is thereby not subject to judgment and thus to misconception, or, in psychological terms: illusion, hallucination and repression do not apply to it. Furthermore, it also evades the division into primary and secondary processes. In fact, we could say that it is nothing other than pure data.

As we have seen, the one factor enabling the psychic mechanism to acknowledge the qualities of things is an explicitly temporal phenomenon, one which Freud calls a period; meaning, the quantity of energy flow, or the periodicity of that flow in the sense of the time period in which a certain quantity of energy is in flow. Adding the temporal duration of energy flow (from the perspective of the psychic mechanism) or of the encounter with the object giving rise to stimulus (from an external perspective) to the process of perception is no mere coincidence. From an epistemological point of view, in order for something to appear as having a qualitative aspect, it must have duration in time. The methodological requirements of explaining the human psyche empirically and, in particular, accounting for sensory perception as a process, preclude any explication of how objects appear to consciousness as possessing duration (in time). In other words, if the representation of physical stimuli is true to its original, we might ask how consciousness is at all capable of observing objects as persisting in time, rather than just gaze at a sequence of momentary representations. In fact, Freud's theoretical model is based on a worldview which posits an eternal, everlasting present existing in an a-temporal dimension. It is only due to the addition of the notion of the period, which is superimposed on Freud's conceptual foundations, that we are finally able to describe and comprehend human behavior in time. In fact, we might say that time, as a phenomenon, is not integral to the Freudian model but is rather imposed as a Deus ex machina on his mechanistic plot.

The existence of the psychic mechanism which Freud introduces in the "Project" is revealed as utterly dependant upon the working assumption, that a period is capable of passing intact through neurone networks and emerging before consciousness as quality. However, this assumption is problematic not only due to the amnesty Freud grants the period vis-à-vis psychic mechanisms, but rather in the implicit assertion it makes about the role of time in the psychic mechanism in general. Actually, in addressing the problem of quality, Freud has already stumbled upon the problem of the period. Now that we are aware of the implicit cardinality of time to the psychic mechanism, we ought to investigate the particular role time has in this system, i.e., its ontological status.

Another way of understanding the ontological status of time in the "Project" is by trying to consider it as an integral part of the cognitive system. We must rule out this possibility, as we have already seen that time is utterly unaffected by the psychic mechanism, nor is it represented in the neurone networks or in consciousness. Another way of construing it is to regard it as a phenomenon which belongs entirely to the objective world. This is precisely what Freud does. In his view, the period supplies consciousness with a kind of neurone-count which corresponds to the duration of the stimulus, granting it immediate access to the temporal aspect. That is, as far as the psychic mechanism is concerned, time functions as a linear sequence of intervals (stimuli), in which each stimulus follows another just as any given moment follows another in the external world. It is in this, in Freud's implicit equation of the phenomenon of time with empirical data, that we find our point of departure for understanding the ontological status of time in the "Project".

Much like Aristotle, who believed time to be that which we count throughout change, Freud implicitly constitutes in his "Project" a notion of time as nothing other than the relation between the quantity of neurones and their rhythm, thereby considering the phenomenon of time and empirical change as one and the same. In other words, Freud reduces the phenomenon of time to the very sequence of intervals. The problem with this approach is that, as we mentioned in the previous chapter, the sequence (of stimuli, in this case) itself cannot account for the phenomenon of the period. Alternately, the sequence of intervals already presupposes the existence of the period as a duration which manifests itself between moments and within each moment. In fact, the theoretical model offered by Freud, much like the Aristotelian notion of time, is imprisoned in a linear view of time which fails to distinguish the phenomenon of time from empirical phenomena. We consequently find, at the root of Freud's "Project", a notion of time based upon a linear temporal axis comprised of intervals that in themselves have no duration. These intervals succeed one another in a manner which, though quantifiable, still remains fundamentally a-temporal. Freud's superimposition of the period on his theoretical model is not an isolated incident, but a symptom of his entire theoretical framework.

It is time to tie our discussion of Freud more explicitly to the Heideggerian question of temporality which lies in the background. We might say that, from Heidegger's point of view, the temporal framework underlying Freudian discourse treats duration in the very same way it treats entities, thereby evoking an understanding of human beings as essentially similar to any other entity. In other words, Freudian theory is unaware of this ontological difference, of the fact that the meaning of the human world is principally conditioned by the way we project ourselves onto our existential horizons of possibilities, as a constant expression of the self-transcendence embedded in the temporal-ecstatic structure of our world. We might argue further, that the notion of time residing at the very heart of the psychoanalytic method is in fact derived from what Heidegger refers to as temporality:

> As the Dasein encounters time, time gets interpreted also as something somehow extant, particularly if it reveals itself as a being in a certain connection precisely with extant nature. [...] The time that is known as the now and as a manifold and succession of nows is an *extant*

> *sequence*. The nows appear to be intratemporal. They come and go like beings; like extant entities they perish, becoming no longer extant (Heidegger, 1982, p. 272).

It is especially interesting to look into an actual encounter between Heidegger and psychoanalysis, as that which took place in the collected lectures of his *Zollikon Seminars* (Heidegger, 1987). Seen against the background of his entire corpus, this anthology is quite out of the ordinary. It is the result of the joint effort of two thinkers who created a dialogue between two disciplines which, at first glance, seem to belong to two distinct fields of meaning: psychoanalysis and philosophy. Medard Boss, a Swiss psychoanalyst who took great interest in the work of Heidegger, saw fit to write to him after the Second World War (1947), asking for clarifications regarding possible relations between ontological insights regarding human existence and the psychological understanding of it. To his surprise, Heidegger met this challenge. Their correspondence and their many meetings led to a series of academic sessions, held in the years 1959-1969, at Boss' home in Zollikon, Switzerland. In this collection of lectures, addressing psychiatry doctoral students, Heidegger discusses the possibility of understanding the human psyche and neurotic behavior in light of his ontological inquiry. This work is unique as in it Heidegger enters in dialogue with the psychological method in general and the psychoanalytic method in particular:

> In any case, much can be presumed already. For instance, the disturbed relationship to time accompanying some forms of mental illness can only be understood from the human background of original, significant, and datable time. This relationship cannot be understood in terms of calculated time, which originates with the idea of sequence of empty, "qualityless" points (Ibid, p. 44).

As we can gather from the above quote, this encounter between philosophy and psychoanalysis, Between Heidegger and Boss, was charged with explicit and penetrating criticism of the manner in which medicine and psychology approach the task of describing, analyzing and treating mental disorders, as phenomena occurring within a pure, homogenous sequence of time intervals.

FREUD AS BRENTANO'S STUDENT

In looking over Freud's biography and examining his first steps in the world of academia and research, we find a small yet particularly qualified group of teachers,[44] who paved the way theoretically for his development of the

[44] I am referring to Ernst Brücke, Theodor Meynert, Jean-Martin Charcot, Hippolyte Bernheim and Josef Breuer; all whom, without exception, saw themselves as pioneers seeking to study and uncover the human being in positivistic terms. Positivism had its sway over academic circles in the late 19th century, originating in the new worldview

psychoanalytic method. Among the first encounters Freud had with the key figures of the academic world of the late 19th century, his encounter with philosopher Franz Brentano (1838-1917) stands out in particular. This section will focus on describing the conceptual connections between Freud and Brentano in the attempt to show that Brentano's epistemology provided Freud with the theoretical framework through which he could forge his ideas. A precise evaluation of the influence of Brentano's epistemology on the Freudian formulation of the structure of human consciousness will show, in the following sections: a. that Freud had integrated Brentano's notion of time into his doctrine and b. how this notion of time came *de facto* to shape his understanding of human existence.

Even though the fact that Freud was a student of Brentano was well known to begin with, a comprehensive and exhaustive study of the extent to which this encounter had influenced the birth of psychoanalysis was carried out only recently. Aviva Cohen (1998) indeed studied the conceptual relationship between Brentano's theory of intentionality and the psychoanalytic method, but she had not elaborated on the perspective which I find central to the Freud-Brentano connection: the notion of time underlying the theoretical framework of the psychoanalytic endeavor. The question of the notion of time fundamental to Freud's structure of the mind and its conceptual proximity to Brentano's, was left altogether unmentioned in her study.

In discussing the birth of psychoanalysis, it is common practice to bring up philosophy as a source of influence, though not as theoretical grounds forming an essential part of Freud's primary motivation to develop psychoanalysis. The young Freud was not only in the right place at the right time in order to learn what contemporary science had to say of the human being, indeed, there was something in his research perspective regarding the findings of his day that was of additional value. As Geerardyn (1997) suggests:

> Freud's psychology neither ensues logically from scientific frames of reference familiar to him nor from what he could learn from Meynert, Charcot, Brenheim or Breuer about neurological and psychological theory. Rather, his theory results from his adoption of a new epistemological view point. Once Freud had well and truly subscribed to the view point on the operation of psychical mechanism, it became possible to speak of a logical dialectic with the clinic (pp. 20-21).

That which set Freud apart from his esteemed contemporaries lies specifically in the epistemological emphasis characteristic of his thinking. That is, the birth of psychoanalysis was made possible due to Freud's ability to reexamine what he had learned from his various teachers in the fields of physiology, neurology and mental pathology in light of his philosophical proficiency in epistemology.

---

provided by 18th century Enlightenment. This new worldview demanded that all research be purged of any trace of the theological or metaphysical thinking which had held the academic reins for centuries.

The ability to conduct his research by relying on his epistemological knowledge is far from accidental: his first years in the academic world provided the perfect environment for the acquisition of such knowledge. In his first year in academy, at the University of Vienna in 1873, Freud (1990) wrote to his friend Silberstein: "Of the next, my first university year, I can give you the news that I shall devote all of it to purely humanistic studies, which have nothing to do with my later field but will not be unprofitable for all that" (p. 24).

THE THEORETICAL CONNECTION BETWEEN FREUD OF 1895 AND BRENTANO OF 1873 - A DISCUSSION OF AVIVA COHEN'S INTERPRETATION

As mentioned above, Aviva Cohen published, following her doctoral thesis, her findings regarding Brentano's immense influence on Freud's thinking. While Cohen (2002) treated several key ideas which have found their way from Brentano's doctrine to the Freudian method (pp. 88-100), we will focus on her treatment of two of the central notions of the "Project": the division of the system of perception into internal and external facets and embracing the intentional link between consciousness and mental representation as the theoretical grounds for describing the inability to distinguish hallucinations from reality.

1. Cohen demonstrates that Freud's (1953) discussion in *The Interpretation of Dreams*, in which he claims that dreams grant better access to unconscious thinking than wakefulness, in fact rests on Brentano's epistemological distinction between internal and external perception: "In waking life the suppressed material in the mind is prevented from finding expression and is cut off from internal perception ['Innere Wahrnemung']" (p. 608).

2. Brentano's concept of intentionality enables him to distinguish between the object appearing in consciousness as an external perception (the product of sensory qualities) and inner perceptions, generally divided into two categories: *realia*, the inner perception of objects, and *irrealia*, the perception of things other than objects, such as thoughts etc. The mental act could be directed at any intentional object, whether real or imaginary, as well as any other mental act, on the sole condition that it is not identical to itself. As each mental act entails an object, the intentional object does not have to exist in the external world. Therefore, mental objects must possess a different status than that of external ones. While we can be certain of the existence of ideas, sensations and emotions, we can never fully determine the validity or falsity of external perception (Brentano, 1973, pp. 10-11). Since our sensory data is misleading, we are utterly incapable of ascertaining whether the true nature of the world corresponds to the way the world appears to us. In fact, sensory perception creates a kind of illusory certainty, which leads us to determine that physical objects are actually real.

This unique epistemological attitude grants mental phenomena primacy over their physical counterparts, establishing a possible state of affairs in which something as particular as a 'unicorn' could be real (Realität), even though it does not exist in the external world. According to Brentano (1973), the experience we gather throughout life teaches us to inspect our inner perceptions and distinguish between real ideas, images or fears and false ones (p. 20).

In the "Project", when Freud discusses the role of the Ego, he is in fact discussing something very similar to what Brentano is thus portraying. In principle, as I have demonstrated, the Ego, according to Freud, is meant to store energy in order to facilitate the proper functioning of secondary processes: "It is accordingly *inhibition by the ego which makes possible a criterion for distinguishing between perception and memory*" (Freud, 1966, p. 326).

The danger which forces the psychic mechanism to make use of the energy stored in the Ego is that of being unable to distinguish an internal representation of a memory from that of an actual object. That is, just as Brentano sees inner representations as possessed of a potential for reality though lacking any external existence, Freud's psychic mechanism is in danger of recognizing internal representations as reality.[45] Alternately, as Cohen (2002) states in discussing Brentano's distinction:

> The same distinction is articulated by Freud. In his 'A Project for a Scientific Psychology' he began to formulate the theory he would later call 'reality-testing'. He explained that an essential function of the ego was its ability to defend itself from the prospect of total belief in hallucinatory fulfilment. There would, for example, be disastrous consequences if one continuously mistook dreams of eating and drinking for reality (p. 95).

Cohen demonstrates how intimately Freud was familiar with his teacher's epistemological thinking. She points out the exact places where Freud clearly utilized Brentano's epistemological assumptions in order to produce a coherent psychological account of the psychic mechanism as a cognitive system, which is capable of explaining human development and behaviour.

Our discussion of the "Project" brought us to the conclusion that the notion of time prevalent therein is not an integral part of the Freudian model, but rather a Deus ex machina, superimposed upon his mechanistic plot.

---

[45] Cohen points out that Freud further develops this issue in a later essay entitled "On Negation" [1925]. Although this text has Freud discussing the pleasure-Ego in a manner corresponding to Brentano's categories of love and hate and despite the fact that Cohen indicates that the pleasure and reality principles can be traced back to this influence, I will not dwell on these subjects as my focus is solely on the manner in which the theoretical framework of the "Project" reproduces the epistemological assumptions set down by Brentano in 1873.

Therefore, it is quite unexpected to find that Cohen's fascinating study contains no reference to the simple fact that, alongside Brentano's epistemology, Freud also took in its underlying notion of time.

BRENTANO'S EPISTEMOLOGY[46]

The Conceptual Framework for Psychology from an Empirical Standpoint

In this section, I wish to demonstrate the manner in which Brentano establishes his epistemology (1871-1876), in order to pave the way for our discussion of how the issue of time became so central to this theory. In the beginning of the first chapter of *Psychology from an Empirical Standpoint*, Brentano (1973) writes:

> We have no right, therefore, to believe that the objects of so-called external perception really exist as they appear to us. Indeed, they demonstrably do not exist outside of us. In contrast to that which really and truly exists, they are mere phenomena (pp. 10-11).

This statement must be read in light of traditional western discourse, which puts the existence of the external world in doubt, turning it into a philosophical problem (the ontological question). This problem outlined a course of thinking employed by philosophers such as Descartes, Hume and Kant, who considered epistemology the proper method for settling this issue and the proper path for providing the natural sciences with sound theoretical foundations. Brentano, as well, believes that we must focus our philosophical inquiry on our way of perceiving the world, rather than the world in itself. Meaning that he finds the philosophical endeavor as, first and foremost, an attempt to answer the epistemological question: how can we know the world?

> Just as in sense perception we encounter phenomena such as warmth, color and sound, in inner perception we encounter manifestations of thinking, feeling and willing. But we never encounter that something of which these things are properties. It is a fiction to which no reality of any sort corresponds, or whose existence could not possibly be proved, even if it did exist. Obviously, then, it is not an object of science. Hence natural science may not be defined as the science of bodies nor may psychology be defined as the science of the soul. Rather, the former should be thought of simply as science of physical phenomena, and the latter, analogously, as the science of mental phenomena (Ibid, p. 11).

Seeing that, according to Brentano, science essentially lacks an immediate access to the manner in which things exist in themselves, he insists on an

---

[46] By this I am referring to *Psychology from an Empirical Standpoint* and the lectures given in the years 1871-1876.

epistemological reform regarding our understanding of the natural sciences and the sciences of the soul. As we cannot consider the natural sciences a method preoccupied with the study of bodies, Brentano suggests that we ought to conceive of it as studying physical phenomena. Accordingly, we are to conceive of the science of the soul (psychology) as a science of mental phenomena. In his opinion, this division does not lead to the establishment of two distinct scientific methods, as both the study of physical phenomena and that of mental phenomena are subjected to the same general rules: the coexistence and succession of phenomena.

> The same thing is true of psychology. The phenomena reveled by inner perception are also subject to laws. […] the laws of the coexistence and succession of mental phenomena remain the object of investigation (Ibid, p. 12).

The philosophical task Brentano takes upon himself in his book is to describe the human psyche (psychology) while relying on the existence of mental phenomena. Although it might be accurate to argue that Brentano sees science as a study not of objects but strictly of phenomena (whether physical or mental), in practicing the science of mental phenomena in order to discuss the psyche, he makes full use of the categories of coexistence and succession. In other words, Brentano genuinely looks upon these categories as the theoretical framework of any science of phenomena, thereby positing his study within the confines of the empirical worldview, as the title of his book, *Psychology from an Empirical Standpoint*, explicitly suggests.

Enclosed within Brentano's thinking (which relinquishes the ontological question) the phenomenological solution seems readily applicable to the natural sciences. Nevertheless, this is not the case for any attempt to apply it to the science of the soul. Employed in regards to the natural sciences, this phenomenological solution enables the researcher to keep using standard methods of investigation, such as the measuring of time and distance, in order to grasp the character of physical phenomena. This is made possible through the extensive and immediate use of the categories of coexistence and succession. In other words, that which is already at hand for the natural scientist is the past, as a coordinate in space and time from which she could theoretically begin to measure the motion of an object.

> All physical phenomena, it is said, have extension and spatial location […] The opposite, however, is true of mental phenomena; thinking, willing and the like appear without extension and without spatial location (Ibid, p. 85).

If extension in space and the ability to be located within it indeed pertain only to physical phenomena, we must ask in what way does mental phenomena become accessible to consciousness. Brentano's last argument is especially troublesome if we fathom it in light of his methodological assertion regarding the subjugation of both natural science and that of the soul to the laws of coexistence and succession. As we shall see, Brentano posits this problem in the context of the question of memory: "In all the experimental sciences memory makes possible the accumulation of observed facts for the purpose of establishing general truths" (Ibid, p. 35).

Could memory function in the science of mental phenomena as it does in the science of physical ones? If we wish to grant memory the same status it enjoys in the natural sciences, we soon discover that as for the science of the soul, we are denied the very possibility of seeing mental phenomena as events taking place in the present.

> To be sure, this procedure, which we could call observation in memory, is obviously not fully equivalent to genuine observation of present events. As everyone knows, memory is, to a great extent, subject to illusion [...] when the phenomena which are retained by the memory are substituted for those of inner perception, they introduce uncertainty and the possibility of many sorts of self-deception [...] (Ibid, Ibid).

Brentano hopes to solve this problem by expanding the borders of empirical psychology to include the consciousness of the other, for which he finds evidence mainly in the phenomenon of language (Ibid, pp. 37-38). In his view, the fact that we are able to learn of the mental state of others through verbalized observations and accounts provides us with indirect knowledge of the existence of mental phenomena in the present. Whether or not we agree with this problematic solution, with which Brentano addresses the issue of the present existence of mental phenomena, we might say that in principal, his method came across this difficulty since it is now paying its dues for providing such a methodological solution to the ontological question. That is, abandoning the inquiry into the conditions enabling the object's unity in the external world generates the problem of temporal unity regarding mental phenomena in the inner world. Consequently, Brentano must account for temporal unity as derived from mental processes themselves.

The Processes of Consciousness: Intentionality and Presentations

As stated, Brentano conceives of the mental process as an empirical procedure based on intentional acts:

> Every mental phenomenon is characterized by what the scholastics of the middle-ages called the intentional (or mental) inexistence of an object, and what we might call, though not wholly unambiguously, reference to a content, direction toward an object [...] every mental phenomenon includes something as object within itself (Ibid, p. 88).

Intentionality is the trademark of all mental phenomena. That is, without intentionality, they were not possible. Mental phenomena are divided into two types: presentations on the one hand, and mental states such as beliefs, desires and judgments, i.e., the cognitive faculties of consciousness. Mental states are derived from presentations, meaning that the latter possess a more primary status among mental phenomena: "We may consider the following definition of mental phenomena as indubitably correct: they are either presentations or they are based upon presentations" (Ibid, p. 85). Any indication of quality appearing among mental phenomena which cannot be labeled as presentation is a product of the cognitive functioning of consciousness. Brentano makes a clear distinction between presentation, the act of presenting and the contents of this presentation: "by 'presentation' we do not mean that which is presented, but rather the presenting of it" (Ibid, p. 77).

Presentation is directed at physical phenomena (objects) while its content exists only intentionally, meaning that it is not part of the presentation per se. The content belongs to the presentation only as part of the intentionality characteristic of mental phenomena. The science of the soul is a science of mental phenomena in which presentation and content are intentionally unified. Presentations themselves are divided in two: outer presentations and inner presentations. Inner presentations are described as acts of reflection regarding mental and emotional contents, while outer ones are constituted by the emergence of physical phenomena into consciousness, in the form of sensory presentations. Presentations are therefore distinguished according to the typology of their contents: while the contents of inner presentations are mental and emotional states, those of outer presentations are sensory data.

According to Brentano, our knowledge of the world is drawn from mental phenomena, which are fathomed in light of intentionality. Intentionality is seen as the most fundamental law of consciousness, connecting presentation, contents and the intentional object. Objects are not perceived as objects in themselves, but as intentional objects, available to consciousness through what Brentano had termed 'outer presentations'. That is, presentations whose contents are sensory qualities such as color, light, sound, scent and temperature. At this stage of his argument regarding the establishment of his epistemology, Brentano warns the reader that even if science is able to break sensations (colors, odors, etc.) down to their primary physical elements, we will still be in need of further laws explaining our ability to encounter these sensations.

> Even if physicists had reduced all the causes which produce our sensations of colour, sound, smell etc. […] any attempt to further reduce the number of such laws would be hopeless and unreasonable (Ibid, p. 47).

In fact, what Brentano means to say is that we are unable to fully comprehend our sensations without initially positing sensory data in the framework of meaning provided by the epistemological structure. Essentially, the structure of consciousness is that which makes possible the intentional encounter with sensory data. At the outset of his third chapter, he writes:

> External perception, therefore, is and always will be unreliable. On the other hand, we are absolutely certain of the veracity of inner perception, because in this case both the presentation and the real object of the presentation exist within us (Ibid, p. 139).

Our acquaintance with objects is, in fact, an internal perception taking place between outer and inner presentations. In other words, the very event of consciousness comes to life in the intentional space between inner and outer presentations. Consciousness does not gaze out at objects in the world but is directed toward the intentional array linking both types of presentations. As a mental phenomenon, the inner process of cognition is comprised of three levels: presentation, judgment and pleasure/unpleasure. As we have seen, it is on the level of presentation that consciousness perceives external presentations. On the second level, a system of judgment is at work, aiming at affirming or denying the existence of objects:

> No one who pays attention to what goes within himself when he hears or sees and perceives his act of hearing or seeing could be mistaken about the fact that this judgment of inner perception [...] consists rather in the simple affirmation of the mental phenomenon which is present in inner consciousness (Ibid, p. 142).

On the third level we find the emotional state related to the object (love/hate or pleasure/unpleasure):

> Experience shows that there exist in us not only a presentation and a judgment, but frequently a third kind of consciousness of the mental act, namely a feeling which refers to this act [...] It may be either pleasure, as when we hear a soft, pure young voice, or of displeasure, as when we hear the scratching of a violin badly played (Ibid, pp. 143-4).

The epistemological structure put forward by Brentano - that of cognition as a mental phenomenon – is graphically demonstrated in the following diagram:

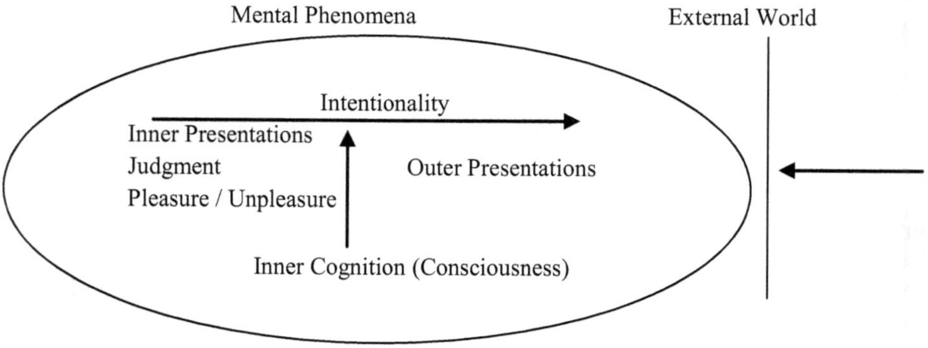

Diagram 1: The Epistemological Structure According to Brentano

Now that Brentano's cognitive array is spread out before us in great detail, we can more readily comprehend his assertion that although the unicorn does not exist, it might still be considered real. By an act of judgment, inner perception can identify the unicorn as an inner presentation. The reality of a presentation is determined by a system of judgments which already operates according to the clear distinction between existence and reality, inside and outside, affirming or denying the imminent presence of intentional objects, rather than their existence.

This description of cognitive processes characteristic of Brentano's epistemology leaves no doubt as to the source of inspiration for the psychic model Freud introduces in his "Project". In the beginning of *Psychology from an Empirical Standpoint*, Brentano states:

> Not only may physical states be aroused by physical states and mental states by mental, but it is also the case that physical states have mental consequences and mental states have physical consequences [...] the psychophysicist, too, will have to investigate the first physical effects of mental causes (Ibid, pp. 6-7).

In response to this very cue, Freud begins his "Project" with the following words: "The intention is to furnish a psychology that shall be a natural science: that is, to represent psychical processes as quantitatively determinate states of specifiable material particles" (Freud, 1966, p. 295). Furthermore, the structure suggested by Freud could also be described graphically:

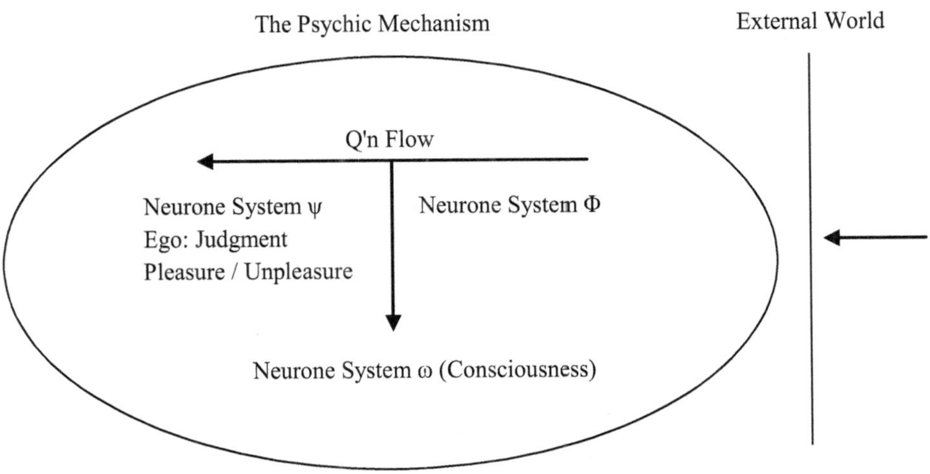

Diagram 2: The Epistemological Structure according to Freud

After observing these two diagrams, we can say that Freud's "Project" reformulates Brentano's epistemological structure in physiological terms, while retaining the quantitative principle. As Cohen indicates, Freud maintained the distinction between inner and outer presentations; the intentional character of the link between consciousness and objects is also maintained, due to the location of consciousness between systems Φ and Ψ; finally, just as Brentano considers objects which do not exist in the external world as real, the same holds true for the psychic mechanism according to Freud. Indeed, Freud's psychic mechanism is analogous to Brentano's structure of consciousness.

So far, we have stayed within the limits of Cohen's discussion of the relationship between Freud and Brentano: we have provided in-depth accounts of cognitive processes and demonstrated that by foregoing the search for the conditions allowing the temporal unity of objects, the same problem resurfaces in Brentano's epistemological account of mental phenomena.

Brentano's work will not furnish us with a deep and detailed description addressing the problem of the temporal unity of mental objects. Nevertheless, Edmund Husserl's (1966) *The Phenomenology of Internal Time-Consciousness* contains a reliable account of Brentano's treatment of the problem of the duration of the temporal object. At the outset of this text, we find a report of the lectures Husserl attended which were given by Brentano at the University of Vienna in 1871 and which dealt with the question of the origin of time. Freud became acquainted with their contents about two years later, having joined Brentano's intellectual circle and having attended his lectures and seminars in the years 1873-1876. This analysis of the notion of duration on which Brentano's epistemological structure is based proves that time functions as the Archimedean point enabling the synchronization of internal and external worlds, that Freud's failure to distinguish the phenomenon of time from empirical phenomena stems from Brentano's conceptualization of time, and finally, that time as a concept, though never explicitly formulated throughout Freud's thinking, operates implicitly as the precondition for the existence of his epistemology.

TEMPORAL CONSCIOUSNESS IN BRENTANO'S THOUGHT ACCORDING TO HUSSERL

In order to explain the problematic nature of the phenomenon of time, Brentano chooses to analyze the way we listen to a melody. This choice exemplifies the issue of object duration, as music is a paradigmatic instance of an object persisting in time. The problem of the duration of temporal objects comes to the fore when we try to explain the cognition of music.

In our attempt to account for the cognitive process involved in listening to music along the lines of Brentano's theoretical framework (that is, an epistemology grounded in empirical elements), we are faced with two essential options: the first suggests that after each note is played and perceived by a listener, it altogether vanishes from the system of perception; the second sees it as preserved within this system. Brentano rules out the first option, as having no conscious trace of notes played precludes us from hearing the interrelatedness of consecutive notes. In this case, we would have heard a new note each time, unable to put together the melody comprised by their juxtaposition. Hence, and we are now embracing the second option, while the melody is played, the single notes which make up the tune do not disappear but leave a mark (trace) which allows us to follow their interaction. Brentano must now account for the manner in which notes remain available to consciousness. In discussing a note's presence in consciousness, we are actually discussing its presentation, or outer presentation to be exact. Nevertheless, not even the existence of such a presentation in consciousness provides a full guarantee for the existence of an object possessing temporal qualities. As long as the presentation remains absolutely identical to the presented phenomenon and internally unchangeable, the only available model for the perception of music would facilitate the hearing of bits and pieces that are essentially cacophonic. As Husserl articulates in describing Brentano's explanation:

> Were they to remain unmodified, then instead of melody we should have a chord of simultaneous notes or rather a disharmonious jumble of sounds such as we should obtain if we stuck all the notes simultaneously that have already been sounded (Ibid, p. 30).

This leads us to the conclusion that any outer presentation of physical phenomena (notes) must itself be susceptible to constant change. The problem is therefore two-fold: on one level we might say that since the epistemological system is principally established within an empirical framework of meaning which maintains a parallel relationship with sensory data, it is unclear on what terms this internal change supposedly attributed to mental objects is even possible. On another level, we might say that not only are presentations required to maintain symmetry with physical phenomena, they also presuppose the possibility of simultaneous acts of consciousness. Returning to our musical example, we find that no sequence of consciousness, as closely bound to note presentations as it may be, could originate any consciousness of the sequence itself. A continuous consciousness of any enduring note already entails the simultaneous consciousness of various parts and aspects of that note. Thus, presentation and the consciousness thereof cannot provide the origin of temporal consciousness. Were consciousness itself the source of the mental object's temporal aspect, this would have required an impossible cognitive process through which presentations, already conscious and appearing in relation to other conscious presentations, would require a consciousness of their consciousness and so forth, ad infinitum. Any comprehension of time, therefore, already presupposes or requires a comprehension of duration.

> For the comprehension of a sequence of representations (A and B, for example) it is necessary that they be the absolutely simultaneous objects of referential [beziehended] cognition which embraces them completely and indivisibly in a single act. All representations of a direction, a

> passage, or a distance–in short, everything which includes the comparison of several elements and expresses the relation between them–can be conceived only as the product of a temporally comprehensive act of cognition. Such representation would all be impossible if the act of representation itself were completely merged in temporal succession (Ibid, pp. 40-41).

Brentano finds his solution for the problem of mental object duration through a psychological law he terms "the law of primordial associations", as Husserl puts it, quoting his teacher:

> Brentano believed he had found the solution to the problem in the primordial associations, in the "genesis of the immediate presentations of memory [Gedächtnisvorstellungen] which, according to the law that admits no exceptions, are joined to particular presentations of perception without mediation" (Ibid, pp. 29-30).

Consequently, the notion of duration stems from "the law of primordial associations" and outer presentations are divided into two types: immediate and non-immediate. While immediate presentations, those of sensory data, are analogous to the latter, representing phenomena quantitatively, non-immediate presentations represent the temporal aspect of sensory data, facilitating the access to the qualitative aspect of mental objects. Termed "phantastic presentations" by Brentano, these non-immediate presentations *de facto* create the temporal aspect of mental objects.

> We arrive at the idea of succession only if the earlier sensation does not persist unaltered in consciousness but in the manner described is specifically modified, that is, is continuously modified from moment to moment. In going into phantasy, the sensation preserves its constantly varying temporal character; from moment to moment the content thus seems to be shoved back more and more. This modification, however, is no longer the business of sensation; it is brought about through the stimulus. The stimulus produces the actual content of sensation. If the stimulus disappears, the sensation also disappears. But the sensation itself now becomes productive. It produces a phantasy idea [Phantasievorstellung] like, or nearly like, itself with regard to content and enriched by temporal character (Ibid, p. 32).

Brentano's notion of time upholds the empirical foundations of the epistemological structure as it appears in consciousness as the product of cognitive processes in which immediate presentations engender phantasy presentations. In other words, a sonic stimulus leads to a sonic presentation, which leads to a phantastic image of duration in consciousness. Phantasy presentations facilitate the link between various presentations of sensory data. Whenever we are conscious of perceiving data from the senses, a phantastic presenting is taking place, producing presentations which linger but a little while in consciousness before fading away. The result of this process is that the mental content of the perceived object is continually produced, while the vividness of its perception, from the perspective of consciousness, gradually decreases. Explicitly, Brentano on the one hand maintains his empirical presuppositions in allowing sensory data to be perceived sequentially, assuming that physical phenomena also follow sequentially along a linear axis of time; on the other hand, in order to solve the problem of temporal object duration, he creates a system which, following the rules of empirical epistemology, manufactures a sense of duration through association. Implicitly, the epistemological consequence of the associative procedure is that the phenomenon of temporal duration itself (being the very phenomenon of time) is not a real, independent phenomenon, but an array of cognitive images interwoven into the matrix of immediate presentations and revealed to consciousness in the form of temporal awareness.

SUMMARY

The solution Freud introduces for the matter of qualities in a system of consciousness established on quantitative principles is inspired by Brentano. Freud, who, according to my argument, took it upon himself in the "Project" to formulate Brentano's epistemological structure in physiological terms, ran up against the same problem as his teacher – that of duration. Developing the physiological aspect of the epistemological structure, Freud referred to this very problem, and with a good deal of sense, as the problem of quality. As stated above, Freud sees quality as information reaching consciousness through what he termed the period of energy flow: a measurement which, while not passing through the neurone system in the same manner as Q'n, is still available to consciousness. Freud could not explain just how this temporal data goes through; he could only indicate that it does. That is, just like Brentano, Freud was careful not to equate this period with strictly sensory data, granting the cognitive process the possibility of perceiving its information as it reaches consciousness.

Both thinkers made attempts to resolve the problem of mental object duration or quality by adding another factor into their system: Brentano added phanatsy presentations and Freud introduced the period of energy flow. However, these solutions do not fully address the problem: in both cases, duration is the direct result of the flow of sensory data. In fact, duration is superimposed upon sensory data, described as a succession of consecutive facts, revealing that this information is already arranged along a linear timeline. The notion of duration in which the epistemological structure is grounded proves, in both cases, to be an Archimedean point enabling the coordination of internal and external worlds. Had this information not been added to the cognitive mechanism, the system of consciousness would have remained isolated from any knowledge of the world, and furthermore, it would have been functioning without any idea about its own existence. By establishing his model of the psyche according to Brentano's epistemology, Freud unconsciously incorporated its underlying notion of time. From this moment on, the further development of Freudian psychoanalysis was routed along a specific path, from which it was never diverted, not by any of its creator's writings. Along this path of development, psychoanalysis explains the phenomenon of temporality, construed by the phenomenological tradition as the most fundamental phenomenon in human existence, as the product of a cognitive system of presentations, as a necessary side-effect within an inner world founded upon a mechanistic and linear notion of time. As I concluded in my discussion of the "Project", artificially imposing the period on the theoretical model is no isolated incident, but a symptom pertaining to Freud's entire theoretical framework, originating in Freud's wholesale incorporation of Brentano's solution to the problem of temporal awareness. Freud refrains from dealing with the notion of time in any extensive manner, neither in the "Project" nor in any other text, as he maintains that time is simply one more piece of information among others available to consciousness, and must, therefore, correspond to the nature of the external world.

Finally, I would like to validate the claim that Freud acknowledged Brentano's solution for the problem of temporary objects by quoting from *The Philosophy of Brentano*, edited by one of Brentano's students, Linda McAlister. In the first chapter, McAlister (1976) describes her teacher's frame of mind, confirming that in January and February of 1873 (a time period encompassing over twenty lecture hours), Brentano discussed one of the most important and innovative subjects of the 19th century – "original associations". This subject was included in the lectures attended by Freud, a regular student and admirer of Professor Franz Brentano.

> To the question of the origin of the idea of space Brentano devoted no less than twenty hours and lectures in January and February 1873 [...] At that time Brentano described time consciousness as follows: at every moment of an (inner or external) perception, a presentation is produced of the content of the perception which is qualitatively the same but which is temporally more remote to a certain extent. For him the characteristic of time was a determination of content whose regular alterations are subject to the very laws of consciousness. He called the process an 'original association' as opposed to the 'acquired association' of memory. If several impressions, *a,b,c,d,* follow one after another, we see that at the entrance of the second one the first has already been pushed back in the above-stated manner, and so on (p. 38).

Thus far, we have focused our discussion on the implicitness of the question of time in Freud's theoretical conceptualization of the human psyche, on the imminence of the notion of time in the theoretical structure of this model of the psyche and on Freud's incorporation of Brentano's conceptualization of time. I will now seek to demonstrate, through a close reading of a text depicting the course of one of Freud's analyses, the manner in which the linear notion of time underlying the analytic method reduces the human phenomenon of duration to a causal succession of data. I will further demonstrate how this reduction engenders the symptomatic concealment of the temporal aspect in the analyst's encounter with the world of the patient.

Five

Freud's Concealment of Temporality

Ida Bauer ("Dora") as a Case Study

Freud's case studies provide a suitable point of departure for uncovering the manner in which his method systematically conceals the phenomenon of temporality.[47] In reading purely theoretical texts, the reader finds herself dropped into the thicket of Freudian concepts and led toward the drive related psychic structure they unveil; case studies, through their narrative character, allow readers to trace the connections Freud makes between clinical conceptualizations and the human narrative. In fact, by adhering strictly to theory, we are unable to discern the unique manner in which Freudian interpretations address the patient's life story, thereby lacking a complete understanding of the analytic setting. Combining patient history and analytic theory, patient-analyst interaction and clinical technique, case histories open up a new, unique perspective. Such depictions grant a more intimate insight into the way the analytic method constitutes the analytic setting and shapes the course of events in the patient's private world.

THE CASE OF IDA BAUER

I have chosen to delve into the case study of "Dora" (the pseudonym Freud gave his patient, Ida Bauer), seeing that this is the first report Freud published[48] during the period in which he acknowledged his method as a psychoanalytic one (following 1900). I will first present the sequence of events chronologically, recounting the course which brought Ida to Freud's analytic

---

[47] Freud had written ten case studies. Four short ones were published in *Studies on Hysteria* [1895]: the case of Emmy von N., that of Miss Lucy R., that of Katharina and that of Elisabeth von R. Each of the six remaining case studies was published individually and they could be divided into two categories: case studies of patients and those of persons who were not treated clinically by Freud. The first category includes four: Dora's case ("Fragment of an Analysis of a Case of Hysteria", [1905]), the rat-man ("Notes upon a Case of Obsessional Neurosis", [1909]), the wolf-man ("From the History of an Infantile Neurosis", [1918]) and the case of a homosexual woman. The second category entails the case of little Hans ("Analysis of a Phobia in a Five-Year-Old Boy", [1909]) and that of Schreber ("Psycho-Analytic Notes on an Autobiographical Account of a Case of Paranoia", [1911]).

[48] Freud, "Fragment of an Analysis of a Case of Hysteria", 1953 [1905].

couch. Thereafter, I will provide a general description of the story as I understand it.

The Sequence of Events Leading to Publication

Ida Bauer, "Dora", underwent a short analysis with Freud in late 1900, when she was in eighteen. She was born in Vienna to a Jewish family: her father, Philip Bauer, was an intellectually inclined textile industrialist and her mother, Katharina Bauer, was a housewife who developed a compulsive need for cleaning to which she subjected the entire family. Ida's brother, Otto Bauer, was only fourteen months her senior.

1892 – Following the father's illness (tuberculosis and syphilis), the family leaves Vienna in favor of the Meran health resort, in Tyrol.

1894 – In Meran, a love affair burgeons between the father and Mrs. K. Ida, twelve at the time, develops various symptoms: headaches, loss of voice and coughing. About two years afterwards (1896), when she is thirteen and a half, Mr. K makes an attempt to kiss her.

1900 – The family returns to Vienna and Ida threatens suicide. From October to December, Ida, now eighteen, undergoes analysis with Freud.

1901, January – Freud puts the case down in writing.

1902 – Ida requests to resume analysis, but Freud declines.

1905 – Freud publishes his case study.

The Contents of Events Unfolded in Detail

In the town of Meran, Ida's family forms friendly relations with Mr. and Mrs. K. Mrs. K. took care of Ida's father during his illness, throughout which time Mr. K. treated Ida very amiably: he regularly went out on walks with her, sent her flowers when he was away on business and brought her presents upon his return (no one in the family saw anything wrong in this behavior). Ida looked after the K.'s two small children with great devotion and was like a mother to them. In addition, she was Mrs. K.'s friend and confidant regarding her failing relationship with her husband.

At one point, Ida and her father went to stay with the K's at their summer home, and Ida was to remain with them, by herself, for several more weeks after her father left. However, as the father began preparing for his departure, Ida insisted that she was going with him. It was only after several days have passed that she explained things to her father: after sailing in the lake, while taking a stroll, Mr. K. dared to offer her his love. Mr. K. denied this altogether and accused Ida of fabricating the entire story and of being exclusively preoccupied with sexual matters. Following this, Ida decided to end her relationship with Mr. K. Unfortunately, her father did not believe her, preferring Mr. K.'s version to hers. Ida demanded that he stop all contact with Mr. and Mrs. K. She began exhibiting the symptoms mentioned above and brooded obsessively about her father's relations with Mrs. K. It is at this point that her father decided to have her treated by Freud.

The Plot

Ida grew up with parents who were alienated from one another, quarreled often and were intentionally indifferent to each other's basic needs. While her father travelled much on business, her mother occupied herself in cleaning the house, ignoring everything else, her husband's exploits in particular. The father contracted a sexually transmitted disease as well as tuberculosis, forcing the family to move about to accommodate his health and his need for clean air. The changes in location to which the family was subjected provided the father with an ideal setting for his love affairs. Ever since she was twelve, Ida found herself caught in a dynamic social web which was utterly indifferent to her needs, her age and her expectations of the central figures in her life. Thus, for example, her father had an affair with Mrs. K., while Ida served her as a confidant and helped tend her children. Mr. K. was aware of his wife's infidelity, but turned a blind eye to the matter, courting Ida instead. Ida's role in this romantic quartet bred in her a sense of self which Freud describes in the following manner: "When she was feeling embittered she used to be overcome by the idea that she had been handed over to Herr K. as the price of his tolerating the relations between her father and his wife" (Freud, 1953, p. 34).

This description paints a very clear picture: Ida felt betrayed. The feeling of betrayal grew even deeper in light of her parents' disbelief after she had told them that Mr. K. tried to kiss her and offered her his love. Ida grew up within a tangled web of infidelities – her father cheated on his wife, Mrs. K. cheated on Mr. K., her mother betrayed their relationship in choosing to disregard her claims and so did her father, who not only used her as a commodity to be bartered to further his own affairs, but also diagnosed her as mentally ill and handed her over to Freud's care. Before ending up in analysis, Ida was submitted to the harsh, abusive treatments common at the time, such as being tied down, beaten and hosed down with cold water while naked. These strengthened her conviction that her family betrayed her, denouncing her very existence. Another aspect of this betrayal was that in spite of Ida's close relationship with Mrs. K., the latter chose to side with her husband and deny any wrongdoing, whether involving herself and Ida's father or her husband and Ida. Mr. K. himself betrayed her doubly, in a way: first, by portraying her as delusional, and moreover, in his doing so after having confessed his love to her. His declarations of love, followed by his perfidious lies, constitute the basic structure of Ida' relationships with those around her. Ida grew up in an environment where love existed only in the form of mutual exploitation. Her father's love for her lasted only as long as she kept from meddling in his love affairs. Mr. K.'s love endured as long as it remained secretive, coercive and compensatory. Mrs. K's love also turned out to be nothing more than a cover for her meetings with Ida's father. Finally, her mother's love required that Ida refrain from disturbing her ignorance of what was going on under her roof. This web of betrayal brought Ida to a severe mental state and the unequivocal demand that her father end his affair with Mrs. K. Unlike the apathy of her friends and family, Freud was genuinely interested in what she had to say (and indeed believed that Mr. K. tried to kiss her). But as analysis progressed, Ida found that Freud, too, was unable to listen to her story or comprehend her delicate condition. Ida, feeling betrayed once again, put a stop to analysis after about three months.

CONTEMPORARY PSYCHOANALYTIC COMMENTARY

Ida Bauer's case study has been the subject of countless discussions in contemporary analytic literature. I will note here some of those which I find representative of the common approaches through which the case is addressed. It is important to indicate that even though these commentaries greatly contributed to understanding this case and reshaping analytic theory, not one of them examines the role of time in the clinical method employed by Freud.

Erik Erikson

Erikson's (1962) critique of the case study revolves around the claim that psychotherapy should facilitate a dialogue between different kinds of truth. In the following example, the truth Freud has in mind is that of science and research.

> It is clear from his description that Freud's original way of working and reporting was determined by his first professional identity as a physiological investigator: his clinical method was conceived as an analogy to clean and exact laboratory work (p. 455).

In contrast, Ida was interested in corroborating a historical truth, in having the people around her acknowledge the truthfulness of her account as to what took place.

> Freud's report indicates that Dora was concerned with the historical truth as known to others, while her doctor insisted on the genetic truth behind her own symptoms. At the same time she wanted her doctor to be "truthful" in the therapeutic relation, that is, to keep faith with her on her terms rather than on those of her father or seducer (Ibid, p. 456).

Erikson, speaking on behalf of developmental psychology, claims that Freud had failed to understand that Ida's demand to bring historical truth to light does not stem from revenge (against the people who abused her trust) or stubbornness, nor is it a symptom camouflaging repressed feelings; rather, it is a legitimate demand appropriate to her particular stage of life (adolescence). In his view, from a therapeutic perspective, such total involvement with the past (which Freud construed as a symptom of hysteria) is simply the legitimate concern characteristic of Ida's age group (eighteen) regarding the possibilities their future has in store.

> It is probable that Dora needed to act as she did not only in order to vent the childish rage of one victimized but also in order to set straight the historical past so that she could envisage a sexual and social future of her choice; call infidelities by their name [...] before she could utilize more insight into her inner realities (Ibid, p. 460).

Jules Glenn

Glenn advocates the analytic critique which sees Freud's difficulties in treating Ida as the result of counter-transference. Glenn bases this critique on the following arguments:

1. Freud tended to offer sexual interpretations too early in analysis, failing to realize that a girl in her teens might experience them as acts of seduction on his part.
2. When addressing Ida, Freud assumes an authoritative and paternal character, presenting his interpretations of the hidden symbolic meaning of Ida's dreams and words in a didactic fashion.
3. Even though Freud states that the girl had made a good impression on him, he tended to push her away. This trend reached its peak during their final session, in which, instead of trying to support those parts of Ida that wanted to remain in analysis, Freud accepted her decision to leave and spent the rest of their last session together furthering his interpretations.

Furthermore, Glenn notes that the pseudonym Freud chose for Ida Bauer, "Dora", is the name of one of his sister's maids. This indicates that Freud had introjected Ida's fears about being used as a servant by her father and Mr. K. It also recalls Freud's self-analysis, in which he discloses that the maid who took care of him as a child was the first cause for his neurosis.

According to Glenn (1986), the failure of analysis, its premature termination and Freud's reaction to this termination, prove the key role of the counter-transference.

> Dora's quitting was a blow to Freud, for without her the work had to come to an end. True, he could carry on without her to some degree, but what he could accomplish alone in his writing the paper on Dora had to be limited. She had "deprived [him] of the satisfaction of affording her a far more radical cure for her troubles" and of contributing more to science than the fragment of an analysis (p. 603).

Coming to see Freud six months after termination, Ida had asked him to resume analysis due to a partial paralysis which affected her face. Freud not only refused to do so, he used this meeting as well to reinforce his interpretations. Ida had told him that two weeks beforehand she had decided to go back to analysis. Freud, on his part, was trying to gather whether her paralysis resulted from seeing his picture in the paper a fortnight earlier. In fact, Freud was examining whether her transference feelings toward him, which he uncovered by analyzing what caused the treatment to fail, still had a major role in her life: "There can be no doubt that Freud was deeply hurt by Dora […] we can see that, invoking reversal, Freud deserted Dora as she had deserted him. He refused to take her back into treatment" (Ibid, pp. 603-604).

Steven Marcus

Marcus (1976), a literary scholar, analyzes the style of Freud's writing, pointing out that it is replete with techniques reminiscent of Ibsen's drama, with one principal difference: "Freud is not only Ibsen, the creator and playwright; he is also and directly one of the characters in the action, and in the end suffers in a way that is comparable to the suffering of the others" (p. 403). The author's presence as a character in the story, repeated addresses aimed at the imagined reader, his tendency to warn the reader against the kind of material she is about to read, his sermons regarding the difficulty involved in remembering the details of analysis as he forbade himself to write throughout it, his complaints about its short duration (three months) – all these and more call attention to Freud's style of writing, forcing it upon the reader, revealing Freud to be a modernistic author. Identifying Freud's writing as manifesting modernist conventions uncovers two important issues:

1. Marcus sees in Freud's writing a categorical distinction, evaluating patients according to the manner in which they tell him their stories. Regarding his patients, Freud (1953) writes:

> They can, indeed, give the physician plenty of coherent information about this or that period of their lives; but it is sure to be followed by another period as to which their communications run dry, leaving gaps unfilled, and riddles unanswered; and then again will come yet another period which will remain totally obscure and un-illuminated by even a single piece of serviceable information. The connections—even the ostensible ones—are for the most part incoherent, and the sequence of different events is uncertain. […] The patients' inability to give an ordered history of their life in so far as it coincides with the history of their illness is not merely characteristic of the neurosis. It also possesses great theoretical significance (pp. 16-17).

This division leads Marcus to conclude that Freud associates lack of mental wellbeing with the inability to generate a coherent, well composed life story, which constitutes a proper sequence of causes and effects.

2. Positing the reader as a fictional character and utilizing the character of the fearless man of science as part of the text's structure paves the way for Freud's character (complete with fears, thoughts and desires) to take over the text entirely. Little by little, the reader witnesses a

tragic scene in which Ida's character (the object of analysis) is pushed aside, leaving her world and her visions of truth without a listener.

> Yet it must be emphasized that the "reality" Freud insists upon is very different from the "reality" that Dora is claiming and clinging to [...] The demon of interpretation has taken hold of him, and it is this power that presides over the case of Dora. In fact, as the case history advances, it becomes increasingly clear to the careful reader that Freud and not Dora has become the central character in the action (Marcus, 1976, p. 432).

Assuming that the text does indeed express the clinical dynamics prevalent between Freud and Ida, it is small wonder that under these conditions, Ida refused to play by the analytic rules and to be a character in the story authored by Freud. On the other hand, we discover that Freud, in operating according to the equation which identifies a healthy mind with a coherent story, is more concerned with creating such coherency for his story (for reasons involving his character) than with providing the proper conditions for analysis. Moreover, in a way, we might say that the very relationships which plagued Ida and brought her to analysis bear that same sign of subjugation: the stories made up by those she trusted have taken over her own life story.

Additional Commentaries

Another critique originating in the synthesis of psychoanalysis and literary theory was formulated by Jacques Lacan (1952). According to Lacan, Freud fails to understand that the source of Ida's trouble is not in repressed memories, but in her inability to accept her being the object of a man's desire. Freud is unable to identify the source of her suffering as her homosexual affinity toward Mrs. K. which entails an identification with her father and Mr. K. The reason for this inability is that Freud himself identifies with the father. This counter-transference prevents him from interpreting her behavior correctly, obliging him to insist upon her love for Mr. K. This line of interpretation is the eventual cause for Ida's choice to leave the analytic couch.

Historian Hannah Decker (1981) highlights several details which, though known to Freud, were not taken into account. The general atmosphere in Freud and Ida's day was imbued with anti-Semitism. Jews from all over the Austro-Hungarian Empire were emigrating to Vienna. Between 1897 and 1910 the mayor of Vienna was the declared anti-semite Karl Lueger: show trials were often held in which Jews were accused of murder – an accusation which amounted to nothing more than a blood-liable. Ida was not only a Jew, living in particularly troublesome times, she also had to deal with being a woman in a society which considered women inferior. Ida, depicted by Freud as a bright young woman, was perfectly suitable for university studies, but had to make do with the minimal education offered by a convent. Such conditions were the ideal grounds for evoking feelings of dissatisfaction and unsettling one's self-confidence. While Freud's analysis indicates specific interpersonal events as responsible for Ida's suffering, Decker sees its source as lying beyond the scope of the analytic drama.

These critiques, as well as many others like them, highlight, each in its own turn, different aspects of Ida's case study, illuminating various flaws in Freud's theory and in his relationship with Ida: Erikson acknowledges that applying scientific norms to the world of a teenage girl is bound to result in therapeutic failure; Glenn sees Freud's counter-transference as the source of his poor conduct in analysis; Marcus demonstrates, by closely examining Freud's text, that he was utterly preoccupied with his own needs, ignoring those of his patient; Lacan claims that Freud did not even find the source of Ida's emotional distress; finally, Decker reveals the social and political conditions which could provide a complementary – if not altogether alternative – interpretation to Freud's.

Even though these critiques diagnose some crucial errors in Freud's attitude toward Ida, it seems that they are reluctant to examine the method itself and more inclined to fill in its gaps and refute its underlying premises, or alternately, to try and save Ida. It is my intention to set out on a different kind of inquiry regarding the case, by asking which element in Freud's method is responsible for overlooking such major portions of Ida Bauer's emotional world. Since the very capacity of the clinical setting to provide patients with treatment, depends on the manner in which the analyst listens to the life story each patient relates, the analyst's own understanding of the human manner of existence in the world is central to his way of listening. The first part of the book, focusing on Heidegger's philosophy, had shown that any understanding of human existence presupposes a notion of time. In the following section I will attempt to show that it is principally the notion of time embedded in Freud's method which causes his interpretative technique to overlook cardinal facets of Ida's world.

WHY HAS THE FREUDIAN METHOD OVERLOOKED IDA BAUER'S EMOTIONAL WORLD?

Freud's introduction to his case study has a certain air of apology about it, pervading it from beginning to end. In my opinion, this air is an attempt to divert the reader's attention away from a fundamental problem relating to therapeutic technique and toward the difficulties of putting the details of the case in writing. The introduction could be divided into three parts: the first is devoted to clearing Freud's name and warranting his decision to publish the case vis-à-vis possible accusations such as exposing the patient's identity and violating her privacy (breaching medical confidentiality), treating sexual matters for sheer entertainment and conversing about improper matters with a teenage girl.

> The presentation of my case histories remains a problem which is hard for me to solve. The difficulties are partly of a technical kind, but are partly due to the nature of the circumstances themselves. If it is true that the causes of hysterical disorders are to be found in the intimacies of the patients' psychosexual life, and that hysterical symptoms are the expression of their most secret and repressed wishes, then the complete elucidation of a case of hysteria is bound to involve the revelation of those intimacies and the betrayal of those secrets. It is certain that the patients would never have spoken if it had occurred to them that their admissions might possibly be put to scientific uses [...] In such circumstances persons of delicacy, as well as those who were merely timid, would give first place to the duty of medical discretion [...] But in my opinion the physician has taken upon himself duties not only towards the individual patient but towards science as well (Freud, 1953, pp. 7-8).

The second part seems like a professional discussion of the problem of setting the course of analysis down in writing, and it begins with the following statement: "I will now describe the way in which I have overcome the technical difficulties of drawing up the report of this case history" (Ibid, p. 9). Freud complains of having been unable to take notes during his conversations with the patient and that he is thus precluded from publishing any case study depicting analysis in great detail. Immediately afterwards, he argues that the case in hand is different, entailing two factors which enabled him to overcome these difficulties. The first is the short duration of analysis, the second is that the material which surfaced in analysis -

> was grouped around two dreams [...] The wording of these dreams was recorded immediately after the session, and they thus afforded a secure point of attachment for the chain of interpretations and recollections which proceeded from them (Ibid, p. 10).

Indeed, it would be wrong to underestimate the problem Freud has brought up. Even the brief analysis dealt with here entails, in fact, seventy-eight days of treatment, equivalent to seventy-eight hours of conversation.[49] These amount to no less than three consecutive days of conversing. It is quite difficult to imagine how one would go about furnishing a precise account of these sessions without the aid of written accounts. Nevertheless, even an analysis which is not destined for publication must involve reference to the material which has surfaced at one time or another throughout the many sessions comprising it. We may therefore conclude that the problem of the reliability of memory, which Freud relegates to writing technique alone, also pertains to the reliability of interpretation within analysis. Freud's problem is not exclusive to the technical difficulties of producing a report but is also pertinent, even particularly so, to the application of reliable analytic interpretation to the material surfacing in

[49] Freud and Ida met six times a week for about three months.

analysis. I contend that the apologetic air, focusing uniquely on the problem of memory during the process of writing, is no coincidence: it serves, in fact, to conceal a more essential problem relating to analytic technique.

Regarding the case study as a whole, Freud states:

> The case history itself was only committed to writing from memory [...] Thus the record is not absolutely—phonographically—exact, but it can claim to possess a high degree of trustworthiness. Nothing of any importance has been altered in it except in some places the order in which the explanations are given; and this has been done for the sake of presenting the case in a more connected form (Ibid, Ibid).

It is important to note that in the above quote Freud explains in advance that the sequence of the material presented in this case study might be altered, rushing to assuage the reader's concern by labeling these changes unimportant and claiming that they serve the text's 'connected form'. Much like his attempt to paint the problem of memory solely as a matter of writing technique, Freud is endeavoring to suggest that changes were made for the single purpose of making the text more legible. While it would appear that in discussing the sequence of events to which he applies his analytic interpretation Freud is referring to the actual course of events underpinning the case, reading the next paragraph, the third part of his *apologia*, indicates that this is far from true.

The third part begins with Freud explaining his choice to publish this particular case. We learn from this explanation that this text comprises a sequel to *The Interpretation of Dreams*, serving Freud to elucidate the manner in which "dream-interpretation is woven into the history of a treatment and how it can become the means of filling in amnesias and elucidating symptoms" (Ibid, Ibid). If we may indeed refer here to an actual sequence of events, this sequence is altogether not the one which brought Ida to analysis nor the order in which things occurred during analysis, it is rather a different kind of sequence. Let us try to define this particular timeline, which manifests the order of occurrences after it has been subjected to Freud's 'unimportant' changes. We might argue that this is a sequence of gaps in the patient's memory, but this kind of timeline could never be recounted by the patient and is thereby not part of either the actual order of things or the problem of writing the material she presented. Rather, it is part of the manner in which the analyst notices these gaps by applying his interpretation. We might also consider the order of things as they are laid out in the case study, after Freud has applied his technique and filled in the gaps. But, same as before, the timeline created by the analyst is not based on any firm recollection of events, but on the technique of interpretation. In fact, the sequence of events outlined in the case study is not derived from more or less accurate memories, neither Freud's nor Ida's. Nor is it the result of whatever minor changes were made to serve the reader. Rather, it is the product of the manner in which Freud enforces the contexts provided by the analytic technique in order to fill in the blanks left in the story.

As we read on through the third part of his introduction, Freud presents a more comprehensive discussion of his analytic technique. He argues that without an understanding of the technique of dream interpretation, the case study will remain opaque.

> Since, therefore, this case history presupposes a knowledge of the interpretation of dreams, it will seem highly unsatisfactory to any reader to whom this presupposition does not apply. Such a reader will find only bewilderment in these pages instead of the enlightenment he is in search of, and he will certainly be inclined to project the cause of his bewilderment onto the author and to pronounce his views fantastic (Ibid, p. 11).

Freud's claim that familiarity with the interpretative technique is prerequisite for any understanding of the case study fails to distinguish between the textual and the analytic. It thereby reveals the fact that the details of the case, as expressed in Freud's writing, could not possibly exist other than as a product of the analytic technique. The latter is depicted thus by Freud:

> I now let the patient himself choose the subject of the day's work, and in that way I start out from whatever surface his unconscious happens to be presenting to his notice at the moment. But on this plan everything that has to do with the clearing-up of a particular symptom emerges piecemeal, woven into various contexts, and distributed over widely separated periods of time (Ibid, p. 12).

The technique Freud employs in order to fathom this case is that of free association. The use of this technique establishes a sequence of events derived from multiple references to various periods of time during analysis in which associations are employed. Furthermore, the contents of these associations themselves refer to various episodes throughout the patient's life.

Again, as elsewhere in the introduction – in attributing the problem of memory to the writing process and discussing textual 'form' as the reason for changing the order of events – this part of his *apologia* serves Freud to conceal the fact that the changes in sequence stem from his technique: this is done by stating that any description provided by the patient as to the order or nature of events is unreliable.

> I cannot help wondering how it is that the authorities can produce such smooth and precise histories in cases of hysteria. As a matter of fact the patients are incapable of giving such reports about themselves. They can, indeed, give the physician plenty of coherent information about this or that period of their lives; but it is sure to be followed by another period as to which their communications run dry, leaving gaps unfilled, and riddles unanswered; and then again will come yet another period which will remain totally obscure and un-illuminated [...] The connections—even the ostensible ones—are for the most part

> incoherent, and the sequence of different events is uncertain (Ibid, p. 16).[50]

The difficulties in producing an eloquent and accurate account are not caused exclusively by the incoherence which must have permeated his patients' stories. They also originate from Freud's use of free association, which garners analytic material incongruously. Throughout the introduction and at the outset of the following chapter, Freud makes use of his apologetic tone to hide the fact that his technique is the only source for the sequence of events described in the case. Freud's inability to distinguish between the problems pertaining to writing technique or the actual order of things and those plaguing analytic technique, or between textual and analytic contexts is not accidental. Freud has thereby stumbled upon the pitfall inherent in his method: the psychoanalytic method shapes case histories by eliminating the phenomenon of temporality.

Not only do associations open up a wide range for creating a new order of events, in addition, Freud's manner of interpreting the material provided by association is constrained by a problematic precondition pertaining to textual form. While Freud alters the sequence of events in the name of the clinical goal of symptom resolution, the process of interpretation thus employed is already bound to the production of a coherent, chronological sequence of things (the patient's words, the contents of association, repressed material). Freud describes this in the following quote: "it is only towards the end of the treatment that we have before us an intelligible, consistent, and unbroken case history" (Ibid, p. 18). The specifics of the analytic session per se do not amount to a case study. Only when these are coherently reorganized according to a technique of interpretation applied equally to the said and the unsaid is the case study produced. The contents of the case are existentially dependent upon a movement between times: both in their textual ordering and in their emergence in the course of analysis. The possibility of this temporal motion is derived not from the sequence of events according to memory but originates exclusively in the nature of the analytic technique. In reorganizing the case history, whether for the sake of publication or interpretations within analysis, Freud employs a technique of interpretation which is formally preconditioned to create a history of illness embedded in a sequential timeline free of any gaps. This precondition is thereby responsible for erasing any trace of the essential movement between times. Freud's attempts at providing excuses for his changes in the sequence of events are a symptomatic reaction to his method's systematic neglect of temporality.

---

[50] Both this quote and the following one are taken from the beginning of the first chapter, "The Clinical Picture". However, according to my reading they clearly continue the third part of the *apologia*.

THE CONCEALMENT OF TEMPORALITY BY FREUD'S TECHNIQUE OF INTERPRETATION

The first time we encounter an explicit application of the technique of interpretation in Freud's text is in reference to three symptoms: nausea, pressure in the upper part of the body and the avoidance of men engaged in amorous discourse with women. This interpretation is set against Mr. Bauer's denial of his affair with Mrs. K. and his claim that Ida had made the whole thing up. We must not forget that he also refused to believe his daughter's account of the incident at the lake, in which she claimed that Mr. K. had tried to kiss her. Immediately upon hearing Mr. Bauer's version, without listening to even a single word from Ida, Freud determines that the incident at the lake is the source (the trauma) responsible for Ida's hysteria. Later on, Freud recounts another version regarding this source, this time repeating the words of Ida. According to this version, when she was fourteen,[51] Mr. K. invited Ida and his wife to his store to attend a church festival. He later convinced his wife to remain at home and sent away his workers. When Ida arrived at the store he led her to a dark corner, pressed her body against his and kissed her lips. Ida felt extremely nauseous. She managed to break his hold and ran outside. This is how Freud responded to the story:

> The behavior of this child of fourteen was already entirely and completely hysterical. I should without question consider a person hysterical in whom an occasion for sexual excitement elicited feelings that were preponderantly or exclusively unpleasurable; and I should do so whether or no the person were capable of producing somatic symptoms (Ibid, p. 28).

Based on her story, Freud determines once more that Ida is hysterical. His interpretation relies on another assertion – that anyone disgusted by sexual excitement is hysterical. First of all, regarding Freud's motivation for writing this case study – demonstrating the technique of interpretation through the use of free association – it might be more accurate to state that while this interpretation relies on associations, it relies on those of Freud rather than Ida. While Ida testifies to a feeling of nausea, she makes no reference to any sexual excitement. Determining that the feeling of nausea originated in sexual excitement is thus derived from Freud's own association or is otherwise a biased interpretation. Secondly, the generalizing character of this final assertion leaves little room for any treatment of the specific character of the situation. We can readily imagine sexual situations in which non-hysteric people would feel repulsed. By confining the situation to a single horizon of interpretation – the avoidance of sexual excitement – Freud seems to pave the way to his

---

[51] Freud is here stating the wrong age for Ida as she was actually thirteen and a half at the time the incident at the store took place. I will dwell on this further on.

reconstruction of the course of the events which took place in Ida's private world. However, as I will demonstrate, the consequences are quite the opposite.

It is far from apparent that Ida could have participated in the situation as Freud described it. Even if Ida had any knowledge of the world of desire and sexuality, whether through reading or talking with her maid (as Freud claims), there is still a fundamental difference between reading about sexuality or discussing it and the ability to act as a sexual being, even more so in regard to a thirteen and half year old girl. Above all else, Ida's reaction is indicative of her lacking the emotional capacity to feel sexual arousal (the kind that might lead to sexual responsiveness). From another angle, Ida utterly lacked any emotional capacity to even enter the kind of situation Freud construes. Freud's interpretation of the incident at the store is a clear example of his way of disregarding Ida's world. Let's observe his interpretation:

> I believe that during the man's passionate embrace she felt not merely his kiss upon her lips but also the pressure of his erect member against her body. This perception was revolting to her; it was dismissed from her memory, repressed, and replaced by the innocent sensation of pressure upon her thorax, which in turn derived an excessive intensity from its repressed source. Once more, therefore, we find a displacement from the lower part of the body to the upper. On the other hand, the compulsive piece of behavior which I have mentioned was formed as though it were derived from the undistorted recollection of the scene: she did not like walking past any man who she thought was in a state of sexual excitement, because she wanted to avoid seeing for a second time the somatic sign which accompanies it (Ibid, p. 30).

This "reconstruction" of the course of events in Ida's world according to the technique of filling up memory gaps and the meta-psychological assumption regarding the link between symptom and repression, enables Freud to reorganize the course of events in Ida's psyche in a chronological manner:

T1 – A passionate embrace; T1` - The erect member

T2 – Repressing any awareness of the erect member

T3 – Displacing and replacing sensations in the lower part of the body with pressure in the chest

T4 – Compensating for repressed material and memory gaps through compulsive behavior

T5 – As T1' was repressed, Ida is no longer willing to go near any man in a state of excitement

By confining the situation, Freud gains the opportunity to "reconstruct" the sequence of events and rewrite a consistent case history. However, he forfeits the other contexts embedded in the situation, which do not conform to the chronological schema of Freudian symptomatology. He therefore forfeits the possibility of being attuned to his patient's inner world. The confinement of the situation to a single horizon of interpretation is no coincidence, it is a direct outcome of Freud's method, which is rooted in an interpretation whose horizon of meaning is set along a linear axis of time. Any situation related in analysis thus receives its particular significance within a temporal schema which completely ignores the fact that human beings live time and not simply occur in it.

At this point it is quite justified to seek to uncover the other contexts enfolded in this specific situation, but the readers of this case history find that they can only access whatever details Freud saw fit to recount. The formal prerequisite for his interpretation, i.e., the creation of a chronological history, and his laconic description of Ida's words, limit the reader, together with Ida herself, to a single horizon of interpretation. Freud leaves no room for reappraisal; as far as he is concerned, reader and patient either surrender themselves to his new order of things or fail to grasp the analytic technique.

Thus far we have found that psychoanalytic interpretation leaves out the temporal aspect and that situations and events arising in analysis (whether as real memories, screen memories, slips of the tongue, resistances, etc.) cannot be fathomed on any other terms than those dictated by the technique of interpretation. Freud's case studies remarkably demonstrate not only the psychoanalytic method's concealment of temporality, but also its dependency upon it. It is only possible to push temporality aside in psychoanalytic accounts of symptom etiology and render temporality invisible by the formal precondition for interpretation since the analytic setting itself is founded on a constant motion between times. The more Freud alters the sequence of events in his case study, the more he is given over to the compulsive transition between different times. Let us move on to examine the second chapter: "The First Dream".

IDA'S DREAM

This chapter revolves around a dream that Ida had in the past and which resurfaced during analysis. In her dream, there is a fire: her father wakes her up, she dresses in a hurry but her mother insists upon saving her jewel-case. Her father then tells her mother that he does not wish to be burnt along with his two children just so she could save her jewel-case. They rush outside and Ida awakes. This dream recurred three times since the incident at the lake and Freud had asked Ida for her associations concerning it.

The first association is a memory from a time after she already had the dream: her parents were arguing about whether or not to lock the dining room. Her father was afraid that locking the dining room door would keep her brother (his was the adjacent room) from leaving in an emergency, as "something might happen in the night so that it might be necessary to leave the room" (Ibid, p. 65).

Second association: spending time with Mr. and Mrs. K., Ida took her midday nap on their sofa. When she awoke, she saw Mr. K. standing in front of her (Freud relates this to the manner in which her father woke her up in the dream). Ida asked him to explain himself and Mr. K. argued that he could not be kept outside his own bedroom. In response, Ida asked Mrs. K. for the key to the bedroom. The next day, as she wanted to lie down and rest, she found that the key was missing and assumed that Mr. K. had taken it. Following the key's disappearance, Ida was afraid to be left alone with Mr. K., unattended by her father. The next morning, fearing that Mr. K. might enter her room, she dressed in a hurry. Freud sees Ida's wish to leave the K. residence during her stay there, several days after the lake incident, as the reason for the dream's recurrence.

A third association comes to her mind as Freud inquires about the jewel-case her mother intends to save. She remembers that she too was fond of jewelry once, but had not worn them since her illness, and that four years before that, her mother and father had quarreled because her mother wanted pearl-drop earrings and he had brought her a bracelet. A fourth association is brought about when Freud asks about the case. Ida recalls that Mr. K. had once given her an expensive jewel-case as a gift. Freud then explains that 'jewel-case' is a common expression for the female genital.

The interpretation of the dream: the danger the dream presents her with is Mr. K.'s desire to sleep with her, to enter her 'room'. Her father is the one who brought her to the K. residence and is therefore to blame for putting her at risk. Thus, he appears in the dream in the opposite manner, as a savior. Her mother, once her rival for her father's favors, had declined the jewel (the bracelet / father's favors) while Ida was willing to accept it. Meaning that Ida was willing to grant her father what her mother had denied him. Her father appears in the dream as standing beside her bed, just as Mr. K. had done. Therefore, we ought to replace her father with Mr. K. and her mother with Mrs. K., which was surely present when Ida awoke to find Mr. K. standing about her. According to this endless set of reversals, to which repressed material is subjected, and by employing yet another twist, Freud concludes that Ida is willing to give Mr. K. that which Mrs. K. denies. Therefore, Ida is protecting herself from her love for Mr. K. by resorting to old patterns – her love for her father.

Freud claims that the task of interpretation is still incomplete as the infantile source of the dream is yet undiscovered, as follows from the psychoanalytic rule that "the wish which creates the dream always springs from the period of childhood; and it is continually trying to summon childhood back into reality and to correct the present day by the measure of childhood" (Ibid, p. 71). Freud is now trying to elaborate his interpretation and uncover the source of the dream in some childhood event. In other words, Freud is seeking the original cause for Ida's hysteria. The opposition of fire to water discloses the source of fire in the dream as water in real life. Freud is utilizing Ida's first association in which her father says that "something might happen in the night so that it might be necessary to leave the room", making the connection between the need to leave the room to the bedwetting common to small children. Her father wakes her up in the dream just as a parent would wake up her child in the middle of the night to keep her from wetting the bed.

Freud asks Ida whether she had been a bed-wetter and Ida answers that she does not remember any such condition, save when she was eight and caught a urinary tract infection. Even though Ida had ruled out his interpretation, Freud goes on to conclude that her bedwetting was related to masturbation. Ida rules this out as well but Freud refuses to heed her disavowal and interprets further: in his view, Ida's symptoms (breathing difficulties) could not have appeared until after she abstained from masturbating. As the desire for satisfaction is retained in the unconscious, symptoms serve as a substitute for the satisfaction derived from masturbation. Freud thus declares that Ida's breathing difficulties first began after she stopped wetting her bed.

Regarding the time when she began experiencing difficulties in breathing, Ida relates the fifth association: her father was away for business for the first time since his recovery (from both tuberculosis and syphilis). Freud sees this memory as encompassing the array of causes responsible for her breathing difficulties, offering the following interpretation: seeing that her room was adjacent to her parents' bedroom, Ida listened in on their nocturnal activities; she had heard her father moaning during intercourse and this produced an inclination to anxiety.

> The sympathetic excitement which may be supposed to have occurred in Dora on such an occasion may very easily have made the child's sexuality veer round and have replaced her inclination to masturbation by an inclination to anxiety (Ibid, p. 80).

After some time, while the father was away, Ida, in love with him, longingly recalled his image, reenacting his hard breathing during intercourse by incurring shortness of breath. Freud considers these events as the primal source of Ida's hysteria: the dream situation is an imagined repetition of the bedwetting scenes of her childhood.

In libidinal terms, coughing is an organic condition around which libido gathers, in Freud's words, as the oyster makes its pearls around a grain of sand. The libido becomes fixated through self-accusation and imitating the father's illness. Instead of undergoing the normal course of development, in which the libido finds new objects of desire to be cathected, bringing about discharge, Ida's libidinal fixation caused her to replicate a preexisting libidinal structure in her relationship with Mr. K. Just as she had missed her father and wanted to give him what her mother would not, she now grieved over Mr. K.'s absence, wanting to provide him with that which Mrs. K. withheld. As her libido was withdrawn from Mr. K., back toward her original love for her father, it entailed a symptomatic aspect, by which Ida's wish to sleep with her father caused her to identify with Mrs. K.

THE TECHNIQUE OF INTERPRETATION AS DEPENDENT UPON THE PHENOMENON OF TEMPORALITY

Much like his interpretation of the store incident, Freud's analysis of the first dream involves creating a story formally preconditioned to arrange events both chronologically and continuously:

T1 – Ida wets her bed because she is masturbating.

T2 – Ida listens to her father's hard breathing during intercourse and becomes anxious.

T3 – Prone to anxiety, she abstains from masturbating and represses her satisfaction fantasies.

T4 – Her father departs, her longing for him cause her libido to regress and become fixated on her shortness of breath.

T5 – Her libido becomes more and more fixated, finding expression in imitating her father's illness.

T6 – She competes with her mother over her father's love, developing sexual fantasies about him.

T7 – Ida falls in love with Mr. K., but, neurotic and hysterical since childhood, she represses her feelings: her libido regresses once more toward its familiar love object – the father.

T8 – The incident at the lake.

T9 – The first dream: the libidinal fixation displaces the dream's characters in order to keep her real feelings repressed.

The occurrences in Ida's private world is laid out as a sequential development in time; her current symptoms are depicted as the result of repressed childhood experiences which remained unconscious, keeping her from genuinely responding to reality. Concerning the store incident, we have seen that Freud confines the situation to a single horizon of interpretation through the (unnecessary) assumption about sexual excitation. In his interpretation of the dream, Freud now inserts, applying his technique of filling in memory gaps, the entire drama of bedwetting, masturbation and listening in on intercourse. Not only are these occurrences not implied in Ida's words, she herself dismisses them altogether. Nevertheless, Freud uses them to limit the events pertaining to the dream to a single horizon of interpretation.

This limitation is not solely the result of inserting the sexual contents congruent with Freudian meta-psychology, it is also the manifestation of the notion of time in which the psychoanalytic method is grounded. The interpretation of the dream discloses the general structure through which Freud confines situations to a single horizon of interpretation – the libido. At the very root of these interpretations lies the libido as a transcendental principle according to which psychoanalytic theory changes the order of events and reorganizes Ida's experiences. Seeing that psychoanalysis posits, at the very foundation of human existence, a libidinal energy which can only move from moment to moment along a linear timeline, the patient's symptoms are compelled to accommodate a chronological scheme of events. Clinically and meta-psychologically, respectively, the formal condition for interpretation and the libido as a transcendental principle in charge of organizing psychic events preclude the analytic method from attaining any understanding of Ida's world unless it conforms to a linear axis of time.

Despite the fact that psychoanalysis is grounded in a categorical concealment of temporality, Freud's text is dependent upon its existence. His interpretation of the particular situations Ida mentions is revealed as a constant motion between several occurrences taking place at different times: between the store incident, the one at the lake, the dream situation, the memory of her parents quarreling and waking up with Mr. K. in front of her. In addition to this temporal motion between the various contents Ida relates, we have the motion between Ida's associations and the filling in of memory gaps: the fire and the bedwetting / masturbation, the felling of nausea and the erect member, her father's going away and her listening in on intercourse. Freudian interpretation is founded on a constant transition between different times and could not claim any validity whatsoever without entering a field of interpretation operating within a temporal dimension. Any situation brought about in analysis serves as a point of departure for an elaborate journey through time. Freud repeatedly replaces Ida's current experiences with her memories and vice versa. The plot of the case study at hand does not move along a constant, linear timeline at all, rather, it takes one step forward and then turns back in a circular motion dependent upon the presence of the temporal dimension. Even though Freud endeavors to present an account of Ida's illness that is consistent through time, his text is first and foremost a motion between times which serves as the ideal platform for any changes in the order of events. The relation between Freud's interpretation of Ida's symptoms and the construction of the course of events, both in the text and in the analysis itself, is one of interdependency: between the possibility of obtaining a coherent case history and the temporal structure in which both the text and the analytic setting reside. Borrowing a Freudian expression, we might say that uncovering the temporal structure of both text and treatment is in fact bringing to light that which psychoanalysis has repressed.

SUMMARY

Although Freud had never explicitly stated that he considers a linear notion of time as the theoretical foundation for psychoanalysis, my reading of Ida's analysis reveals that this is implicitly the case: the technique of interpretation is formally bound to chronology and each situation is strictly confined to a particular horizon of interpretation. The problem in basing the analytic method on linear time is that human nature is thus accounted for, described and analyzed as one empirical object among others. This approach loses sight of everything uniquely human, everything distinguishing the human world from that of objects. To be exact, that which this approach leaves out of human existence is the phenomenon of time as primarily one of duration.

The fact that Erikson, Glenn, Marcus, Lacan and Decker all accept the above case study as a framework for examining Freud's psychoanalytic treatment of Ida reveals that their analyses rely on the same one-dimensional notion of time implicit in Freud's method. Their psychoanalytic and literary critiques do not bear on the question of time as a fundamental element of Freudian interpretation, seeing that their references to Freud's findings remain confined to the inherent concealment of temporality.

Exchanging Ida's life story for a sequence of instances shows that the Freudian method is rooted in a worldview which sees time as a sequence of homogenous intervals. Each instance along the timeline (T1...T9) is formally identical to its predecessors and successors. The existence of each instance is in no way dependent on any of the other instances, but is derived from belonging to a consistent and predetermined time scheme. It is into such a scheme that Freud implants his findings. In fact, Freud perceives time as a sequence of intervals that are, as it were, measurable by an external observer. This scheme of time is grounded in spatial rather than temporal terms so that the sequence of intervals functions as a series of closed off, compartmentalized and measurable spaces, as if they were units of weight or empirical objects. Limiting situations to single horizons of interpretation denotes the fact that the theoretical foundations of psychoanalysis allowed Freud to presuppose that he could take apart the temporal field pertaining to each situation, reducing it to its primary elements: homogenous intervals of time, existing regardless of the specific contents or events life pours into them. Time, in Freud's method, is not studied as a phenomenon possessed of independent characteristics, but is presupposed as empirical data existing in the objective world.

The linear timeline, functioning as a single horizon for interpretation and as the basis for perceiving time intervals homogenously, engenders a symptomatic concealment of temporality and paves the way for a systematic neglect of considerable parts of Ida's inner world. In light of the above, it seems that Ida terminated analysis not without reason: Freud insisted on presenting her with a consistent account of a fragmented character. The means of treatment he had to offer were equivalent to the complete abandonment of any personal experience inconsistent with his congruous scheme of events.

Although Freud's method relies heavily on a linear time scheme, his writing reveals a temporal dimension which transgresses the boundaries of a consistent 'history of the illness'. Ida's case study is replete with transitions between different times, exposing the cardinal significance of temporality to psychoanalytic treatment. Freud's use of the movement between times creates a sense of continuity regarding the many segmented interpretations he scatters about the text. We find the same temporal dimension that was concealed by the linear depiction of the illness in the textual qualities of the case history. Freud's compulsive motion between various periods of time uncovers that which was lost in founding psychoanalysis upon a linear notion of time – the phenomenon of time itself, or, in Heidegger's words, "Temporality". This notion of time is unique in that it comprehends the field in which things appear in the world in light of a temporal unity in which past, present and future are not set apart. This notion of time leads us to construe human existence not according to scientific categories which presuppose a linear time, but in keeping with an ontology grounded in the unified temporal fabric characteristic of human existence. Acknowledging human existence in the world as occurring within the horizon of meaning provided by temporality reveals that time in human life is a phenomenon existing through the profound connectedness and interdependence of different periods of time. It is therefore a phenomenon essentially open to change. Past, present and future are not commensurate, homogenous instances spread along a timeline, but interwoven layers dynamically interacting with each other.

Had Freud theoretically acknowledged time as an independent phenomenon, that is, as one already unifying, by its very existence, the interaction of different temporal layers, his technique of interpretation would not have been able to exchange life situations for homogenous points in time, as it does, for example, in the interpretation of the fire dream.

Let us recall this interpretation. According to Freud, the fire that broke out at the Bauer's home was the result of repressed memories of childhood masturbation and bedwetting. Ida's desire to run away from the fire is in fact the wish to escape the K. residence, but this wish is an outcome of her repressed desire to respond to her longing for Mr. K. Ida indeed wants to sleep with him, but replaces him with her father as her libido regresses to her primary love-object. Her desire to become reunited with her father is reinforced by Freud's analysis of the third association. Her mother, once her rival for father's attention, refuses to sleep with the father (to accept the jewel) and Ida, libidinally fixated on him, is willing to take her mother's place and accept father's jewel. Since in Freud's method, time is presupposed as a necessary, predetermined and unchangeable sequence of intervals, Ida's behavior is explained by a conjectured succession of psychic events that is rooted in a linear flow of energy (libido). The dream situation is uncovered as a jigsaw of events coming to form a clear picture on the condition that interpretation provides them with consistent causal connections. Freud dismantles the dream situation into isolated images and these come together again to form a coherent storyline whose protagonist is the libido.

Freud is so preoccupied in putting together the linear puzzle in which his method is rooted that he fails to read the dream as the keen depiction of Ida's emotional world that it is, ignoring the manner in which it encompasses the temporal formations unfolded in analysis. Paying attention to the dream in a way which does not seek out the primary linear components of each situation but rather aims at understanding the structure of dream situations within the temporal unity characteristic of Ida's world might give rise to an alternative interpretation. In my opinion, the fire is a manifestation of the way Ida experiences the consequences her parents' conflicts have for her and her family (their constant quarreling sets the house on fire). Her father has no intention of dealing with the destructive implications his relationship with his wife carries for his family (the fire might consume his children). Instead of facing these conflicts head on, his solves the problem by running away (to Mrs. K.). Ida's mother still sees her relationship with her father as dear to her (a jewel), insisting on staying inside (ignoring the terrible price her children will have to pay).

Ida's dream situation is not an isolated event, nor could it be translated into a single, coherent temporal sequence of contiguous events. It is intimately related to other situations in a temporal fusion, expressing Ida's attempt to tell herself (for the fourth time) and Freud (by dreaming this dream once more during analysis) that her parents' conflict had left her homeless and emotionally drained. She is torn between her determination to make her family whole again and her desire to see her father happy (in his lover's arms). In her dream, Ida does not run out willingly (as Freud's interpretation implies); it is her father who awakens her and rushes her to escape. In fact, her father's actions in the dream testify to her own desire to escape the situation she is in (the fire / parental struggle). As her father chose to run away from the hardships of his home to the company of Mrs. K., Ida was facing a similar alternative – escaping her own feelings through the love of Mr. K. Her mother's willingness to sacrifice herself for the things she holds dear expresses Ida's desire to stay put, to try and save what is dear to her (her family). This interpretation casts a different light on her behavior toward Mr. K., which Freud had dubbed hysterical. In shunning Mr. K., Ida chooses to deal with the family conflict, instead of running away like her father. Ida's insistence that her father refrain from seeing Mrs. K. and her refusal to respond to Mr. K.'s amorous propositions are the result of her choice to fight to ensure her family's existence.

Unlike the manner in which Freud employs time as a mold into which he could pour any psychological content, this alternative interpretation sees the phenomenon of time as already an integral part of the way these contents appear or surface, if you will, in analysis. Heeding these contents is first and foremost heeding the manner in which temporality enables the particular existence of each and every one of them. Temporality, the dynamic unity in which past, present and future are interdependent, is the very mode by which time is perceived as open to change. The past is open to the present and the future, the future is open to the present and the past, etc. Understanding Ida's personal point of view psychologically requires that we attend to its unique existence in time, meaning, to the way in which the situations Ida mentions are open to the different times that make up her world. Freud could not have put forward such an analysis to the fire dream as his analytic efforts were blind to any emotional structure that could not be transcribed as a frozen instance in time.[52]

[52] Relying on Heidegger's notion of temporality, or more accurately, on the way Heidegger describes the dynamics characteristic of the relationship between the three ecstases – past, present and future – I will elaborate, in the concluding chapter,

At this point of our discussion, a methodological question arises: is the problem with Freud's interpretation actually related to his notion of linear time, or is his interpretation flawed regardless? In other words, to what extent does the linear time scheme fundamental to Freudian thinking obstruct interpretation? Interpretation is a motion which advances from the partial aspects of meaning (Ida Bauer's case study) toward the whole; from the immediate to the composite. This motion is essentially temporal. Interpretation is a temporal process which manifests the internal structure of understanding. That is, interpretation is an action taking place in a temporal horizon and which is intrinsically open to a future which carries along its own past. In this sense, if both interpretation and interpreter are confined to a worldview disclosed through linear time, interpretation is unable to uncover the human situation as constituting and embodying a life story, but is rather restricted to revealing it as a more or less reasonable sequence of events. The case of Ida Bauer is a clear-cut example of how the notion of linear time fundamental to psychoanalysis *de facto* reduces the human phenomenon of duration and symptomatically conceals the temporal dimension in the encounter between the analyst and the world of the patient. But does the same hold true for the rest of Freud's writing? Is the linear time scheme characteristic of his thinking as a whole? Finally, does it persist in concealing the temporal dimension?

The current chapter examined a particular case study which included clinical mediation in order to demonstrate and confirm the conclusions arising from our reading of the "Project". In the sixth chapter, I intend to show that the linear notion of time clearly apparent in Freud's early writing is indeed carried on into his middle and late periods and continues to generate the symptomatic concealment of temporality.

---

regarding the manner in which the ecstatic structure of temporality could function as a theoretical foundation to psychoanalytic interpretation.

Six

From Neurosis to the Structure of the Mind

The Question of Time in Freud's writings, 1905-1937

"THREE ESSAYS ON THE THEORY OF SEXUALITY" [1905]

In his "Three Essays on the Theory of Sexuality", Freud (1953, pp. 123-246) establishes the theoretical link between neuroses and sexuality.[53] As he considers neuroses to be the outcome of modifications in pathways of libidinal flow, the conceptual framework sustaining their depiction is already limited to the horizon of meaning opened by a linear time-axis.

At the outset of this text, Freud distinguishes between the narrow sense of sexuality, as specific activities characteristic of the sexual act, and sexuality in its broader sense, as a long line of sensations and developmental processes, both physical and psychic.

> It has been brought to our notice that we have been in the habit of regarding the connection between the sexual instinct and the sexual object as more intimate than it in fact is. Experience of the cases that are considered abnormal has shown us that in them the sexual instinct and the sexual object are merely soldered together—a fact which we have been in danger of overlooking in consequence of the uniformity of the normal picture, where the object appears to form part and parcel of the instinct. We are thus warned to loosen the bond that exists in our thoughts between instinct and object. It seems probable that the sexual instinct is in the first instance independent of its object; nor is its origin likely to be due to its object's attractions (Freud, 1953, pp. 147-148).

This augmentation of the notion of sexuality allows Freud to account for sexual behavior and its variety of normal and abnormal choices. Facing ostensibly abnormal cases of sexual object-choice, Freud suggests that we should make a distinction between the sexual instinct and the sexual object. This distinction facilitates the discussion of the relationship between sexual development (the various forms of the instinct throughout several developmental stages) and sexual object-choice (the instinct's final goal). This ties the sexual instinct together with neurosis by pinpointing the instinct (in its various forms) as its cardinal energy source.

---

[53] These essays were written not too long after Freud's analysis with Ida (1901), going along the same lines of interpretation which Freud employs in the above treatment. In the course of time, Freud had added several segments and comments to these texts.

In essence, the psychosomatic system Freud puts forward as the basic structure of the psyche operates according to a principle of stimulus and tension discharge. The primary motivation for the discharge of tension is the desire to sustain life. When the system is forced to handle an overload of tension, the process of discharge becomes active. Freud describes this process as occurring as part of the activity of the self-preservation instinct. Throughout the infant's development, the process of discharge becomes immeasurably intricate, particularly as the sexual instinct takes part in it.

The origin of the instinct is an "Erotogenic" zone, in which an internal stimulus is evoked; the aim of the sexual instinct is to remove this stimulus. The manner in which erotogenic zones develop is crucial to a person's psychic growth. These zones function as primary mechanisms for determining and recognizing patterns of experience (which Freud will later refer to as instincts). Each of these zones is related to a vital somatic function. As examples, Freud mentions the mouth and the anus. The mouth is involved with eating and the anus with excretion. When the mouth receives food, one feels a pleasant sensation in it. Internalizing the pleasurable pattern evokes the need to feel such satisfaction regardless of the bodily function associated with the erotogenic zone. As for the mouth, thumb-sucking arouses it, bringing about satisfaction without providing any nourishment. From this point on, even external stimuli could be used to discharge tension from the erotogenic zone, thus attaining the accompanying pleasure.

> Our study of thumb-sucking or sensual sucking has already given us the three essential characteristics of an infantile sexual manifestation. At its origin it attaches itself to one of the vital somatic functions; it has as yet no sexual object, and is thus auto-erotic; and its sexual aim is dominated by an erotogenic zone. It is to be anticipated that these characteristics will be found to apply equally to most of the other activities of the infantile sexual instincts (Ibid, pp. 182-183).

Freud here reveals the origin of sexuality as lying in the rift between the initial form of satisfaction – as a pure response to the instinct for self-preservation – and the resulting form of satisfaction, which occurs in response to pleasure-patterns. However, since in early childhood the sexual instinct is distributed among several erotogenic zones and is yet to organize itself around one dominant pattern of pleasure, the conflict between a system aspiring to discharge tension in order to sustain life and one aiming to discharge tension for the attainment of pleasure becomes inevitable. According to this developmental scheme, only once the dominant pleasure pattern in the psychosomatic system is derived from the erotogenic zone of the genitals (the genital stage), is the system able to achieve a balance between the sexual and self-preservative instincts. Until the genitals possess such pleasure-pattern dominance, the sexual instinct encounters quite a few obstacles which might keep it from reaching its goal.

At the erotogenic zones of the genitals, the sensation of pleasure is inevitable. It is sensed in voiding urine or in nocturnal secretions and through contact, whether accidental or intended, while being bathed or by friction during motion. This acquired pleasure pattern leads the child, already in infancy, to the first stage of masturbation. The second stage of masturbation[54] involves a renewed arousal of the genital zone by which masturbation is either suppressed or continues uninterrupted, depending on the child's environment. This period is of great importance to human development, since, as we have seen, the erotogenic zones responsible for the creation of patterns of pleasure, repression or discharge establish different modalities of experience and behavior.

As formative factors in human development, these patterns of pleasure and their suppression are joined by the occurrence of seduction, which introduces an early sexual arousal in the erotogenic zones, facilitating the formation of a perverse personality structure. The barriers against sexual lasciviousness (shame, disgust and morality, which according to Freud are developed throughout the latency period) are still insubstantial in childhood and are unable to generate more than little resistance. The premature introduction of the sexual object, well before the sexual instinct is capable of utilizing it to attain satisfaction through discharge, alters the course of libidinal development.

Freud mentions two other events taking part in the ensemble of processes constituting a turn for the worse in libidinal development. The first is witnessing sexual intercourse at an early age: children construe adult sexual acts as sadistic abuse or subjugation and are thus led to develop sadistic sexual behavior. The second is the unavoidable failure of infantile sexual research, which Freud links to the investigation of childbirth. Joined together, these two events create an atmosphere of alienation between the child and its adult environment.

The integration of component instincts, dispersed among various erotogenic zones, leading to genital primacy, occurs only partially in childhood and achieves its final form only once the genitals are organically capable of reproduction: this constitutes the difference between infantile and adolescent sexuality. Therefore, sexual object-choice takes place during two periods. The first spans between the ages of two and five, when it is halted during latency; the second period commences after latency, once the genitals become functional. This attribute of sexual object-choice indicates the vital importance of childhood events in shaping adult sexual choices.

The onset of puberty is first of all a process of change for the sexual instinct: from its autoerotic state, in which it operates according to various pleasure patterns, to a unified state in which it is directed at finding a sexual

---

[54] The description of this second stage and the recapitulation of the discussion of infantile masturbation were added in 1915, as part of the changes made as part of the third edition of the text.

object. This change is manifest in the primacy of the genitals over other pleasure patterns. Finally, sexual stimulation occurs through one of three paths:

> from the external world by means of the excitation of the erotogenic zones with which we are already familiar, from the organic interior by ways which we have still to explore, and from mental life, which is itself a storehouse for external impressions and a receiving-post for internal excitations (Ibid, p. 208).

The course of development leading from the autoerotic stage to the stage in which sexual satisfaction is possible, that is, to the initiation of the third path, entails the distinction between the pattern of pleasure as sexual satisfaction and the pattern of fore-pleasure as erotogenic stimulation. This graded structure, in which sexuality depends on the developmental transition between fore-pleasure and pleasure per se, constitutes what Freud refers to as a libidinal fixation. Should the experience of fore-pleasure become too powerful at any stage in childhood, the sexual instinct would become fixated at this stage, dissipating the instinctual energy designated to facilitating the sexual act. In this case, normal pleasure patterns are replaced by perversion. Neurotic symptoms are in fact substitutes for repressed wishes and desires which are precluded from attaining the instinctual satisfaction normally available through conscious psychic activity. This means that at the root of every symptom, we find repressed perverse material. These are the grounds for Freud's famous saying that "neuroses are, so to say, the negative of perversions" (Ibid, p. 165).

Neurosis originates in the repression of perversion and perversion results from the flow of libido through pathways deviating from the natural course of libidinal development. According to Freud, there is no such thing as a flawless sexual development; the individual always encounters one of the aforementioned reasons for diverting libido off its natural course in one way or another: "Thus the extraordinarily wide dissemination of the perversions forces us to suppose that the disposition to perversions is itself of no great rarity but must form a part of what passes as the normal constitution" (Ibid, p. 171). We are thereby prompted to inquire which factor in Freud's theoretical structure makes perversion an integral part of sexual development. In order to address this inquiry, I will dwell again on the initial awakening of the sexual instinct through my reading of Jean Laplanche's (1976) notion of the origin of sexuality.

Laplanche, relying on the Freudian assumption that infantile sexual manifestations are based on vital bodily functions, argues that the origin of human sexuality lies in what he terms 'the leaning of the sexual instinct' upon the instinct for self-preservation:

> The phenomenon Freud describes is a leaning *of the drive*, the fact that emergent sexuality attaches itself to and is propped upon another process which is both similar and profoundly divergent: the sexual drive is propped upon a nonsexual, vital function or, as Freud formulates it in

> terms which defy all additional commentary, upon a 'bodily function essential to life' (Ibid, p. 16).

Laplanche is claiming that the sexual instinct both resembles the instinct for self-preservation and essentially differs from it at the same time. This resemblance is the result of its leaning. This means that the energy sustaining it is the same energy sustaining the instinct for self-preservation – a sequence of energetic motions seeking to discharge tension in order to enable life. The two instincts are essentially different seeing that the motivation of the sexual instinct to discharge tension is not derived from any vital need; rather, it operates through the pathways established by a succession of acquired pleasure patterns which seek to discharge tension for pleasure. If, according to Freud, it is the instinct for self-preservation (the aspiration to sustain the organism by discharging tension) which governs the actions and choices of the psychosomatic system in early childhood, the awakening of the sexual instinct posits an alternative source capable of governing the psychic system. Therefore, sexuality is not just one additional step in human development. Once the sexual instinct has awakened to form part of the psychic array, sexuality becomes an alternative framework of meaning for the psychosomatic actions and choices characteristic of individual life.

As long as the demands made by the sexual and self-preservative instincts coincide, discharge of internal tension proceeds unhindered. However, when the conflict between the two instincts generates more tension than discharge, the psychic system rejects the 'superfluous' demand by releasing the hold of the sexual instinct on the instinct for self-preservation. This is the root of Freud's assertion that every neurotic symptom hides repressed perverse material. This perverse material is that part or demand relating to the sexual instinct that is denied entry into consciousness or expression through action in the world by the instinct for self-preservation upon which it leans. As we have seen, the Freudian method conceives of sexuality not in the narrow sense of activities pertaining to the sexual act, but as a psychic array that is vital to human life, providing it, in fact, with a framework of meaning for choice and action.

In keeping with this analysis, when observing the world of the neurotic, we might construe the repression of perverse material in the following manner: the life of the neurotic manifests a split between two legitimate sources of selfhood or two legitimate sources facilitating action in the world – the sexual instinct and the instinct for self-preservation. The act of repression always applies to sexual (perverse) contents, as the instinct for self-preservation is capable of liberating itself from the hold of the sexual instinct which leans upon it. Seeing that Freud stipulates that a full human encounter with reality depends on the joint activity of both instincts, any instance of repression limits any such encounter, rendering it partial. Repressed representations are kept in the unconscious, losing their direct link to reality. This means that part of the way human beings encounter reality is repressed and hence removed from the sequence of events committed to memory.

As we have seen, a clear example is found in Freud's interpretation of Ida's recollection of the chain of events taking place in Mr. K's store:

> I believe that during the man's passionate embrace she felt not merely his kiss upon her lips but also the pressure of his erect member against her body. This perception was revolting to her; it was dismissed from her memory, repressed, and replaced by the innocent sensation of pressure upon her thorax, which in turn derived an excessive intensity from its repressed source (Freud, 1953, p. 30).

Freud states that the event was removed from consciousness because Ida found it revolting. Nevertheless, as aforementioned, disgust and morality are cultural constructions established during latency and operating to restrict the sexual instinct. Repression occurred at this precise moment, manifesting the struggle between the sexual and self-preservative instincts. According to Freudian theory, were Ida possessed of a healthy personality, she should have responded, in this situation, to the sexual instinct awakened through such stimuli (as Freud had argued in his interpretation). However, as Ida was hysterical, the instinct for self-preservation detached itself from its sexual counterpart, causing its repression. Repression was executed at this very moment as the demand made by the sexual instinct to respond to Mr. K's advances generated excessive tension in the psychic system, an excess which spelled danger for the instinct for self-preservation. After repression took place, Ida failed to remember not only the feeling of K's erect member against her body, but her desire to respond to it as well.

Freud's theoretical account produces a split in the relationship between the inner world and the timeline in which it exists. When the interaction between the sexual and self-preservative instincts is in order, human beings encounter the world 'normally' – as a linear sequence of successive events. When repression occurs, the sequence of objective phenomena is disrupted and a split is manifest along the timeline of human existence. On the one hand, the individual's world exists as a conscious sequence of events which contains certain gaps in memory; on the other hand, the contents relating to these gaps are stored outside the sequence of events, in the unconscious. According to this analysis, neurotic behavior is first and foremost an expression of a disrupted sequence of time. As human beings and their behavior are conditioned by libidinal economy, their existence is equivalent to the flow of energy along a linear time axis. When someone's behavior fails to match the links between various points in time, Freud construes this behavior as neurotic, that is, as abnormal. The split in the timeline is indeed revealed with the emergence of neurosis, but seeing that the sexual instinct is dependent upon the instinct for survival, this temporal split is already present as an inherent disposition, pertaining to every individual's personality. In contrast with the way Freud understood the psychic model he formulated, we may now affirm that the temporal split is not the result of neurosis but rather that the very existence of neuroses is already a manifestation of a split structure of time embedded in the foundations of the theoretical account of the psyche.

> Thus the extraordinarily wide dissemination of the perversions forces us to suppose that the disposition to perversions is itself of no great rarity but must form a part of what passes as the normal constitution (Freud, 1953, p. 171).

In general, we might consider the three essays as a Freud's tremendous intellectual effort to provide a theoretical framework which accounts for the manner in which infantile sexuality shapes adult life. At the end of his text, after enumerating the causes of libidinal fixations Freud admits that the precise reason linking infantile manifestations of sexuality to the life of the adult, shaping his character as neurotic or perverse, had remained a mystery. Nevertheless, he further explains that the reason that these, rather than other manifestations of sexuality, are bound to adult life and its neurotic inclinations is related to an element he terms 'memory-traces', viewed as distinct from more recent sensory data. Infantile sexual experiences deemed responsible for deviations in libidinal development persist in the psychic structure as memory traces of the fixation-generating event, unconsciously controlling the neurotic's behavior. Memory thus has a cardinal role in constituting libidinal fixations, since these fixations are in fact bound to memory traces of past events. Freud comments thus about these traces:

> This factor is clearly dependent on intellectual education and increases in proportion to the degree of individual culture. The savage has been described in contrast as 'the hapless child of the moment'. In consequence [there is an] inverse relation holding between civilization and the free development of sexuality [...] (Ibid, p. 242).

This quote is particularly instructive as Freud casts the blame for the existence of neurosis on the fact that civilized (intellectually developed) human beings live beyond the moment, that is, beyond their instincts. This reference to the temporal aspect of neurosis indicates that Freud was well aware that neurosis entailed an alternate relation to time. In fact, we might suggest that Freud knew full well that the problem neurosis poses for a biologically oriented account is that as a phenomenon, it seems to eradicate the linear sequence of events which he posited as governing the entire psychic system. In order to account for neurosis in his description of sexual development, he had to form a theoretical structure capable of explaining a phenomenon which exceeds the linear order of things. Using a more Heideggerian phrasing, we might say that the phenomenon Freud was trying to account for was nothing other than the phenomenon of temporality. However, since he perceived it as temporal disruption, his account is a reductive one, obviating the ontological meaning of temporality.

Seeing that in inspecting neurosis in agreement with Freudian theory we uncover it as first and foremost a disruption of time, we cannot fully accept the distinction between the savage, as the hapless child of the moment, and the civilized person at face value. In a way, Freud rightfully considers the savage as able to respond to his instincts without any cultural restrictions, living the moment to an utmost extent, and the civilized person as indeed suspending her momentary needs. However, the theoretical framework Freud posits in order to explain the phenomenon of neurosis is also utterly bound to the moment. The history of object-choices in which individual development is rooted is the history of the conflict between the sexual instinct and the instinct for self-preservation. While Freud's definition of neurotic behavior relies on this conflict, the conflict itself does not exceed the framework of meaning provided by linear time. The presence of the past in the moment of conflict does not exceed the moment as a present. The past is present in the conflict as just another moment in a series of moments along a temporal axis. This moment is related to the past as a flow pattern through which the libido regresses to previous stages in its development. Much like the savage, confined to her momentary needs, the civilized person is revealed to be imprisoned in a sequence of moments, all of which are always the present. Every change occurs at a present moment in which the flow of libido manifests some kind of pattern. From this perspective, we might say that neurosis according to Freud is not a real disruption of time, only an ostensible one. In other words, we can see that Freud, in a way, possesses the notion that one could go beyond the moment. While it might have been reminiscent of an ecstatic temporal structure, this insight eventually collapses and remains unrealized, seeing that Freud's distinction between the savage and the civilized is actually based on their differing positions along the linear timeline.

In fact, the Freudian worldview and the manner in which the analyst listens to the patient's world only seemingly construe neurotic responses as outside the linear sequence – the patient had lost her 'yellow brick road' and in order for her to come home, the analyst must reposition her steps along an amended timeline. The analyst's analysis of libidinal flow in relation to past events uncovers a new order of events (the original one), other than that previously apparent, one in which the disruption in the sequence of events (in time) is rectified. Freud indeed recognized the phenomenon of neurosis as a problem articulated in temporal terms. However, as his account of sexuality is grounded in libidinal flow, neurosis was explained in terms immured within a world of linear time. Furthermore, given the analysis of the structure of neurosis as an apparent temporal aberration, we ought to mention that as far as Freud is concerned, the very identification of a temporal phenomenon is equivalent to diagnosis of neurosis.

THE TOPOGRAPHIC MODEL OF THE MIND [1913]

As we have demonstrated, time in the "Project" is not some secondary event, as one would have thought at first glance, rather, it functions as the ontological link between the internal and external worlds. Moreover, we have seen that Freud's (1957) account of the phenomenon of neurosis presupposes a splitting within the timeline. I will now endeavor to describe the status of 'unconscious' time in Freud's discussion of the unconscious in the context of the topographic model of the mind (pp. 159-215).

Much like the "Project", in which Freud implements Brentano's distinction between inner and outer presentations, "The Unconscious" postulates the epistemological primacy of the internal world over the external one as fundamental to the structure of consciousness: "[…] the correction of internal perception will turn out not to offer such great difficulties as the correction of external perception—that internal objects are less unknowable than the external world" (Ibid, p. 171). This primacy is grounded, indeed, in the division to internal and external worlds. The system of consciousness is an occurrence which operates on the level of representation, which is joined by the emotional and instinctual aspects, as well as an ensemble of judgments. While "The Unconscious" does not address the problem of duration characteristic of mental objects, seeing that the fundamental nature of the epistemological structure remained the same, the specific functioning of the unconscious in the epistemological array still bears the mark of the linear notion of time. Freud divided the system of consciousness into three parts: conscious, pre-conscious and unconscious, all three of which harbor mental representations. In Freud's words:

> I am in fact of the opinion that the antithesis of conscious and unconscious is not applicable to instincts. An instinct can never become an object of consciousness—only the idea that represents the instinct can. Even in the unconscious, moreover, an instinct cannot be represented otherwise than by an idea. If the instinct did not attach itself to an idea or manifest itself as an affective state, we could know nothing about it. When we nevertheless speak of an unconscious instinctual impulse or of a repressed instinctual impulse, the looseness of phraseology is a harmless one. We can only mean an instinctual impulse the ideational representative of which is unconscious, for nothing else comes into consideration (Ibid, p. 177).

When the psychic mechanism represses a wish, it is not the instinct that is repressed; rather, it is its inner representation which is expelled to the unconscious. As for the temporal aspect of this topographical division, we may already implicitly gather the nature of the relation between time and the unconscious. Seeing that repression does not apply to the instinct itself but to the fabric of instinctual representations, the biological-energetic aspect of the epistemological structure is retained as an occurrence which maintains the unity of the temporal succession. Freud needs this succession to provide him with a standard which affirms or denies the correlation between thoughts and emotions and external events. While the "Three Essays" have shown us that neuroses manifest a splitting in the time axis, this text allows us to discern the manner in which the unconscious functions as a repository for those events that were detached from the chronological sequence.

> The nucleus of the Ucs. consists of instinctual representatives which seek to discharge their cathexis; that is to say, it consists of wishful impulses. These instinctual impulses are co-ordinate with one another, exist side by side without being influenced by one another, and are exempt from mutual contradiction [...] There are in this system no negation, no doubt, no degrees of certainty [...] (Ibid, p. 186).

Whenever the conscious system decreed that a certain event is unacceptable as part of the sequence of actual events, this event is repressed into the unconscious, where the chronological facet becomes insignificant. In other words, the split we encountered in the analysis of neurosis is now transposed onto the topographical modality in the form of the unconscious. On the one hand, the psychic structure exists on a conscious, chronological level (though certain gaps may occur); on the other hand, it exists unconsciously and a-temporally.

> The processes of the system Ucs. are timeless; i.e. they are not ordered temporally, are not altered by the passage of time; they have no reference to time at all. Reference to time is bound up, once again, with the work of the system Cs. (Ibid, p. 187).

Even though the epistemological structure was elaborated by Freud's topographical division, and although the unconscious part of consciousness contains numerous non-linear aspects, the linear time scheme continues to provide the theoretical framework by which psychic functions are fathomed. The data pertaining to consciousness are either sensory data or instinct representations perceived as internal representations. Internal representations exist in consciousness as a kind of memory which could potentially be perceived as part of the individual's past (conscious) or as divorced from it, being repressed into the unconscious. While the connection between the topographical structure and the external world is both physiological-biological on one level and mental on another, time, as a linear sequence of intervals, functions as a link between internal and external worlds on both levels. Freud indeed comprehends the unconscious as timeless in itself, but seen against the psychic structure as a whole (when we examine the topographic model of the mind from the perspective of time), the unconscious is that part of the psyche which enables us to understand symptom etiology. Although the representations of wishes which compromise the reality principle are repressed out of consciousness, they continue to exert their influence upon the individual's behavior unconsciously, in the form of symptoms. When we are unable to grasp the connection between symptoms and the sequence of events wherein they appear, the unconscious functions as the theoretical framework and the very field within the epistemological structure which enables the disruption of time and opens the possibility of restoring symptoms to the linear timeline.

The epistemological structure Freud employs in unfolding the topographic model leaves no room for us to fathom human beings as temporal entities. Alternately, it prevents us from seeing time as an integral part of human existence. Time is thus always the selfsame sequence of events, its disruption always the result of tribulation (trauma, undermining wishes, anxiety, etc.) or otherwise a problematic stage belonging to normal development. The depiction of the unconscious as transgressing the boundaries of time does not entail any complex notion of time but involves only detachment, only removal from the flow of time. Even though Freud never explicitly claims so, time is a kind of standard by which the entire psychic system is calibrated. In other words, Freudian theory employs time as an essentialist and objective measure. While Freud is aware of the fact that the human structure is open to the possibility of temporal disruption, he does not allow this fact to serve as an actual relation between human beings, their world and themselves.

In general, we might argue that beginning approximately with "Beyond the Pleasure Principle" [1920], the center of attention in Freud's research shifts from the study of repressed material to the uncovering of those factors and forces which cause the repression (Freud, 1955, pp. 1-64). This reformulation of the forces operating upon the psyche results in a new structure of consciousness which relinquishes the topographic model in favor of a new formation. This trend reaches its peak in "The Ego and The Id" [1923], where the psychic mechanism and repression are reorganized in keeping with the structural division into Super-Ego, Ego and Id. In the following section, I wish to demonstrate that the conclusions we have thus far formulated in our reading of Freud regarding the notion of time and the manner in which it encompasses the etiology of neurosis likewise apply to his later articulations of the psychic mechanism.

"BEYOND THE PLEASURE PRINCIPLE" [1920]

So far we have seen that Freud interprets the psychic structure in light of the confrontation between the sexual instinct and the instinct for self-preservation (the Ego). Freud posits the reality principle as the counterpart to the pleasure principle, the former operating to regulate the demand for discharging the tension built up in the system. We have encountered this fundamental dynamics in the "Project" as well: Freud had distinguished between the quantity of energy flow (Q) and the principle of constancy. These principles (regulation and discharge), as they are formulated in Freud's early and middle periods, are characterized by the interdependency and correlation of the elements seeking discharge (energy / instincts) and those regulating that discharge (the principle of constancy / the instinct for self-preservation). This dependency is manifest in the fact that the regulators (the ego-instincts) rely upon sexual energy. In other words, before 1920, the depiction of the psychic structure had failed to properly discriminate between the sexual instinct and the ego instinct.

Freud was indeed mindful of this shortcoming when he endeavored to account for the phenomenon of aggression, as in "Instincts and their Vicissitudes" [1915]. In principle, Freud set down three criteria defining instincts: source, aim and object. The source is the factor constituting and governing the instinct's behavior (erotogenic zones). In expressions of violence (sadism, masochism), the source is usurped by the aim as the element governing the instinct and its actions. Freud saw the root of the problem not in aggression as an isolated event, but in the fact that the phenomenon of aggression is related to the ego-instinct, which in turn is discovered (regarding sadistic and masochistic behavior) as dependent upon the sexual instinct.

In order to provide a theoretical / meta-psychological foundation which could facilitate a clearer distinction between instincts regarding phenomena such as aggression, Freud depicts in "Beyond the Pleasure Principle" the structure which regulates energy in a manner which exceeds the interdependence both of the pleasure and reality principles and of the demand for discharge and the system's accumulation of energy. In 1920, he argues that the psyche often functions as if it is capable of eliminating tension altogether. That is, the regulating element does not aim merely at modifying the levels of tension in the system but also at eradicating the system itself. This tendency sheds new light on psychic life as it enables us to account for actions that we see as aimed at self-destruction, through the introduction of a new force: the death instinct.

The above change in meta-psychological conceptualization stems first and foremost from a need for change arising in Freud's clinical work. Freud saw his analysis with Ida as a failure seeing that, according to him, he had not noticed that his interpretations evoked in his patient a resistance which expressed itself through the transference. Ever since, Freud began shifting his clinical focus from the attempt to pinpoint the role of the repressed in the patient's world, to a more detailed study of transference and the role of the analyst in the patient's world. In 1912, Freud writes "The Dynamics of Transference", in which he explains the process through which the libido, in response to the work done in analysis, regresses and reawakens past objects and images. As far as the general notion of the human psyche in concerned, we might say that Freud believes that only few of our feelings can be fully developed, that is, can reach a state in which they are facing reality and remain at the disposal of our conscious personality. The rest of our libidinal emotions become halted during development, failing to reach consciousness, and are thus not perceived as part of reality. Instead, they are redirected into fantasy or the unconscious. *The precondition for any psychoneurotic illness is the introversion of libido*. That is, it is the diminution of that part of the libido which faces reality and is potentially conscious, and the augmentation of the part which is unconscious, which turns its back upon reality and is likely to engender fantasies. According to this model, *the role of analysis is to liberate the libido*. Such release occurs through bringing unconscious instincts and fantasies back from repression. When the patient feels that his repression of unconscious instincts fails to handle the material arising in analysis, resistance emerges as the expression of the patient's desire to maintain the libido's regression, thus responding to the pleasure principle rather than the reality principle. Freud refers to this kind of resistance as "transference neurosis". On his part, transference is a defense mechanism protecting the patient from the analytic work of interpretation which exposes his infantile world. This course of events leads to a state in which all conflicts will be dealt with in the context of transference.

In "Beyond the Pleasure Principle", Freud portrays transference as one of the most important parts of psychoanalytic technique.

> Twenty-five years of intense work have had as their result that the immediate aims of psycho-analytic technique are quite other to-day than they were at the outset. At first the analysing physician could do no more than discover the unconscious material that was concealed from the patient, put it together, and, at the right moment, communicate it to him. Psychoanalysis was then first and foremost an art of interpreting. Since this did not solve the therapeutic problem, a further aim quickly came in view: to oblige the patient to confirm the analyst's construction from his own memory. In that endeavor the chief emphasis lay upon the patient's resistances: the art consisted now in uncovering these as quickly as possible, in pointing them out to the patient and in inducing him by human influence—this was where suggestion operating as 'transference' played its part—to abandon his resistances.
>
> But it became ever clearer that the aim which had been set up—the aim that what was unconscious should become conscious—is not completely attainable by that method. The patient cannot remember the whole of what is repressed in him, and what he cannot remember may be precisely the essential part of it. Thus he acquires no sense of conviction of the correctness of the construction that has been communicated to him. He is obliged to repeat the repressed material as a contemporary experience instead of, as the physician would prefer to see, remembering it as something belonging to the past. These reproductions, which emerge with such unwished-for exactitude, always have as their subject some portion of infantile sexual life—of the Oedipus complex, that is, and its derivatives; and they are invariably acted out in the sphere of the transference, of the patient's relation to the physician. When things have reached this stage, it may be said that the earlier neurosis has now been replaced by a fresh, 'transference neurosis' (Freud, 1955. p. 18).

Freud is essentially accounting for the phenomenon of transference as repetition compulsion, as the patient's inner need to reenact that which had been repressed, as if it were a present experience. But unlike the previous formulations of the phenomenon of transference, in which the main resistance for retrieving repressed material was seen as dwelling within the unconscious itself, Freud's account in "Beyond the Pleasure Principle" identifies the source of this resistance primarily in the Ego and only secondarily in the unconscious. The Ego's resistance to the retrieval of repressed material serves the pleasure principle as it reinforces repression in the attempt to prevent feelings of grief (unpleasure). In transference neurosis, however, acting out does not prevent grief but rather gives rise to it. In fact, Freud is here making a considerable change regarding his understanding and description of the principles governing psychic life. Transference neurosis, explained as a manifestation of repetition compulsion, is depicted as causing repressed material to resurface from the unconscious, thus causing the Ego to suffer. In line with this analysis, Freud states that the phenomenon of transference goes beyond the pleasure principle:

> If we take into account observations such as these, based upon behavior in the transference and upon the life-histories of men and women, we shall find courage to assume that there really does exist in the mind a compulsion to repeat which overrides the pleasure principle (Ibid, p. 22).

The need to reenact repressed events does not coincide with the pleasure principle – it contravenes it. Although the very repetition could potentially bring about a state of enjoyment (due to the momentary sense of control over repressed material), as far as the compulsive aspect is concerned, the possibility for enjoyment is revoked and libidinal energy is dissolved entirely. In other words, this discharge does not leave enough energy for life to be sustained – it is a discharge to the death. Freud's discovery of the death instinct enabled him to consider the sexual instinct as one of the life-instincts and to view the Ego's aggression toward itself and others as an expression of the death instinct. The conflicts hitherto explained as confrontations between sexual and ego instincts, are now construed in terms of life and death instincts. Nevertheless, even though Freud amends the inadequate distinction between constitutive principles by adding the death instinct to the arsenal of forces operating on the psyche, the products of psychic conflict are still understood as those parts of the psyche which are repressed into the unconscious.

Transference projects the repressed material of the patient's world onto the analyst. From a temporal perspective, this phenomenon leads the patient to live the past as if it were the very present.[55] As it were, this depiction seems to portray an event possessed of temporal qualities. That is, we notice

[55] Green indicates the crucial link between transference as repetition compulsion and time in his *Time in Psychoanalysis* (2002). I will elaborate on his views in the seventh chapter, in my discussion of the ontological relatedness of transference and temporality.

that in temporal terms, this process entails looking at the present while seeing the past as a kind of future. However, much like our previous analyses, we see that though we may indeed claim that Freud's thinking possesses considerable intuition regarding temporal aspects, this intuition does not come to fruition. Transference neurosis is only accounted for in terms of the libidinal fixations embedded in the psychic system in general and in the unconscious system in particular as the result of the Oedipus complex. The past, as it is manifest in Freud's account, is nothing other than external and internal events projected onto the present. The connection between past and present is made possible seeing that the past is stored in the unconscious, which is essentially located outside time. This connection is indirect rather than direct, and its foundation supposedly lies beyond the phenomenon of time itself. Much like the way it was described in his early and middle writings, Freud now depicts the unconscious as that part of the psychic structure which exceeds time.

> At this point I shall venture to touch for a moment upon a subject which would merit the most exhaustive treatment. As a result of certain psycho-analytic discoveries, we are to-day in a position to embark on a discussion of the Kantian theorem that time and space are 'necessary forms of thought'. We have learnt that unconscious mental processes are in themselves 'timeless'. This means in the first place that they are not ordered temporally, that time does not change them in any way and that the idea of time cannot be applied to them. These are negative characteristics which can only be clearly understood if a comparison is made with conscious mental processes. On the other hand, our abstract idea of time seems to be wholly derived from the method of working of the system Pcpt.-Cs. [perception-conscious] and to correspond to a perception on its own part of that method of working (Freud, 1955, p. 28).[56]

Even though this essay radically alters the meta-psychological structure, Freud's epistemological structure remains untouched and, at bottom, no different than the one outlined in the "Project". The distinction between an internal and an external world, related through a system which perceives stimuli, still generates a theoretical framework founded on a linear axis of time and relying on the unconscious to represent and contain repressed events. Indeed, Freud considered transference as a form of resistance or a manifestation of the death instinct. Even though in both cases he describes transference as establishing a temporal motion, it remains no more than a neurosis whose existence is permitted by the analyst as it leads to the release of repressed

[56] Freud's choice to present the Kantian notion of time as the background for discussing his notions regarding the existence of the unconscious is all but unexpected. It strengthens my claim which applies Heidegger's critique of the western notion of subjectivity to Freud's thinking and reveals that the latter is indeed entrenched in the western tradition which considers the metaphysical foundation of the subject as external to the phenomenon of time.

material. In Freud's view, it is a temporal deviation serving a compulsive repetition which is aimed toward a temporal plain in which the psychic process never actually takes leave of the present.

THE STRUCTURAL MODEL OF THE MIND AND TIME (1923-1937)

In congruence with the same line of thinking prevalent in "Beyond the Pleasure Principle", in which Freud's focus is shifted from repressed material to repressing forces, his "The Ego and The Id" [1923] transforms the structure of consciousness, reformulating it as revolving around those repressing forces (Freud, 1961a, pp. 1-66). Beforehand, it was the topographic model's division into conscious, pre-conscious and unconscious which created the static spaces within which the sexual and self-preservative instincts could operate. Now, it is the various parts comprising the structural model which have become the key characters in psychic dramaturgy. The unconscious, portrayed topographically as a horizontal center, is radically transformed – it is now depicted vertically, becoming an integral part permeating all elements of consciousness. Freud comments on the inherently problematic nature of his topographic accounts for neurosis:

> From the point of view of analytic practice, the consequence of this discovery is that we land in endless obscurities and difficulties if we keep to our habitual forms of expression and try, for instance, to derive neuroses from a conflict between the conscious and the unconscious. We shall have to substitute for this antithesis another, taken from our insight into the structural conditions of the mind—the antithesis between the coherent ego and the repressed which is split off from it (Ibid, p. 17).

Freud thus locates the phenomenon of neurosis between the coherent Ego and the repressed Ego, thereby exposing the dynamic structure of the unconscious. In contrast with the topographic model, in which the functioning of the unconscious was limited to a single, circumscribed portion of consciousness, the current depiction sees the unconscious as an active element which is already embedded in the system. This change in the relationship between the structure of consciousness and the unconscious transforms our understanding of the correlation between the unconscious and repressed material: "We recognize that the Ucs. does not coincide with the repressed; it is still true that all that is repressed is Ucs., but not all that is Ucs. is repressed" (Ibid, p. 18). That which has been repressed indeed becomes unconscious, but the unconscious shapes psychic life regardless of repression. In fact, Freud insinuates that the new structural model maintains that the unconscious is involved is psychic life from several angles at once, with respect to its role in the Id, the Ego and the Super-Ego.

Id, Ego and Super-Ego

In the structural model, the Id represents the animal aspect, that which refuses to abide by any law. Phylogenetically, the Id is that part of the system of consciousness which preserves the link to the primitive sources of the human psyche. Economically, the Id is responsible for the discharge and expenditure of energy related to animal instincts. When it is not capable of such discharge, tension forms in the system, leading to the onset of symptoms. Responding to discharge on the part of the Id is equivalent to responding to the pleasure principle. In his "New Introductory Lectures on Psycho-Analysis" [1932], Freud describes the Id as a dark realm where the laws of reason do not apply and instincts and their psychic manifestations reign:

> It is the dark, inaccessible part of our personality [...] we call it a chaos, a cauldron full of seething excitations. We picture it as being open at its end to somatic influences, and as there taking up into itself instinctual needs which find their psychical expression in it, but we cannot say in what substratum. It is filled with energy reaching it from the instincts, but it has no organization, produces no collective will, but only a striving to bring about the satisfaction of the instinctual needs subject to the observance of the pleasure principle. The logical laws of thought do not apply in the id, and this is true above all of the law of contradiction. Contrary impulses exist side by side, without cancelling each other out or diminishing each other: at the most they may converge to form compromises under the dominating economic pressure towards the discharge of energy (Freud, 1964, pp. 73-74).

In depicting the Id from a cognitive perspective, it is fathomed as shaping the initial mental image of any object which addresses our basic needs. However, at the level of the Id itself, we are still incapable of differentiating the mental image of the object from the object itself. This accentuates the evolutionary orientation of Freudian theory, which considers the infant's development as reflecting its ability to delay the satisfaction of its basic needs. The distinction made by the infant between its needs and the possibilities available in the external (real) world, thereby granting the image its independence of the object, is facilitated by the Ego.

The Ego is positioned at the seam between the infant's needs and the possibilities made available by the external world. Its role is therefore to stand guard, disentangling the Id from the conditions enabled by reality. Consequently, in contrast with the basic impulse of the Id, which obeys the pleasure principle, the Ego adheres to the reality principle.

> The relation to the external world has become the decisive factor for the ego; it has taken on the task of representing the external world to the id—fortunately for the id, which could not escape destruction if, in its blind efforts for the satisfaction of its instincts, it disregarded that supreme external power. In accomplishing this function, the ego must

> observe the external world, must lay down an accurate picture of it in the memory-traces of its perceptions, and by its exercise of the function of 'reality-testing' must put aside whatever in this picture of the external world is an addition derived from internal sources of excitation (Ibid, p. 75).

If the Id is characterized by primary processes, the Ego represents secondary processes, described as thoughts in which fantasy and reality are clearly distinguishable. That is, from a cognitive perspective, the Ego is responsible for our ability to grasp reality at the conceptual and categorical level with which we are familiar in everyday life. Therefore, the proper functioning of the Ego enables us to think rationally, thus coming between the conditions of reality, the desires which irrationally imperil our existence and the sound functioning of the psychic structure. In "The Ego and The Id", Freud (1961a) describes their relationship in the following manner:

> Thus in its relation to the id it is like a man on horseback, who has to hold in check the superior strength of the horse; with this difference, that the rider tries to do so with his own strength while the ego uses borrowed forces (p. 25).

The difference Freud highlights in this comparison with the horse and its rider is manifest in the fact that the Ego, in its attempt to 'straddle' the Id, actually employs the Id's instincts, whereas the rider is independent of the horse, controlling it and subjecting it to her own strength. From the Ego's vantage point, it is bound up in a paradox, by which the very instincts it endeavors to restrain or repress are part and parcel of its particular structure and even its ontological source. This formulation teaches that the Ego is indeed part of the Id, a part which had learned that in order to comply with the pleasure principle in an enduring fashion, external circumstances must be rationally inspected. In other words, the reality principle is resulted or derived from the pleasure principle.

For human beings to be able to live in society, they must acquire a set of values that are internalized through their interaction with their parents. This interaction is made up of various actions emblematic of the parents' expectations of their child. The child's chief endeavor is to avoid any conflict with her parents and their ability to punish. This child-parent dynamic is embedded into our lives and our ability to identify with our parents creates an introjective mechanism, which, upon the resolution of the Oedipus complex and the determination of individual sexual preferences, pours the formation of the Super-Ego into our private world.

> The ego ideal is therefore the heir of the Oedipus complex, and thus it is also the expression of the most powerful impulses and most important libidinal vicissitudes of the id. By setting up this ego ideal, the ego has mastered the Oedipus complex and at the same time placed itself in

> subjection to the id. Whereas the ego is essentially the representative of the external world, of reality, the super-ego stands in contrast to it as the representative of the internal world, of the id (Ibid, p. 36).

We may grasp the notion of a Super-Ego from a different angle by noting the distinction Freud makes between the stage in which thought and world are undifferentiated (Id) and the stage in which the Ego distinguishes wish from reality. The latter stage includes the Super-Ego which introduces categories and injunctions addressing the existing separation between Ego and Id. Freud writes the following:

> The mental apparatus is composed of an 'id', which is the repository of the instinctual impulse, of an 'ego', which has been modified by the influence of the external world, and of the 'super-ego', which develops out of the id, dominates the ego and represents the inhibitions of instinct that are characteristic of man (Freud, 1959, p. 265).

The application of Super-Ego's injunctions and categories to the Ego forms a relationship which Freud describes as a feeling of guilt, which, if it is functioning normally, is called a conscience:

> An interpretation of the normal, conscious sense of guilt (conscience) presents no difficulties; it is based on the tension between the ego and the ego ideal and is the expression of a condemnation of the ego by its critical agency (Freud, 1961a, pp. 50-51).

The structural model, as it is manifest in Freud's late writings, presents a structure in which each component is both in conflict with the other parts of consciousness and dependent upon their normal functioning in order to exist. The system of consciousness is portrayed as a constant struggle between the Id's desire to discharge tension, complying with the pleasure principle, and the Super-Ego's attempt to convince the Ego that it would be better off investing the energy originating in the Id in a process of identification and introjection, in order to attain the perfection emblematic of meeting the demands of society. Freud's account of consciousness is replete with constant tension, manifest in the desires of the Id. However, it seems that the structure as a whole is unable to release this tension once and for all. On the contrary, as the structural model is elucidated, it appears that tension keeps bouncing back and forth between its various components, creating different kinds of tension which evoke different kinds of defense mechanisms (on which I will refrain from elaborating in this section). The Ego, in charge of stabilizing the system is doing battle on three fronts at once: that of reality, that of the Super-Ego and that of the Id.

> Thus the ego, driven by the id, confined by the super-ego, repulsed by reality, struggles to master its economic task of bringing about harmony among the forces and influences working in and upon it; and we can understand how it is that so often we cannot suppress a cry: 'life is not

> easy!' if the ego obliged to admit its weakness, it breaks out in anxiety—realistic anxiety regarding the external world, moral anxiety regarding the super-ego and neurotic anxiety regarding the strength of the passions in the id (Freud, 1964, p. 78).

Time and the Unconscious

In general, we might say that the structural model of the mind posits the Id as that part of it which takes on the attributes previously related to the unconscious in the topographic model. As we have seen, Freud's structural model equally assigns the unconscious to other levels of consciousness (Ego and Super-Ego) but limits the primordial and primitive qualities, which preclude any hierarchy or order in unconscious material, to the Id alone.

> You can see, incidentally, that we are in a position to attribute to the id characteristics other than that of its being unconscious, and you can recognize the possibility of portions of the ego and super-ego being unconscious without possessing the same primitive and irrational characteristics (Ibid, p. 75).

In fact, Freud's portrayal of the Id as the source of primitive and irrational qualities is first and foremost a portrayal of those same qualities which rule out the existence of time in the realm of the Id. In other words, we might say that the structural model uncovers the Id as having inherited the very same roles Freud accorded the unconscious in his 1915 essay, "The Unconscious".

> There is nothing in the id that corresponds to the idea of time; there is no recognition of the passage of time, and—a thing that is most remarkable and awaits consideration in philosophical thought— no alteration in its mental processes is produced by the passage of time. Wishful impulses which have never passed beyond the id, but impressions, too, which have been sunk in to the id by repressions, are virtually immortal; after the passage of decades they behave as though they had just occurred. They can only be recognized as belonging to the past, can only lose their importance and be deprived of their cathexis of energy, when they have been made conscious by work of analysis, and it is on this that the therapeutic effect of analytic treatment rests to no small extent (Ibid, p. 74).

Regarding the notion of time, the structural function of the Id is identical to the topographic function of the unconscious. It acts as a repository for all those moments that have been repressed from the conscious sequence of moments, keeping them outside of time. The recurrence of this pattern in the Freudian system of consciousness leads to the conclusion that linear time, as the theoretical framework in which Freud has grounded his models of the mind, has remained untouched by the transition from a static model to a dynamic one. Furthermore, seeing that the "New Introductory Lectures" comprise a summary of sorts, encompassing thirty-seven years of research, the following quote is of particular interest. Freud is here amazed by the fact that theoretical research had gained no new insights regarding the immutability of repressed representations, claiming that he himself failed to advance beyond this initial assertion.

> Again and again I have had the impression that we have made too little theoretical use of this fact, established beyond any doubt, of the unalterability by time of the repressed. This seems to offer an approach to the most profound discoveries. Nor, unfortunately, have I myself made any progress here (Ibid, Ibid).

Freud acknowledges time, or, more precisely, the timelessness characteristic of the unconscious and the Id, as a cardinal issue holding great promise for further discovery. According to Freud, if we were to gain a greater understanding of time we could shed much light on the key objects of psychoanalytic research. Nevertheless, Freud was not able to do so. As I have argued throughout our reading of his works, time runs as a golden thread through his entire corpus of fascinating ideas, but does so implicitly, since it is perceived (due to the influence of Brentano) as a flow of moments which succeed each other chronologically.

CLOSING TIME: THE NOTION OF TIME IN FREUD'S THOUGHT

The second part of this book discussed time as it is manifest in Freudian theory. I have called this specific manifestation a 'temporal lacuna' as I believe Freud's psychoanalytic theory lacks the ability to understand and interpret human beings as entities whose being is temporality. Aviva Cohen provided the direct theoretical link between Freud and Brentano, but, as I have demonstrated, she neglected to address the implications of this link regarding Freud's notion of time and the cardinal role of time in the foundation of the psychoanalytic system as a whole. Brentano's notion of time was deemed problematic on two levels: first, on the level of consciousness, it retains the empirical element characteristic of the epistemological structure, seeing that it appears in consciousness as the result of cognitive processes in which immediate representations are the cause for the very possibility of the phantastic representations of duration. Second, conscious representations of time operate under the erroneous assumption that the phenomenon of time is a linear, homogenous sequence of moments.

Brentano indeed portrayed consciousness as empirically connected to data arising from the world, providing a detailed account of the manner in which consciousness processes these data to form a notion of the world, but he left behind quite a few problems regarding the relationship between subject, world and time. As aforementioned, Brentano's philosophy relies on the categorical distinction between subject and object. However, unlike Kant and Descartes, who grant the subject an a-temporal status, Brentano's primary argument positively thrusts the subject into linear time, thus stripping it of any trace of transcendence. For this reason, Brentano is consequently in need of "the law of primordial associations", as a position exterior to the linear flow of time, in order to enable the phenomenon of duration to emerge into the human world.

In the very first chapter of the book, when discussing the problem of the subject and time in the western tradition, I have demonstrated that Descartes and Kant depict the subject as external to the world and to the sequence of time. At first glance, Freudian theory seemed to position the human subject within the world, allowing it to emerge from the field of temporality. Nevertheless, our reading of Freud had shown that his attempt to explain the psyche in physiological terms, according to Brentano's epistemology, had created a method centred on a linear notion of time. Through this, Freud was indeed able to represent psychic events along a timeline, but, in contrast, as Heidegger would say, this method depicted the human subject as one more object among others in the world. Positing the linear notion of time at the foundation of the psychoanalytic method left Freud with no alternative but to fathom human existence through the horizon of meaning appropriate for the existence of objects, thus interpreting any temporal phenomenon as neurosis or as a transgression of the actual sequence of phenomena.

The Freudian subject is customarily seen as the product of the various stimuli operating on the living organism: immediate (external) stimuli, transitory (data-bearing) stimuli, to which the organism responds through reflexes, and continuous, incessant stimuli which require the organism to respond in a more intricate manner than tension discharge. The Freudian subject presents itself whenever continuous stimuli cannot be removed through the workings of reflex. The organic interior, which Freud calls Ego ('I'), is seen first and foremost as an experience of duration. Silvana Dalto (2002) also portrays the Freudian subject as an entity constituted by the contiguity of psycho-physical relations in the organic body: "The formula is thus not *if it is interior, then it is constant,* but rather *if it is constant, then it is interior, it is I.* This is where the famous *Real Ich* comes from, the 'real I' which Freud situates at the origin of subjectivation" (p. 217).

As shown in the three chapters comprising this part of the book, the Freudian notion of duration (the period), which Dalto construes as the source of Freudian subjectivity, is altogether incapable of constituting the subject, as the very phenomenon of duration is unaccountable in Freudian terms. The phenomenon of duration is presupposed in the same way the existence of the subject is. The Freudian subject does not emerge through the phenomenon of duration which enables it to discover the internal and external worlds. Rather, the linear notion of time establishes the subject's existence in advance, alongside the partition generating internal and external worlds. The psychoanalytic method is described as unveiling the various ways through which the subject is formed and as operating within a field of meaning which precedes the subject. However, practically, in psychoanalytic terms, it operates within a theoretical scheme presupposing the existence of the subject in a manner that enables psychological contents to be poured into it. At the root of Freudian thinking we find a worldview confined to what Heidegger termed the metaphysics of presence: phenomena, objects and the many facets of the internal world are accounted for exclusively through the horizon of meaning of the present (Praesens). The linear notion of time characteristic of Freudian thinking throughout its many stages is the paradigmatic expression of how psychoanalysis is constrained by a metaphysics of presence. Examining the status of time by reading Freudian texts throughout the fourth, fifth and sixth chapters, we have shed light on the temporal lacuna inherent in the psychoanalytic method and the manner in which linear time had shaped its theoretical structure: the splitting of the timeline as an inbuilt disposition of the relationship between the sexual and life instincts; neurosis as a manifestation of temporal splitting; transference as a temporal disruption and the unconscious as a container for events and instances derailed from the timeline by repression.

Three

Psycho-Ontology

Introduction

The first part of this book treated Heidegger's critique of the notion of the subject in the western tradition, demonstrating how this notion led to a systematic concealment of the phenomenon of temporality. Throughout the second part, we criticized the notion of linear time implicit in Freud's method, showing that the Freudian subject is a presupposed axiom which serves as the underlying condition enabling the psychoanalytic worldview. In light of the conclusions derived from our critique of Freud's notion of time, I would like to examine, throughout the third part of the book, the reformulation of the psychoanalytic method as we replace the meta-psychological assumption which sees consciousness as the product of neuro-biological processes with the ontological understanding which construes consciousness as resulting from temporal structures. More specifically, I would like to investigate the manner in which the key concepts of psychoanalysis may be reformulated in light of the phenomenon of duration, as a manifestation of the temporality embedded in our very being, rather than derived from processes positioned along a linear timeline; to rethink the cardinal psychoanalytic concepts we have discussed in light of the alternative provided by Heidegger's Temporality. In particular, I wish to return to psychoanalysis possessing the insight that human beings exist, first and foremost, in light of the horizon of meaning of temporality.

In the seventh chapter, I will seek out the specific point in psychoanalytic theory where ontological concepts may be acknowledged as a potential theoretical background for such notions as Ego, unconscious, repression, projection, identification, etc. In the eighth chapter I will return to the story of Ida Bauer in order to demonstrate how those same concepts utilized by Freud to account for Ida's behavior could be reread as manifestations of the phenomenon of temporality. I resort once more to Ida's case study, not only because it had served me throughout the entire book as a prism illuminating those parts of psychoanalytic theory that often go unnoticed at first glance, but also because the endeavor to portray psychoanalytic concepts through the lens of temporality could never be accomplished by abstract and structural formulations alone.

Seven

An Ontological Reading of Narcissism

THE ROLE OF ONTOLOGICAL THOUGHT IN RELATION TO PSYCHOANALYTIC THEORY

Although Freud depicts the human subject as the chief object of research of psychoanalytic theory, we have already seen that the latter's theoretical foundations are embedded in the ontic layer of human existence. Therefore, psychoanalysis, as a method aiming to describe and account for human nature, ought to investigate human beings as ontic-ontological entities. In other words, it ought to explain the psychological phenomena disclosed in the analytic setting and depicted in professional literature as manifestations of ontological relations which are, as aforementioned, essentially temporal relations.

Throughout this chapter I will seek out those parts of psychoanalytic theory by which ontological concepts may provide the theoretical background for such notions as Ego, unconscious, repression, projection, identification, etc. Although I have hitherto demonstrated that the psychoanalytic method is founded upon theoretical foundations constrained by the metaphysics of presence, we can indeed find, within the vast array of theoretical conceptualizations of human conditions characteristic of psychoanalytic research, the kind of accounts which enable us to acknowledge ontological concepts as an alternative to the theoretical foundations set down by Freud. I would like to reexamine the way in which Freud describes the link between human beings and the world, between Ego and reality, in order to locate the particular point in psychoanalytic thinking in which the concepts it employs could be reinterpreted as manifesting ontological relations. That is, before delving into the description of key psychoanalytic notions and ideas from a temporal perspective, I shall discuss the very possibility of converting such concepts from the psychoanalytic to the ontological layer.

The Relation between Reality and the Psychic Structure

Since Freud discusses the world in terms of scientific truth and objectivity, and seeing that we are in search of the place where ontological concepts could provide a theoretical alternative, we ought to focus on those sections of psychoanalytic theory in which this aspect of the Freudian view of reality had not yet overwhelmed his understanding of the individual's presence in the world.

According to Freud, the mature Ego possesses the ability to relinquish the pleasure principle in favor of the reality principle, to the extent that it is not governed blindly by instinct, but chooses its actions in light of their possible consequences. In his "The Ego and the Id" [1923], Freud depicts the mature Ego as mediating between the external world and the internal one (Id). The existence of the Ego in the psychic system is thereby essentially connected to the distinction between internal and external worlds. The stages preceding the full maturation of the Ego are those in which the world does not appear in the infant's experience as some external object clearly distinguished from its internal world. Chronologically, regarding the development of psychoanalytic theory, Freud first introduced the Ego as a repressing factor and only later on came to consider it a faculty in charge of organizing the various psychic components.

> The ego is an organization characterized by a very remarkable trend towards unification, towards synthesis. This characteristic is lacking in the id; it is, as we might say, 'all to pieces'; its different urges pursue their own purposes independently and regardless of one another (Freud, 1959, p. 196).

As his method developed further, Freud was more and more inclined to see the Ego as an organizing faculty, though its defensive role was never fully abandoned and still lingered on in the background. The role of the Ego could be defined, therefore, through three characteristics:

1. Mediating between external and internal worlds.
2. In charge of organizing the internal world vis-à-vis the Id.
3. Protecting the psychic mechanism.

As Freud conceives of the Ego as mediating between the external and internal worlds, reality is revealed as strongly connected to the Ego.[57] The more the Ego is mature and its flow of libidinal energy free of inhibitions and fixations, the more objectively reality is perceived, according to Freud. However, as we have seen, reality is perceived as objective when it is construed as a coherent sequence of homogenous instances, i.e., when it is conceived in light of a linear notion of time. In order to liberate the Freudian Ego from linear time, we must find a way to disentangle it from the hegemonic objective aspect this notion of time entails. This is possible by reexamining the Ego: a. by investigating its source; b. by studying the manner in which the world is present before the Ego is fully established; and finally, c. by uncovering the status of time at these early stages.

From Freud's famous dictum "where Id was there Ego shall be", we gather that the origin of the Ego is the Id itself. In fact, Freud conceives of the

[57] At this stage I will only relate to the first characteristic, as I see it as a milestone in psychoanalytic theory capable of paving the way toward ontological thought. I will discuss the other characteristics further on.

Ego as that part of the Id which became separate due to internal and external stimuli. He states so in "The Ego and the Id":

> It is easy to see that the ego is that part of the id which has been modified by the direct influence of the external world through the medium of the Pcpt.-Cs.; in a sense it is an extension of the surface-differentiation (Freud, 1961a, p. 25).

In "Civilization and its Discontents", Freud links the psychological development of the Ego with the ability to acknowledge reality, in describing the infant's sense of self in relation to its mother: "An infant at the breast does not as yet distinguish his ego from the external world as the source of the sensations flowing in upon him. He gradually learns to do so, in response to various promptings" (Freud, 1961b, pp. 66-67). Among the various stimuli experienced by the infant, are those internal stimuli, which are not always instantly satisfied, as when the mother's breast is not available to feed it at the exact moment it is hungry. As for stimuli, Freud argues:

> […] other sources evade him from time to time—among them what he desires most of all, his mother's breast—and only reappear as a result of his screaming for help. In this way there is for the first time set over against the ego an 'object', in the form of something which exists 'outside' and which is only forced to appear by a special action (Ibid, p. 67).

The repeated feeling that something is lacking in its original world, or that something is occasionally absent, produces the distinction between inside and outside, leading up to the separation of the Ego from both the Id and external reality. In keeping with Freud, we might say that the Ego detaches itself from the external world, seeing that in principle it originally senses itself as omnipotent (Ibid, p. 68). As feelings of lack and their accompanying responses recur time and again, the Ego abandons such illusions of grandeur, allowing reality to gradually emerge from 'within it' and alongside it. The psychological condition in which the Ego is still indistinct from the world is termed by Freud the narcissistic stage.

The Narcissistic Stage

Freud explains this stage in terms of libidinal energy and its capacity for cathecting actions and objects. What will later develop into the mature Ego is, for the time being, a libido-Ego, in which libidinal energy cathects the mother to an utmost extent, as an entity indistinguishable from the infant's own existence. The development of the Ego entails the withdrawal of libidinal energy from the primary narcissism by which energy is stored exclusively in the Ego. This comprises the transition to the secondary stage, that of object-libido, in which the Ego utilizes libidinal energy to cathect objects. The process through which libido is withdrawn from its primary state to one in which the Ego functions as a container for the libidinal energy used to cathect its surrounding objects is the beginning of the journey from infancy to adulthood and toward the ability to acknowledge objective reality.

This account is of great import regarding the development of psychoanalysis, as it depicts the transition from a period in which the world appears pre-objective to one in which it is disclosed through the prism of objective reality. Meaning that at the narcissistic stage, the world appears without the categorical division into subject and object, inside and outside, and the encounter with reality as objective is revealed to be an essentially egocentric event. Therefore, I find the narcissistic state, in which the infant's encounter with the world is not yet dominated by categorical modalities, to be, at the very least, a conceptualization of an existential situation which may potentially be construed in ontological terms. From another angle, we might argue that in Freudian thinking, the narcissistic stage is a situation which is naturally free from subjugation to a framework of meaning generated by a linear notion of time. In the following sections, I wish to study more closely the process through which the human subject emerges from primary narcissism, examining whether this process is comprehensible in light of the phenomenon of temporality.

The recourse to a narcissistic psychological stage and its reformulation is prevalent in the works of the major theoreticians which have contributed to psychoanalytic theory after Freud. A clear focus on the interpretations of Lacan,[58] Kohut[59] and Winnicott[60] regarding the narcissistic stage would demonstrate the extent to which each of their psychoanalytic visions are founded on their manner of rereading primary narcissism and the subsequent formation of the individual.

THE RECOURSE TO PRIMARY NARCISSISM IN POST-FREUDIAN PSYCHOANALYSIS

Jacques Lacan

Much like Freud, Lacan advocates the assumption that the early stages of the infant's life are profoundly narcissistic, lacking any clear distinction between the child and its mother or surrounding environment. When the infant is six to eighteen months old, it undergoes what Lacan (1997) terms "the mirror stage".

---

[58] French psychoanalyst, theoretician and philosopher, advocated the reinterpretation of Freud in line with the linguistic structuralism characteristic of mid-twentieth century.

[59] Born in Vienna but practiced in the United States, where he founded the 'Self-Psychology' school; also served as president of the American Psychological Association.

[60] British psychoanalyst and theoretician, founded the 'Middle Group' in response to the disagreements between the followers of Anna Freud and those of Melanie Klein; held the position of chairman at the British Psychoanalytical Society.

During the process of separation from its primary environment, there comes a moment in which the infant looks in a mirror and notices its own reflection (imago).

> The *mirror stage* is a drama whose internal thrust is precipitated from insufficiency to anticipation— and which manufactures for the subject, caught up in the lure of spatial identification, the succession of phantasies that extends from a fragmented body-image to a form of its totality that I shall call orthopedic— and, lastly, to the assumption of the armour of an alienating identity, which will mark with its rigid structure the subject's entire mental development (p. 4).

On the one hand, the discovery of its own reflection enables the infant to fathom its own boundaries (Gestalt), unifying its fragmentary bodily sensations around the presence of an image; on the other hand, this discovery facilitates the distinction between self and other. The reflection in the mirror heralds the existence of a self which is actually a reflection of itself, rather than the self proper. In other words, it belongs to a self which is an other. This otherness which dwells at the root of any possible existence as a self, engenders what Lacan refers to as the "fragmented self". Within this tension between self and other, embedded in the self's very possibility for being itself, the drama of desires which governs psychic life unfolds. The attempt to satisfy desires necessarily leads to failure, as at the bottom of this psychic turmoil lies an essentially unattainable wish: to return to a state of primary narcissism, in which self and other are still undifferentiated.

Heinz Kohut

Kohut's Self-Psychology is founded upon Freud's notion of primary narcissism. However, unlike Freud, who considered narcissism a mere step on the way to discovering the object by means of libidinal cathexis, Kohut saw narcissism as encompassing any libidinal investment which contributed to the growth of the self. That is, as far as Kohut is concerned, this is not just a primary stepping stone in human development, soon to be replaced by object-love, rather, it is a fundamental developmental axis which accompanies us throughout our entire lives. Seeing that Kohut's Self-Psychology shifts the psychoanalytic center of gravity from the drives toward the self, neurosis (originally construed as the result of castration anxiety or some other unconscious fantasy) is now understood as a narcissistic disorder, principally derived from a possible regression or fragmentation of the self. The model of neurotic conflict is substituted by that of deficient self-organization. This model views the self as a dynamic, integrated entity which is characterized by selfobject relationships, unlike the classic relationship between Ego and object (in which the drive-Ego is separated from its object). This means that the object, as a selfobject, is perceived as an integral part of the narcissistic array of the psyche. Positing the narcissistic stage as the very heart of psychoanalytic theory and embracing the other as an essential part of the self's existence, has shaped a notion of the self which exceeds the boundaries of the Ego and even, at times, of the individual. Kohut (1966) argues:

> The general definition of narcissism as the investment of the self might still be compatible with a transactional approach; but the self in the psychoanalytic sense is variable and by no means coextensive with the limits of the personality as assessed by an observer of the social field. In certain psychological states the self may expand far beyond the borders of the individual, or it may shrink and become identical with a single one of his actions or aims. The antithesis to narcissism is not object relation but object love (p. 245).

Since the self as an integrated entity is open and vulnerable, the appropriate environment for achieving wellbeing ought to include other people capable of functioning as selfobjects. These relationships are indeed characteristic of psychic life in childhood but de facto they continue to exert their influence upon the adult psyche in the form of such selfobjects as intimate relationships, works of art, etc. The notion of the self and its emergence through primary narcissism reveal empathy as a key means of communication between human beings, especially in the analytic setting. Regarding the primary bond between mother and infant and the way this bond endures within the structure of the self, Kohut writes:

> The groundwork for our ability to obtain access to another person's mind is laid by the fact that in our earliest mental organization the feelings, actions, and behavior of the mother had been included in our self. This primary empathy with the mother prepares us for the recognition that, to a large extent, the basic inner experiences of people remain similar to our own. Our first perception of the manifestations of another person's feelings, wishes, and thoughts occurred within the framework of a narcissistic conception of the world; the capacity for empathy belongs, therefore, to the innate equipment of the human psyche and remains to some extent associated with the primary process (Ibid, p. 262).

Donald W. Winnicott

According to Winnicott, the very transition from living within the maternal environment to a life led beside the mother and eventually to independence (i.e. leaving the narcissistic stage) is a process grounded in transitional phenomena. Transitional phenomena exist from the stage in which the breast (which provides nourishment and warmth) appears as soon as the infant fantasizes it and up until the stage in which the mother is perceived as existing outside the infant's omnipotent space. One of the transitional object's key attributes is its being the infant's discovery rather than an object imposed upon it. The infant must feel that the transitional object in not an internal fabrication or fantasy, without feeling that it is external to it, that is, beyond its control. Any object which answers these two conditions in the infant's eyes serves as a transitional object. Winnicott (1971) addresses transitional phenomena, writing thus:

> This third area has been contrasted with inner or personal psychic reality and with the actual world in which the individual lives, which can be objectively perceived. I have located this important area of experience in the potential space between the individual and the environment, that which initially both joins and separates the baby and the mother when the mother's love, displayed or made manifest as human reliability, does in fact give the baby a sense of trust or of confidence in the environmental factor (pp. 101-102).

Regarding the metaphysical foundation of psychoanalytic theories, the transitional object, as a phenomenon, possesses an "intermediary status". In other words, its field of appearance lies midway between subject and object.

Summary

Utilizing the notion of narcissism, Freud's piercing gaze into the structures of the human psyche located and conceptualized an existential condition in which the division into subject and object is not yet in effect. Nevertheless, the general orientations of his psychoanalytic theory, its focus on drives and the Ego and its principal rootedness in a notion of linear time, precluded it from comprehending human nature against the horizon of more primordial psychic structures, keeping it altogether bound to the metaphysical distinction between subject and object. Glancing at the recourse each of the above thinkers has to the narcissistic stage demonstrates that we can indeed uncover structures more primary than those depicted by Freud, thereby reconstructing the cardinal concepts of psychoanalysis.

Lacan shows the extent to which the other is embedded in the structure of the self, accounting for the human propensity to neurotic states as a futile attempt to return to the narcissistic stage. Kohut demonstrates that the self is a dynamic entity, exceeding the structure of the Ego, claiming that narcissism should not be understood as a mere phase in psychic development, but as an occurrence that is fundamental to the structure of our self throughout life. Winnicott resorts to primary narcissism, insisting that the human world is utterly unimaginable without applying the "intermediate area" to the whole of psychoanalytic theory and to the human condition in its entirety. Winnicott thereby surpasses both Lacan and Kohut, supplying the much needed link to the ontological aspect of our existence. The inability to locate an experience in either the subjective or objective domains requires Winnicott to demarcate a third field of existence possessing its own ontological status. Even though all three theoreticians notice the problems involved in maintaining an egocentrically oriented method, their depiction of the subject's process of individuation fails to address the relationship between the narcissistic condition and the temporal dimension directly.

NARCISSISM AS A MANIFESTATION OF A NON-LINEAR FLOW OF TIME

According to Freud, the encounter with reality is an egocentric occurrence. However, as we have seen, reality itself is conceived as objective only if it is perceived as posited along a linear timeline. Observing the Ego from a temporal perspective, we notice that a mature Ego is equivalent to the individual's ability to regard the sequence of events chronologically while the regression characteristic of the Ego in certain psycho-physical states, such as neurosis, is tantamount to the inability to maintain one's grasp of the objective (linear) timeline. This reading comprehends the Ego as a precondition for the encounter with objective reality, which manifests itself as a linear sequence of intervals. We may further conclude that when the world is unmediated by the Ego, as it is in the narcissistic state, the encounter with it (in the sense of pre-objective reality) occurs in a principally a-chronological temporal field. The narcissistic state is that section of Freudian theory in which we may still, essentially, recognize the temporal phenomenon as not yet subjugated to the linear paradigm, neither in order to provide the subject with a coherent and persisting structure, nor in order to shape reality as a sequence. Consequently, we ought to try and gather the psychological manifestations related to this state against the horizon of meaning provided by temporality. In other words, since the narcissistic stage exists within an a-chronological temporal framework, I suggest that we ought to consider it the particular place in Freud's thinking through which the phenomenon of temporality could be acknowledged as the ontological horizon of possibility through which psychological characteristics emerge.

FROM NARCISSISM TO REALITY: FREUD AND LOEWALD

In order to comprehend how temporality may be seen as a phenomenon inherent to the narcissistic stage, we must gain a clearer understanding of the relation between the narcissistic stage and reality; we must understand the exact nature of the process of individuation, as it proceeds from primary narcissism toward the ability to encounter reality; finally, we ought to elucidate the manner in which the very aptitude for undergoing this process is bound up with temporality to begin with.

According to Freud, the capacity to transcend primary narcissism is dependent upon the infant's ability to acknowledge its own separateness from the mother, that is, to acknowledge the mother's existence as external to its own. As soon as the mother begins to be perceived as a separate entity, a libidinal relationship, as Freud terms it, is commenced, reaching its peak during the phallic stage. At this stage, the child is in the very midst of the Oedipus complex which is eventually resolved, as aforementioned, through the establishment of the Super-Ego. We find a fascinating reading of these stages and their temporal context in the writings of psychoanalyst Hans Loewald.

Loewald is an exceptional American psychoanalyst and theoretician, whose thinking is not reducible to normative psychoanalytic schools such as Ego Psychology, Object Relations or Self-Psychology, seeing that it succeeds in encompassing all of them. Loewald fled Nazi Germany and came to the United States in mid-twentieth century and his work, in many ways, combines psychoanalysis and philosophy, ontology and depth-psychology. During his student years in Germany, Loewald studied philosophy under Heidegger, while cultivating an interest in Freud's psychoanalytic method as well. As the Nazis came into power, Loewald left Germany and came to the United States, where he denounced his teacher, Heidegger, for his part in the Nazi regime and proceeded to study Freudian theory.[61] Loewald is indeed one of Freud's most insightful commentators, but his writing exceeds, as I will endeavor to demonstrate, the theoretical framework propagated by Freud. Throughout this chapter, I will attempt to show that he conceives of the structural model as possessing temporal facets and that he reveals, through his discussion of the processes relating to the Oedipal triad, the crucial importance of the narcissistic state to the formation of the structure of consciousness. This treatment of Loewald's commentary of Freud will enable us to follow the traces of non-linear temporal structures in the workings of the mature mind.

Two Fundamental Models for Reality

Loewald interprets the castration anxiety at the heart of the Oedipal drama in broader terms than the concrete fear of having one's genitals severed. He depicts it as a paradigmatic representation of the reality principle, construed as the demand the infant is faced with to forego the mother as a libidinal object. At the same time, Loewald asks his readers (in "Ego and Reality" [1951]) not to conceive of psychological terms such as castration anxiety and the Oedipus complex as actual events but as metaphors for psychic processes. That is,

---

[61] In the introduction to his collection of papers, Loewald (1980) writes the following regarding his relationships with Heidegger and Freud:

> Philosophy has been my first love. I gladly affirm its influence on my way of thinking while being wary of the peculiar excess a philosophical bent tends to entail. My teacher in this field was Martin Heidegger, and I am deeply grateful for what I learned from him, despite his most hurtful betrayal in the Nazi era, which alienated me from him permanently. Freud is close enough to my generation to have been a commanding living force as I grew up and become a psychiatrist, although I never met him in person. He has remained for me, through his writing, that living presence (p. ix).

Loewald seeks to understand these concepts as the essential patterns comprising the individuation process.

> If we understand the Oedipus conflict and the castration threat as the prototype of the demands of realty, it should be clear how strongly for Freud the concept of reality is bound up with the father. [...] Reality, then, is represented by the father who as an alien, hostile, jealous force interferes with the intimate ties between mother and child, forces the child into submission, so that he seeks the father's protection. The threat of the hostile reality is met by unavoidable, if temporary, submission to its demands, namely to renounce the mother as a libidinal object, and acknowledge and submit to parental authority (Ibid, p. 7).

Relying on the psychoanalytic scheme of infant development, Loewald argues that the narcissistic stage is that stage in which the infant experiences internal reality as secure while external reality is deemed threatening. This account uncovers that at the foundation of psychoanalysis as it was formulated by Freud, there are two models of reality: one seen as essentially threatening, represented by the father and one construed as essentially safe, represented by the mother. The model governing Freud's conceptualizations is that of threatening reality, of reality in its masculine-paternal sense. This model of reality as a threat serves as the grounds on which the Ego is described as a faculty mainly striving to protect the psyche from reality. Loewald, proclaiming the existence of the second model, claims that regarding maternal reality, the Ego's role is primarily to organize the psyche, rather than protect it from external forces.

> The relatedness between ego and realty, or objects, does not develop from an originally unrelated coexistence of two separate entities that come into contact with each other, but on the contrary from a unitary whole that differentiates into distinct parts. [...] It is from here that the synthetic, integrative function of the ego can be understood. The ego mediates, unifies, integrates because it is of its essence to maintain, on more complex levels of differentiation and objectivation of realty, the original unity (Ibid, p. 11).

Defense as Psychic Organization

According to Loewald, if we fathom the Ego as an organizing faculty, defense mechanisms, construed by Freud as the Ego's means of defense against reality, are disclosed as mechanisms acting against a possible loss of reality. But what does Loewald mean by such 'loss of reality'? Seeing that the depth and complexity of reality perceived by the individual depend on the level of Ego organization, the latter's defensive functions amount to abandoning existing levels of organization and current possibilities for arranging reality. Castration anxiety, disturbing primary unity, calls the structures of Ego and reality into being. Were the primary unity left intact, the complex structures of Ego and reality would never have come to exist. Facing the castration anxiety manifesting the threatening aspect of reality, Loewald posits a castration anxiety expressing maternally perceived reality: the fear of being engulfed and drawn back into the womb, back to primary unity.

The dangers facing the Ego are not just the growing frustrations and hardships accompanying the attempts to cathect objects in order to substitute the primary link between the libidinal Ego and the mother. The Ego is also imperiled by the other end of the Oedipal equation, i.e., by the mother which envelopes the infant, blurring the boundaries of its individual existence. As Loewald states: "The original unity and identity, undifferentiated and unstructured, of psychic apparatus and environment is as much of danger for the ego as the demand of the 'parental castration threat' to give it up altogether" (Ibid, p. 14). At this point, Loewald resorts to the structure which precedes the Oedipal complex, highlighting the ability to identify with the father as a counter-force, sustaining the infant and keeping it from being immersed in an unbounded narcissistic experience with the mother.

> Against the threatening possibility of remaining in or sinking back into the structureless unity from which the ego emerged, stands the powerful paternal force. With this force an early identification is attempted, an identification that precedes and prepares the Oedipus complex (Ibid, Ibid).

Evoking defensive measures on the part of the Ego, loss of reality takes place regarding the two forms of anxiety mentioned above. Reality is lost when the Ego is detached from its object (castration anxiety) and when the boundaries between it and reality vanish (womb anxiety). Loss of reality, as mentioned earlier, is not a state in which a certain part of reality is missing, rather, it is a regression regarding the level of Ego-reality integration, revealing reality in its pre-objective form. Between these two kinds of anxiety which represent the limits of its possible existence, the Ego organizes various levels of reality. Essentially, the limits of reality and the Ego's growing separation are the result of identification with the unified narcissistic state – the mother, on the one hand, and with the separate, distinct state – the father, on the other.

This account suggests that preceding both the Ego and the Oedipal complex are primary systems of identification with the mother and the father, constituting the two possible models of reality: threatening and secure. These systems of identification are composed of introjective and projective processes, upon which Loewald comments:

> The various processes of infantile aggression, the various stages of incorporation and projection are considered as early stages of the activity of the primitive ego, whose synthesizing and differentiating is still a much more concrete action than the comparatively abstract activity of the fully developed ego. Introjection and projection are such early stages of ego activity (Ibid, p. 18).

The Infant's individuation is commenced once the Ego is differentiated from the narcissistic state. However, the primary stages of this process are the introjections and projections which Loewald describes as concrete acts of unity and separateness, distinct from the introjections and projections of the mature Ego, which performs these activities as mostly abstract. The particular element of the psychic structure which makes it possible to acknowledge introjections and projections as activities belonging to abstract thought is the Super-Ego. Without the addition of the Super Ego to the structure of the mind, abstract projections and introjections, i.e., secondary processes, could not have been performed, leaving the Ego unable to acknowledge reality in its cultural, objective sense.

The Relationship between Super-Ego and Reality according to Freud

So far we have seen that Freud considers the Ego to be a faculty in charge of mediating, organizing and protecting as far as the encounter with reality and its perception are concerned. It now appears that the Super-Ego is another faculty which conditions our perception of reality. In this context, we ought to inquire as to which particular quality on the part of the Super-Ego enables human beings to encounter the world they inhabit culturally and objectively.

In Freudian terms, the Super-Ego is the psychic consequence of the resolution of the Oedipus complex. When the struggle between the libidinal attachment to the mother and the ambivalence toward the father (castration anxiety and primary identification) reaches its peak, the child relinquishes his libidinal attachment through his identification with the father. As a result, the father-image is introjected into the psychic structure, allowing the child to feel in control of the father's anger. Moreover, as this introjection also entails a certain erotic disposition toward the mother, the child is also compensated for losing his libidinal attachment to her. The incorporation of the paternal image into the psychic structure is equivalent to an official adoption of the reality principle while giving up the mother as a libidinal object is tantamount to declaring the Ego's maturity and ability to negotiate with the pleasure principle. Accordingly, in "The Ego and The Id", Freud describes the establishment of the Super-Ego as a faculty in charge of the prohibitions and injunctions characteristic of civilized life and as generating the feeling of guilt endemic to the tension between the orders to be X or to cease to be Y and the Ego's actual achievements.

> It is easy to show that the ego ideal answers to everything that is expected of the higher nature of man. As a substitute for a longing for the father, it contains the germ from which all religions have evolved. The self-judgement which declares that the ego falls short of its ideal produces the religious sense of humility to which the believer appeals in his longing. As a child grows up, the role of father is carried on by teachers and others in authority; their injunctions and prohibitions remain powerful in the ego ideal and continue, in the form of

> conscience, to exercise the moral censorship. The tension between the demands of conscience and the actual performances of the ego is experienced as a sense of guilt. Social feelings rest on identifications with other people, on the basis of having the same ego ideal (Freud, 1961a, p. 37).

In order to be able to live in society, the infant must acquire a set of values internalized through its interactions with its parents, characterized by acting in keeping with their expectations. The importance of the Super-Ego to acknowledging reality mainly concerns its role within the structural model, as applying its categories and injunctions to the separation between Ego and Id.

> The mental apparatus is composed of an 'id', which is the repository of the instinctual impulse, of an 'ego', which has been modified by the influence of the external world, and of the 'super-ego', which develops out of the id, dominates the ego and represents the inhibitions of instinct that are characteristic of man (Freud, 1959, p. 266).

In conclusion, the structural model embodies a constant struggle between the Id's desire to discharge tension and appease the pleasure principle and the Super-Ego, which strives to convince the Ego that it is better off investing the energy originating in the Id in a process of identification and introjection through which it may attain the perfection pertaining to the demands of society. The existence of the Super-Ego in the system of consciousness is revealed as archetypical to the process of acknowledging objective reality. Objective reality and social structures are acknowledgeable seeing that the psychic mechanism had been socialized through a process of identification centered on the ability to recognize external elements within itself. Once this ability is acquired, the system of consciousness can acknowledge abstract projections and introjections as well. The Super-Ego serves as the condition for acknowledging reality as its very existence in consciousness manifests the system's adherence to the reality principle, after having incorporated reality.

Super-Ego and the Capacity for Acknowledging Reality according to Loewald

Throughout our discussion of the relation between the Super-Ego and reality in Freud's thinking, we learned that the Super-Ego is that faculty which enables the processes of introjection and projection to operate abstractly, thereby allowing us to live a normal life. Furthermore, we learned that this possibility is founded on more primary introjective and projective processes which are not abstract. Loewald's analysis of the role of the Super-Ego reinforces the Freudian account and my reading of it while adding yet another layer, which elaborates on the status of introjection in the psychic system and introduces the cardinal link between the Super-Ego, the temporal dimension and the process leading to an acknowledgement of reality.

In his "On Internalization", Loewald (1980) comments on the role of introjection in the psychic system, viewing it as a constantly active component which precedes the establishment of the Super-Ego. This reveals introjection as a significant primary psychic component, preceding both the existence of an internal world and the ability to represent portions of reality within it:

> My own use of internalization refers to the processes involved in the creation of such internal world and structural resultants, and not to the construction of inner models, schemata, or maps, which are representations of the external world of objects and their relations. The latter I will tentatively consider as mental functions possible by creation of that internal world (p. 73).

This reading of introjection processes facilitates Loewald's understanding of the establishment of the Super-Ego from the Ego's perspective: this is seen not as a defensive measure addressing the Oedipal complex nor a repression of it, but as a state in which the Ego opens itself up for a possibility of growth and change (Ibid, p. 75).

The tendency to fathom the Ego according to the paternal model of reality presents it as a faculty whose chief function is to provide protection from reality. This kind of understanding, while indeed allowing us to regard the Ego as protecting against reality, forfeits a considerable portion of life in which the link between human beings and their world is still maintained. Further on, Loewald introduces a distinction between the Ego's defensive function, repression, and its growth and change producing function, introjection, as particular states of psychic organization:

> Repression tends to keep object representations and object relations on an infantile level. Internalization, on the other hand, is a process by which, in the example of superego formation, oedipal object relations are renounced as such, destroyed, and the resulting elements enter into the formation of higher psychic structure, leading in turn to the development of object relations of a higher order of organization (Ibid, p. 76).

In addition to the above distinction, which considers repression as preserving primitive or primary psychic states and introjection as leading to higher levels of psychic organization, Loewald indicates that while repressed material takes no part in the formation of the Ego, introjected material is assimilated into its structure. Freud's notion of repression in the context of the structural model suggests that something is repressed not by being assigned to the unconscious, but due to not being integrated with the Ego, thus remaining separate from it. The appearance of the Super-Ego in the psychic system, following the resolution of the Oedipal complex, transforms the Ego in a way which cannot be construed as splitting off unintegrated material but rather as a splitting off of material that had already been assimilated, leading to a higher degree of separation within the Ego itself.

The tendency to regard the two stages of psychic development – the pre-Oedipal stage, in which the world appears pre-objectively and the post-Oedipal stage in which it appears objectively – as two hierarchical layers creates too dogmatic a notion of the psychic world, failing to reflect the complexity of human reality. While mature object relations are only possible at the Oedipal stage, before which reality is perceived as pre-objective, projection and internalization occur at varying levels of development. Loewald mentions several adult-life situations such as intense desire and ecstatic states, which, though uncommon, are not pathological and which still dissolve the subject-object distinction: "We are dealing here with the fact that early levels of psychic development are not simply outgrown and left behind but continue to be active, at least intermittently, during later life including adulthood" (Ibid, p. 81). At the narcissistic stage, or, more accurately, as this stage is transcended, introjections exist as part of pre-objective reality. Nevertheless, they are never simply past events which have paved the way for human consciousness to meet objective reality. Rather, their continuous effects on the entire structure of consciousness are present at any given moment. This claim cannot be restricted to its narrow sense, as regarding extreme or pathological cases; Loewald is here arguing about the nature of the entire psychic structure:

> But even where the subject–object distinction seems firmly established, where there seems to be no question of a weakening or loss of ego boundaries as we may observe it in exceptional or pathological states, the situation is less clear than we often assume. Any close, intimate object relationship has narcissistic features [and] identifications are involved (Ibid, p. 82).

Any significant encounter with the other necessarily entails certain elements of intimacy, which, in turn, involve narcissistic elements. Seeing that primary introjections and projections are always in the background throughout each meaningful encounter with the other, the subject-object distinction is never fully sustained: primary introjections and projections preserve that existential space in which human beings and their world are inseparable.

Super-Ego and Time

When the Super-Ego appears, at the end of a process replete with pre-objective identification and introjection, to complete the structural array of the psyche, the internal world is fully established. In other words, the individual is fully capable of living in a world which has both an inside and an outside. In "Superego and Time" (1962), Loewald examines the relationship between time and the psyche according to the structural model. Relying on Freud's account, in the *Interpretation of Dreams*, of psychic occurrence as belonging to the present, Loewald writes thus:

> In passing it is worth mentioning that Freud thought there was no need to assume a spatial arrangement of psychic systems, even though he speaks, by analogy, of the idea of psychic locality, but that it would be sufficient to assume, as he puts it, "that in a given psychical process the excitation passes through the systems in a particular temporal sequence" (S.E. 5:537). The concept of time involved here is that of objective time, not of psychic, active time (Ibid, p. 45).

Loewald distinguishes between objective time (prevalent in consciousness as Freud described it) and what he calls psychic time. The time which is of interest to Loewald and which he discusses in relation to the structural model is the dynamic time of human life, depicted as a form of psychic organization rather than a sequence of moments. As part of the attempt to comprehend the components of consciousness in relation to psychic, dynamic time, Loewald presents the following account of the Super-Ego:

> Insofar as the superego is the agency of inner standards, demands, ideals, hopes, and concerns in regard to the ego, the agency of inner rewards or guilt, the superego functions from the viewpoint of the future ego, from the stand point of the ego's future that is to be reached, is being reached, is being failed or abandoned by the ego (Ibid, Ibid).

In the previous section, we learned that the Super-Ego is the result of identifications and introjections which have been reorganized by the Ego and separated from it to form a new faculty. When we examine this faculty from the perspective of time, from the Ego's vantage point, the Super-Ego is uncovered as the Ego's future. Meaning that within the structural model, the Super-Ego manifests the temporal modality of the future.

The Ego, in charge of the direct link with reality, preoccupied with representing reality and constructing a system of immediate responses as means of protection against it, is associated with the modality of the present: "When we speak of the object representation, drive representation, a concept of time is implied in which 'present' is understood as an active process— to present something" (Ibid, p. 44). Now that we are aware of the link between Ego and present, between Super-Ego and future, we can observe the system of consciousness from a point of view more attuned to temporality. Thereby, we may notice that the manner in which the Ego is disclosed through the Super-Ego and manifests the present in relation to it as it is revealed through the perspective of the future. The Super-Ego, as the last faculty to be established in consciousness, embodies a certain relation toward the other components, including the Id. The Oedipal introjections comprising the Super-Ego are not structured solely by reality, rather, their particular character is determined in relation to the intensity and quality of the libido. Thus, they are representative of drives themselves inasmuch as they represent their objects. The Id, that faculty which contains our genetic past and the primary organization into which we are born, stands for the modality of the past. In this context, the Super-Ego, whose very existence serves to mediate between external reality and the Id, contains the Id as it is supposed to be organized, thereby encompassing the past as it emerges through the perspective of the future: "The superego than would represent the past as seen from the future, the id as it is to *be organized*, whereas the ego proper represents the id as organized at present" (Ibid, p. 45). The establishment of the Super-Ego completes the individual's internal world by achieving the temporal unity within which the past manifests itself in the future, alongside its potential reorganizations, and the present is manifest in the future, along with its ability to reorganize the past.

Summary

The departure from the narcissistic stage (the infant's individuation) toward acknowledging objective reality and the many cultural facets embedded in it is a process strewn with projection and introjection. This process, during which the Ego is differentiated from pre-objective reality, culminates in the emergence of the Super-Ego.

While Freud's account of the relation between the Super-Ego and reality stresses the role of the Super-Ego as the representative of culture and the socialization process and as applying categories and injunctions to the boundary between Ego and Id, Loewald explains this link in terms of the temporal relations prevailing in consciousness.

Uncovering the temporal aspect inherent at the very core of the structural model demonstrates that the establishment of the Super-Ego is both a precondition for abstract thinking and a factor facilitating the objective and cultural encounter with the world:

a. The Super-Ego, whose very existence represents the unique presence of Ego and Id in consciousness, enables the modalities of the present and the past to become integrated and reorganized, thereby producing a higher level of reality perception (more objective).

b. The Super-Ego, in opening the Ego to the future aspect, opens us to the variety of possibilities in light of which our individuation is attained.

The ability to reorganize the past and the present in light of the future is a precondition for abstract thinking as well as for the individual's admission into the social order. This is due to the fact that it enables consciousness to discover and acknowledge the world not only through the limited contexts of whatever facts are present at a given moment but through those contexts that are generated by human existence as well. The ability to organize the relationship between past, present and future opens the infant-subject to the possibility of knowing itself not only in relation to the world it encounters but also regarding what has-been, what might be, what never was and what could never be.

Loewald's reading of the structural model and of Freud's account of the establishment of the Super-Ego successfully identifies the centrality of the phenomenon of time to the very existence of consciousness. Furthermore, this reading demonstrates that at the heart of the Freudian structure, through operating within a linear time scheme, there lies a more fundamental temporal structure, in which the future aspect gains precedence over the past and present aspects.

THE TEMPORAL-ONTOLOGICAL STRUCTURE OF NARCISSISM

As we have seen, the narcissistic stage is itself divided into two stages: the first, in which infant and mother are still undifferentiated, and the second, in which the Ego is already somewhat distinct, and serves as a repository for libidinal energy withdrawn from the cathected mother. Freud's account of this second stage, in which he analyzes the individual's possible sexual identities, relies on the presence of the Ego. Prior to this stage, the budding emergence of world and Ego is manifest through primary projections and introjections.

The transition from the first to the second stage of narcissism entails a shift from a state in which the infant's encounter with the world takes place within a non-linear field, to a state in which the world can be encountered in light of a linear time scheme. Our discussion of Loewald's account of the narcissistic stage teaches that primary psychic states are not evolutionary steps left behind in the past, but primal layers that are constantly reintegrated into the psychic array as a whole. In essence, these primary stages are part and parcel of the psychic structure at any given moment. This assertion suggests that at the root of the psychological structure lies a non-linear temporal element, constantly present throughout every psychic activity.

The primordial processes characteristic of the emergence from primary narcissism are those of identification and introjection. Primary identification is the manner in which the infant identifies with the mother, narcissistically seeing itself in her. From Freud's perspective, we identify with an other which is later on incorporated into the psychic structure, that is, introjected. Loewald's account of the structural model shows that alongside Freud's linear depiction, consciousness is also permeated by a non-linear temporal aspect. I would now like to link this aspect and primary projection and introjection by describing the particular temporal relations they exhibit.

In general, we would not be mistaken in indicating that the narcissistic relation is that state in which the mother, whose psychic structure is far more organized than that of the infant identifying itself with her, through her responses and behavior, shapes the infant's possibilities for future existence. This preliminary depiction of the way in which time is manifest in this process indicates a future which is not-yet-now and therefore does not exceed the nature of time as it is manifest in Freudian thinking. From another angle, one more attuned to the possibility that these processes are essentially temporal, we may suggest the following: the infant's very identification with the mother, as its future, is a state in which, through identification, its very being is being ahead-of-itself. For example, the infant might identify with the mother as providing a sense of security, although this sense of security is not of its own making (though one day it could be). This sense of self, originating in identification, opens the infant to the future aspect through its self-transcendence toward the possibility of being itself embodied and actualized in the mother's identification with her infant. In Heideggerian terms, the psychological notion of identification is the most primary manifestation of the future ecstasis, while introjections, respectively, constitutes that manner in which identification is retained within the psychic structure once its future possibility, sustained by the mother, ceases to exist. That is, introjection is the infant's relation to its has-been self, it is its self-transcendence towards what has-been and is therefore the most primary manifestation of the ecstasis of the past.

Alongside these processes of identification and introjection, the Ego is becoming more and more distinct as a faculty, which, according to both Freud and Loewald, represents the events of the present. The vantage point of temporality would describe the Ego as the particular manner (present) in which the infant discovers its possibilities for being itself (future) as a part of itself (past). This structure becomes fully formed once the structural model is completed by the establishment of the Super-Ego. According to this reading, the present is never a full external presence but rather, it is the infant's ability to exist in relation to the field of its past possibilities, of what it has-been. Observing the Ego through the prism of temporality reveals that it could be fathomed as manifesting the infant's openness to its own present dimension – to the ecstasis of the present. In his discussion of the formation of the Ego, Freud depicts this process as libidinal withdrawal from a state in which it is utterly identical to reality: "originally the ego includes everything, later it separates off an external world from itself" (Freud, 1961b, p. 68). This account leaves the formation of the Ego shrouded in mist; what does Freud mean by stating that the Ego includes reality? Are we to understand that before reality receded Ego reigned supreme? This final conclusion raises much difficulty as the Ego is a faculty in charge of organizing, protecting and repression, none of which are possible before reality recedes. Grasping human beings as temporal entities sheds considerable light upon this claim: seeing that the primordial state linking infant and mother is a narcissistic state, characterized by non-linear temporality and seeing that departing from this state involves the infant's recognition of each of the temporal modalities as pertaining to itself, we may construe the lack of differentiation from the mother as a state in which all three temporal modalities are unified. In his "The Experience of Time" [1972], Loewald discusses two possible experiences which he sees as marking the extremities of human existence – eternity and fragmentation. Regarding the experience of eternity, Loewald (1980) elaborates:

> At one extreme is the experience of eternity where the flux of time is stayed or suspended. Eternity is to be distinguished from sempiternity or everlasting time. Scholastic philosophers speak of the *nunc stans*, the abiding instant, where there is no division of past, present and future, no remembering, no wish, no anticipation, merely the complete absorption

> in being, or in that which is. [...] Time as something that, in its modes of past, present, and future articulates experience and conveys such concepts as succession, simultaneity, and duration is suspended in such a state (p. 141).

The lack of differentiation between infant and mother is not to be explained in empirical terms or as an erroneous perception of reality which both sides must overcome. This undifferentiated state manifests the infant's immersion in a unified temporal field in which the links between future, past and present have not yet been revealed as part of its existence. Seeing that the distinctness and the integration of the three modalities of time precondition the appearance of things in the world, the infant is not separate from the mother, as there still isn't anything to be separate from. The departure from this state, in which eternity encompasses everything, leads to the state in which the Ego is distinct as the infant's specific ability to acknowledge the present aspect in consequence of his openness to the future (identification) and the past (introjection). In this context, we can reexamine Freud's assertion regarding the Ego as including reality. As far as the temporal aspect in concerned, the Ego was indeed present before reality receded and was indeed identical to it since eternity, as a temporal unity, is a perpetual present. As long as the infant remains in this state of temporal unity, it cannot be differentiated from the mother, only identical to her. Primary narcissism is a manifestation of temporal unity, while secondary narcissism indicates that the infant is beginning to acknowledge itself through time. It recognizes itself since it has been opened to the aspects of future, past and present as parts of its own being. Its openness to the temporal aspect is not equivalent to introjection, identification or representation; rather, these are made possible since the temporal aspect is already embedded in the infant's existence.

Lacan's formulation of the mirror stage deals with this very stage of the infant's development, emphasizing the impact of the processes characteristic of the narcissistic stage prior to Ego formation. Since the infant identifies with its mirror-image which is something other than itself, Lacan considers primary identification as the psychic act responsible for unifying fragmented bodily sensations into a viable Ego. This account stresses the image as the result of the infant's fantastic, imaginary ability to see itself as other, acknowledging its existence as a subject possessed of an Ego. Lacan sees this occurrence as the source of the self-alienation he finds fundamental to human existence: the subject alienates the Ego as it is, after all, only an imaginary being. Unlike Lacan's reading, I propose not to emphasize the spatial aspect, i.e., the image, but rather the temporal aspect as the prerequisite for identification. That is, I propose to comprehend the moment in which the infant identifies with the other as itself not as an imaginary act in which its selfhood reflects that of the other, but as the moment in which it is opened to the future aspect of its existence. The future, as part of the infant's selfhood, simultaneously contains both its own self and that of the other. Manifesting the future aspect, the infant's field of possibilities for being itself encompasses the other or otherness as part of its temporal structure. In keeping with this reading, the process of identification does not hinge on the image but on the opening of the future as a field within the infant's psychic structure, enabling it to transcend toward its other-self. This transcendence could be perceived as imaginary, if we construe it in light of the linear framework of meaning, or alternatively, as the core of human reality, when we observe it in light of the horizon of meaning provided by temporality

Unaided by the other (the mother as mirror), the infant is incapable of acknowledging the future as part of its own structure. However, the openness to the temporal phenomenon underpinning human existence does not posit the other as preceding self-possibilities but rather allows the future to reflect both alike: the possibility for being its self's-other and its other's-self.[62] Freud's use of the metaphor of Narcissus, who fell in love with his own reflection, as the prototypical structure for psychopathologies, implicitly posits, in keeping with Lacan's interpretation, the other as the core of the subject. Reading the mirror stage in light of temporality suggests that the subject's fixation with itself results from its inability to detach itself from the spectacle of identifying itself in time. The problem here is not only self love (as Freud argues or as we can gather from Lacan's transposition of the Freudian pitfall onto his own notion of desire) but the ontological fear of losing the self, which is constituted as a temporal fabric.

In order to articulate this final point, I wish to make use of Ovid's (1955) version of the myth of Narcissus (pp. 67-73). In the Roman version of the myth, Narcissus is a handsome young man who wouldn't respond to the courting of women and men who admired his beauty. Especially offended by his behavior is Echo, the nymph who, cursed by Hera, is able to speak only by repeating the words of others. As punishment for his arrogant indifference, the gods send Nemesis, the goddess of revenge, to cast a spell on Narcissus so that he cannot fall in love with anyone but himself. Once Narcissus notices his reflection in the water, he is trapped by it and becomes unable to remove his gaze from his own reflection. When Echo speaks to Narcissus, she is compelled to repeat the last words of each sentence he utters. However, instead of hearing her voice repeating his words, Narcissus hears the echo of his own

---

[62] These terms, *Self's-other and Other's-self*, serve to capture the unique intricacies of the encounter between self and other in light of Heidegger's ontological insight and the structure of temporality in particular; together, they constitute the existential structure of the self's being-in-time. A full understanding of the structure of the self discloses the inherently two-faced presence of otherness at the core of the self, which emerges through the past and future ecstases to the present. The *Self's-other* refers to *the potential otherness integral to the self*, to a concrete possibility of the self among the myriad possible selves comprising its available field of possibilities for being-itself; the *Other's-self* refers to *the inherent potential of the self to be permeated by other selves*, to that particular presence of the other in our world which manifests itself also in terms of our possible selves, expanding our field of self-possibilities.

voice. Nemesis' curse turned out to be devastating since Narcissus' inability to distinguish between himself and his own image left him without the ability to acknowledge any reality principle and caused his death. Narcissus' rejection of his courters was interpreted by the gods as a refusal to identify with the other, and thus they literally deprived him of the ability to see himself in the other. Regarding the moral of the myth, there is wide consent that in order for the subject to recognize reality, the other must be somehow present to her; but in what way, and to what extent is the other present for the subject, there is, evidently, a great dispute.

Taking the myth of Narcissus as a point of departure for a new reading of the Narcissistic drama, I would like to propose that if we would be able to put our finger on what it is exactly that Narcissus cannot recognize when Echo approaches him, we could gain a better understanding of what the psychoanalytic reading of Narcissism lacks. Note that Echo's repetition of Narcissus' words is not an exact duplication of them; in fact, uttered in Echo's voice, it is already a modification of his words. Thus, Echo's repetition presents Narcissus with an aural (sonorous) reflection of his self. Drawing a distinction between Narcissus' immersion in his own reflection, and his inability to recognize his reflection in Echo's words, we could argue that while the conditions for the appearance of his reflection and Narcissus' immersion in it are grounded in a space actualized in the present, the condition for hearing his own voice reflected in Echo's is grounded in temporal duration. We could thus conclude that if Narcissus is unable to hear Echo's voice, it would appear that his own mode of being somehow blocks his ability to grasp temporal manifestations.

We could say that, caught up in the lure of his image, deprived of the presence of the other, Narcissus is trapped in a perpetual present that leads to his death. From Narcissus' autopsy we learn that the cause of his death is the absence of any other from Narcissus' self-recognition. Unlike Lacan's interpretation, in which the other generates the self-alienation endemic to the human psyche, my reading considers the lack of the other, which is an integral part of the self's temporal structure, as the etiology of Narcissus' death and the source of the human, all too human, phenomenon of self-alienation. From a different perspective, the moment the self's-other cannot appear as part of the self, the otherness of the self is denied, and the possibility of coming back from its horizon of future possibilities to itself is sealed off.

In conclusion, this reading suggests that the primary processes of the human psyche, which consequently provide the foundation for the entire psychic structure, are already anchored in a temporal structure, seeing that the life of human beings as ontic-ontological entities is a constant manifestation of temporality. Human existence cannot be fully comprehended as long as it is conceived solely as an event occurring alongside a notion of time or within time. Human life is itself a particular mode of living time. Life is always a temporal occurrence and each and every life-event bears the signature of time. To make things clear, I am not arguing that introjection, identification and the

Ego, the paths which open one to the temporal aspect embedded in human existence, are themselves ontological characteristics. I am claiming that, as psychological processes, they manifest an array of ontological relations – the temporal openness underpinning the structure of human existence as the three temporal ecstases: future, past and present. From the perspective of temporality, considering the narcissistic state as accompanying us throughout our entire lives reveals that the future ecstasis opens an existential field in which the other's-self and the self's-other are present as part of the self's structure. The Freudian method, presupposing a subject which is external to time, leaves no room for such an understanding of the psychic structure.

Eight

Back to Ida

Psychoanalytic Concepts as Manifesting Temporal Relations

In light of Heidegger's inquiry, Freudian theory is revealed to be subjected to the framework of meaning provided by a metaphysics of presence, in which the present serves as the ultimate foundation for the appearance of things in the world. The attempt to reinstate temporality within psychoanalytic theory requires that we formulate a new understanding of the latter, one relying on the manner in which temporality constitutes Dasein's existence in the world through the horizon of presence, that is, the present (Praesens). Freud's 'objective world' is one in which the present, emerging from the horizon of presence, has come to dominate all reality. My attempt to return to psychoanalysis and reformulate its tenets in light of the perspective provided by temporality entails, first and foremost, understanding psychological processes as constitutive not only regarding the present (the objective world), but also regarding the three modalities of time and the ways in which the horizon of presence enables phenomena to manifest themselves in the world.

My reading of Ida's case study in the fifth chapter strived to show the extent to which psychoanalysis had overlooked the phenomenon of temporality. In this chapter, my main interest is to demonstrate that those same concepts Freud employs in his account of Ida's behavior could be interpreted as manifestations of temporality. Any observation of the phenomenon of temporality requires that we allow distinct temporal aspects to co-exist simultaneously, instructing us to consider the symptomatology characteristic of case-study analyses as manifesting an intricate life-story. The very possibility of letting temporality depict human behavior through psychoanalytic concepts lies in our ability to develop a keen sensitivity to the presence of temporal phenomena in Ida's world.

In chapter three, the section entitled "Being-There in Time" discussed the relationship between time and selfhood according to Heidegger. It demonstrated that Dasein is an essentially temporal entity, not to be construed as some pre-existing being simply projected onto time. It is always already, by its very being, simultaneously open to the future, the past and the present. This temporal openness preconditions the phenomenon of the world and any understanding thereof. Human beings are not 'inside' the time by which they are measured, they *are* temporality in their very being. Dasein's relation to its own being is one of its existentiales and its possibility for being-itself (its relation to its own being) is nothing other than the manner in which it *lives* time. I propose that we understand psychoanalysis, as a method employing an array of concepts accounting for human behavior in normal, pathological or psychotic states, in light of the manner in which Dasein lives time, i.e., in light of the presence of temporal structures in its way of life.

One of the central differences between a theory of interpretation founded upon a metaphysics of presence and one derived from ontological insight lies in the theoretical role of nothing or absence. Freud sees nothing as a 'lack', as something once present but now gone: the infant is hungry while the mother is absent and unable to feed it. In contrast, ontological thought considers nothing (Das Nicht) as immanent to human existence. Freudian theory sees nothing as affecting and constituting psychic activity in the sense that the psychic mechanism is capable of acknowledging certain lacks, thus setting out to abate them by acting in the external world or through the appearance of fantasy as an internal activity which acts as a compromise between the reality principle and the pleasure principle. While these two alternatives address nothing merely as a representation of an absent object (either internal or external), Heidegger, as we have seen, conceives of beings as always disclosed in light of the present (Praesens). Since beings indeed manifest themselves as lacking in the Freudian sense (as non-existent beings), Heidegger avows that rather than grasping the representation of some presence which once was or is yet to be, we sense the presence inherent, in a way, in its absence. Being and nothingness are not in binary opposition, in the sense that being exists and nothing does not.[63] Any interpretation advocating a worldview in which being and nothingness are thus opposed discloses the world only through the layer pertaining to the existence of objects, i.e., the ontic layer. In the world of Dasein, being and nothingness appear through an existential field which could never be fully accounted for in ontic terms. Reestablishing psychoanalytic theory upon the tenets and the layered worldview derived from phenomenological ontology allows us to discuss various nuances of presence and absence. Psychoanalysis, when construed in light of Heidegger's temporality, reveals nothing not as a psychological lack but as an existential layer pertaining to the temporal fabric. In this context, fantasy is that manner in which the ecstasis of the future opens Dasein to the world's possibilities. These possibilities, though we may not always be able to actualize them in the present (hence the presence of 'nothing'), still possess, in Dasein's world, a certain reality of their own and are not mere illusions mediating between the pleasure and reality principles. One example of the reality of fantasy lies in the meaning of transference in light of temporality.

---

[63] Heidegger (1993) elaborates this notion in his "What is Metaphysics?", in which he explains human existence as transcending from being to nothingness and back again (pp. 89-110).

TRANSFERENCE, COUNTER-TRANSFERENCE AND TEMPORALITY

As mentioned in chapter six, Freud's "The Dynamics of Transference" [1912] describes the response to the work of analysis as a regression of the libido which revives childhood objects and images. Following Freud's 1920 "Beyond the Pleasure Principle", transference is explained as the patient's internal compulsion to repeat repressed experiences as if they were part of her present (repetition-compulsion). In general, transference projects the repressed aspects of the patient's world onto the analyst, making the patient relive the past as if it were the present, transposing the past onto the present and compulsively repeating repressed material. Freud's explanation for this phenomenon, whether in terms of libidinal regression or repetition compulsion, depicts it as a state in which one looks upon the present objective reality, but, failing to acknowledge it, encounters only the past. In other words, transference keeps the patient from fully experiencing reality, trapping her in a subjective, illusory dimension projected onto the analyst / other. As far as the sequence of events is concerned, it seems that positing the structural component of the unconscious outside the flow of time is the precondition for any projection of the past onto the present. The unconscious, as that psychic component containing repressed / unintegrated images and experiences, serves as the connection between the has-been past and the actual, objective present, creating an illusory encounter in which the patient relates to the analyst as if she were someone else.

The difficulties inherent in Freud's formulation of transference as repetition compulsion are depicted in temporal terms in Andre Green's *Time in Psychoanalysis.* The book devotes considerable attention to transference as repetition compulsion seeing that, psychologically, it maintains an inherent relation to time – one which Freud terms 'Nachträglichkeit' (deferred action).[64] It is, in fact, Green's endeavor in this book to examine the status of such 'deferred actions' in Freudian thought and to attempt to provide them with a new theoretical framework, one more attuned to temporality.

Initially, Green (2002) locates the problem in Freud's account of transference as drive-related (derived from the death-instinct) which essentially leaves the object (the analyst) external to the phenomenon in question. This means that the Freudian account of the phenomenon of transference is founded upon a methodological separation of the object from the drive.

> This, then, was where Freud's error lay. When approaching the question of transference in repetition, he made no mention of its object (the analyst) – apart from simply pointing out that the latter is led,

[64] This refers to the manner in which past events, recollections and impressions are subsequently altered. This means that an event's significance is obtained in retrospect rather than derived from its contemporary circumstances.

> reluctantly, and under the pressure of circumstances, to play the bad role. He did not go far enough (p. 125).

The above quote formulates Freud's error as neglecting the significance of the object in relation to transference. Regarding the development of psychoanalysis from a historical perspective, Green laments the extreme reaction on the part of contemporary approaches – Relational, Object-Relations, Self-Psychology, etc. – to Freud's neglect of the object: a complete abandonment of the instinctual sources of the psyche (Ibid, p. 120). Green formulates his conclusions as an appeal to rethink the objects of psychoanalytic thought in general and of transference in particular, using a method which combines both instinct and object (patient and analyst). He proposes to do so by acknowledging the connection between the time of the subject and the time of the other: "All this requires us to recognize that a path has to be found between the time of the subject and the time of the other: that is, a moment of encounter between the two" (Ibid, p. 140). In other words, when the grounds upon which the phenomenon of transference – as we have seen, a clearly temporal phenomenon - is analyzed bring together object and instinct, transference is reformulated in terms of the subject's and the other's time.

This reformulation of transference in temporal terms raises certain doubts regarding Freud's assertion that the unconscious is a faculty residing outside time. Indeed, Green attempts to grant the unconscious a status which might liberate it from the classic notion of it as a container for repressed material.

> Far from being merely the scrap heap of consciousness or the dumping place of desires, beliefs and effects which do not want to yield to the dictates of reason and logic, the unconscious is first and foremost a treasure-trove of meaning, a reserve that is not only a storehouse of past illusions, but an inexhaustible dynamic source inclining towards the future by virtue of the constant stimulation of forces which dislodge the subject from his centre, displacing him, and sending him 'elsewhere' (Ibid, p. 149).

Green conceives of the unconscious as harboring a dynamic variety of meanings facing the future and capable of de-centering the subject, transporting her 'elsewhere'. A more ontologically inclined formulation would state that Green acknowledges the manner in which the unconscious is bound to the future aspect. Moreover, his suggestion that we should regard the Freudian unconscious through the prism of the future and his indication that it is capable of displacing the subject from her center is in dire need of Heidegger's notion of temporality and the ontology based on Dasein's modes of being. Unfortunately, Green does not develop this intuition further, nor does he provide us with a reevaluation of transference after recognizing the need to acknowledge its existence as grounded in the time of the subject and the other.

This section will present a new understanding of transference in light of the phenomenon of temporality. The next section will deal with the status of the unconscious as examined in the same light.

The phenomenon Freud diagnoses as transference is the projection of the past onto the present. However, since Freud sees time as a homogenous sequence of intervals, he binds these intervals in a way which relies on the ability of the unconscious to serve as their nexus. Unlike the etiology Freud constructs around the notion of transference, the account derived from the phenomenon of temporality already acknowledges the past as preceding the present, considering it as a precondition for the disclosure of time as a homogenous sequence of coherent intervals. At the root of our everyday encounter with our surrounding world, the past is constantly in a process of becoming. This means that a temporal-ontological reading discloses transference, in its Freudian sense, as an integral part of our psycho-existential structure, rather than a disturbance of the normal structure of the mind. Tracing the transference of the past onto the present is not sufficient for diagnosing neurosis, as the human psychological structure is founded upon the phenomenon of time as a temporal unity. By its very essence, the analytic setting (in which the world of the patient encounters that of the analyst) entails an inherent openness to the particular manner in which the patient is present in time including her unique manner of binding together past and present. Consequently, the very transference of the past to the present is an existential phenomenon, not a manifestation of neurosis. Moreover, as far as the existential analytic is concerned, we may also describe how past becomes present in terms of Freud's "repetition-compulsion". Seeing that the structure of temporality, as a future having been which makes present, permeates every single one of the moments positioned along the linear timeline, each present period of time already contains a 'repetition-compulsion' due to the necessary return of the past into the present as part of the temporal motion inherent in human existence. The cardinal matter here is not the return of the past into the present but rather which past made it through to the present and which didn't.

Dasein does not exist in time; it exists as a temporal being. In fact, the very possibility for being human, for having a past, a history, a heritage or, alternately, for having a temporal quality pertaining solely to oneself, is rooted in the existential fact that the human past is a past which makes present rather than simply passing away. From the perspective of temporality we might say that transference, in its Freudian sense, in not equivalent to the phenomenon of past making present, as this state is characteristic of the human condition in general. How should construe, therefore, the phenomenon of transference in terms of temporality? First of all, I would like to claim that transference is the particular manner in which a particular person's past makes present. This manner may indeed differ from person to person even to the point of disclosing the present as manifesting primarily the past rather than functioning as a temporal field bearing its own independent significance. However, this state is chiefly the result of the presence or absence of the future aspect in transference.

As the previous chapter indicated, the psychic structure is founded upon a temporal one, which is rooted in primary narcissism and whose narcissistic qualities are constantly present, underlying every psychic activity. The ontological analysis of narcissism demonstrated that the identification of the subject with the other-as-self is not necessarily explained as an imaginary act in which the subject's selfhood is a reflection of the other. Rather, it could be accounted for as opening up to the future dimension which forms part of its very being. In this sense, the future is that part of the subject's selfhood which simultaneously contains the aspects of self and other. In other words, the self's field of possibility, manifesting the future aspect, always already contains the other or otherness as part of its own temporal structure. As transference is diagnosed within the analytic setting, the making-present of the past already entails the field of possibility from which the other / the analyst may emerge into the world of the patient. Meaning that transference, as an event, also includes the future as having been and making present. This event already harbors the manner in which the possibilities of the other (a parent figure or any other significant figure in one's history) and those of the self appear together as that future having been or as that future which never was but had to be.

Seeing that the future – that horizon of possibility comprised of self's-others and other's selves – belongs to the very nature of transference, the position of the analyst within the patient's world is one of its cardinal aspects. The material projected onto the analyst is not a pure transference, it is not a closed off event or group of events, utterly detached from the analyst's personality. The analyst, letting the patient feel, to a certain extent, inseparate from her, is present within the patient's world as that other's-self which appears alongside the patient's self's-other. Regarding Green's articulation of the need to understand the time of the subject and the time of the other as pertinent to transference, we might say that the analyst which is aware of the interconnectedness of temporality and transference ought to maintain the ecstasis of the future open to the existential field in which the other's-self and the self's-other may manifest. In addition, in examining the presence of the patient in the world of the analyst, we might formulate the structure of counter-transference as that manner in which the patient, as an other's-self, emerges from the future horizon of possibility as part of the structure of the analyst's self.

While Freud conceived of transference as a form of acting-out, marking it as a neurosis which creates a gap between the way the world appears and the way it is perceived, its depiction in temporal terms positions it at the very foundation of any possible encounter between human beings and the world and between them and others. Transference, in its psychological sense as a therapeutic instrument, manifests the manner in which the temporal motion from the future to the past and onto the present, concealed by average everydayness, could be uncovered within the analytic setting.

EGO, REPRESSION, UNCONSCIOUS AND TEMPORALITY

Freud's transition from the topographic model to the structural one made it possible to consider the Ego as a faculty in charge of organizing the various psychic components. Loewald saw this capacity for organization as preconditioning the Ego's ability to function as a defense system. With these insights in mind, I now wish to portray repression as a temporal phenomenon, demonstrating that our understanding of the Freudian unconscious should not be limited to the notion of a container, housing those events which exceed any linear-objective sequence. Rather, we might conceive of the unconscious as one of the unique temporal relations pertaining to human life and belonging to the very heart of the temporal structure. Accounting for the unconscious in temporal terms requires us to understand it as part of a conceptual array including both Ego and repression.

Laplanche and Pontalis (1973) depict the nature of repression in Freudian thought as that activity by which the subject attempts to suppress or restrict certain representations (thoughts, images and memories) to the unconscious (p. 390). In fact, repression occurs whenever conflicting demands within the system lead it to respond to a particular instinct. Repression is that particular manner in which the system pays the price for instinctual satisfaction: although a certain instinct was indeed satisfied, other demands were left unheeded and the psychic system is led to experience more unpleasure than pleasure. In order to avoid this inherent predicament, repression sets in, causing the troublesome representation to vanish from the conscious level, confining it to the unconscious. Thus constrained, it is precluded from participating in the encounter between the individual and her world or in her understanding of her personal history. According to Freud, such acts of repression manifest themselves consciously as symptoms.

The structure underlying the work of repression could be explained in various terms – economic, topographic, linguistic and structural – yet each of these perspectives, in their account of the mechanism in which repression is rooted, portrays the unconscious as a container for repressed material. The manner in which Freud relates repression to the unconscious is problematic seeing that the prevalent metaphor in his depiction of the unconscious and its function vis-à-vis repression is a spatial one. Limited to spatial imagery, the unconscious is already subjected to the reign of spatial relations over temporal ones. Freud indeed defines the unconscious as exceeding the linear scheme but in fact, as we have seen, it lacks any positive characteristics and is comprehended solely as the negation of objective time; as an enclave in which causality and coherence do not apply.

I would like to present the unconscious as a phenomenon belonging to the structure of temporality. My presentation traverses Freud's transition from the topographic model to the structural one, relying on the manner in which this transition leads to a vertical notion of the human psyche. After 1923, it became possible to consider the unconscious as a component pertaining to the Ego, the Super-Ego and the Id. This vertical layout was adopted by Anna Freud and Heinz Hartmann and was further developed to accommodate the fundamental change in the Ego's role within the psychic system: from being in charge of defense, it became responsible for organizing both the psyche and external reality. However, this change does not mean that the Ego had lost its defensive capabilities. This is how Loewald (1980) addresses this possibility in his "Ego-Organization and Defense" [1973]:

> This does not mean that the defense functions of the ego were lost sight of, but that the latter now were understood in the context and from the viewpoint of psychic organization, rather than psychic organization being viewed from the standpoint of defense (p. 175).

Loewald here claims that the defense mechanisms characteristic of psychic activity are in fact derived from the consequences of psychic organization processes. The psyche, or the structure of the human personality, is first and foremost a dynamic structure whose chief attribute is a capacity for organizing itself in various forms. In keeping with the conceptions propagated in Loewald's "The Experience of Time" [1973] and "On Internalization" [1972], we might argue that the forms of organization mentioned by Loewald are clearly temporal formations.

Therefore, in discussing Ego-formation, how are we to construe its particular organization at those stages which precede its full maturation as far as object-relations, identification, regression and introjections are concerned? So far we have linked the Ego to the temporal modality of the present in particular. Now, in order to comprehend the Ego as a form of psychic organization, we must link its forms of organization to the temporal dimension in general. As aforementioned, spatial metaphors dominate Freud's suggested structure of the mind; thus the Ego, as a psychic component, is perceived as a spatial entity. From the perspective of temporality, the Ego, as the faculty responsible for psychic organization, is disclosed as the specific manner in which the present emerges from the temporal unity. In other words, the Ego manifests self-possibilities in the present. Consequently, the Ego is affected (regarding the narcissistic stage) by the self's-other and the other's-self (principally related to the ecstasis of the future) with which it is intertwined as well as by the manner in which this future field has been introjected, has become past and now opens or limits the Ego's present possibilities for being. As the specific manner in which the self emerges into the present, interlaced with past and future, the Ego's very existence entails a unique temporal relation. The Ego is not a psychic entity active in our internal world as Freud suggest, rather, our presence in the present is marked by time, by the particular manner in which our own private temporal unity facilitates or precludes our discovery of the present. In order to complete this revision of the notion of Ego in temporal terms I would like to emphasize that it is not that the Ego encompasses temporal manifestations; rather, the term Ego could apply to the manifestation of the self in the present as emerging from the temporal unity.

Ego and Temporality

The classic Freudian view of the Ego could now be exchanged for an interpretation which considers the Ego as a form of temporal organization. An instructive example of this exchange lies in Freud's depiction and analysis of Ida's reaction to her encounter with Mr. K. As you may recall, Ida was sent to be treated by Freud against her will, following her family's refusal to accept the state of affairs derived by what took place at the lake. After having sailed, while strolling about, Mr. K. dared to offer Ida his love. Afterwards, Mr. K. had denied everything, accusing Ida of being interested only in sexual matters and of fabricating the whole affair. After this incident, Ida decided to refrain from seeing Mr. K., demanding her father, who unfortunately did not believe her, to end his relationship with Mr. and Mrs. K. She began exhibiting the symptoms which Freud depicted as obsessive brooding about her father's relationship with Mrs. K.

Freud's analysis of the incident at the lake led him to conclude that Ida is hysterical, seeing that she failed to respond to Mr. K.'s advances. According to Freud, this hysteria is the result of the regression of the libido to previous stages (an unstable Ego), which brought about the repression of the sexual feelings Ida was supposed to experience in that situation. An alternative reading, one which considers the Ego as manifesting the temporal formations comprising the structure of human existence, might portray Ida's obsessive preoccupation with sexuality or with her Father's involvement with Mrs. K. as an attempt to deal with a feeling of loss. In addition, my analysis of the incident at the store argued that Ida had not yet developed the adequate emotional capacities in order to experience sexual desire toward Mr. K. and to interpret his advances as sexual. His choice to disavow the incident at the lake stranded Ida in an irresolvable psychic state – a trauma. In light of my reading of the structure of the self and the narcissistic state which permeates it, I propose that we ought to view Mr. K.'s unwillingness to acknowledge Ida's story as the event which overwhelmed her, inciting the very behavior which made her family force her into analysis.

Paving the way for my portrayal of the Ego from a temporal perspective, I wish to elucidate Freud's assertion that Ida is in love with Mr. K., and to indicate that this feeling of love stemmed from her true need for him to be with her, the same need he ignored. In order for Ida to construe Mr. K.'s actions as courting, as Freud and Mr. K. himself indeed have, Ida had to successfully undergo a fundamental and impossible transformation on two levels. The first level involves her emotional environment. At this level she had to perform three feats: to relinquish the hope or fantasy that her father will spend time with her instead of Mrs. K.; to allow herself to take Mrs. K.'s place in her relationship with her husband; to give up her friendship with Mrs. K. In other words, Ida ability to interpret Mr. K.'s actions as sexual advances and respond to them in kind, depended upon her willingness to exchange the emotional fabric of her life for another, thus repositioning herself within her emotional-social-familial matrix. It is highly unlikely that Ida, a lonely child, emotionally abandoned by her entire family, could have undergone such drastic changes, including painful compromise, giving up essential emotional needs, emotionally separating herself from her family etc. On the second level, which Freud terms sexual, in keeping with my analysis in chapter five, Ida, a thirteen-year-old girl, could not have responded to Mr. K.'s seduction nor could she have entered any kind of a mature erotic relationship with him. It is my claim that her inability to endow these events with meaning either on the level of her emotional and social environment or on the sexual level, is cardinal to her experience of Mr. K.'s advances. Her inability to grant meaning to the experience of her encounters with him and the implications these had regarding her life is the essence of her traumatic experience.

We might better understand how Ida's inability to give meaning to her experience of meeting Mr. K. produced the kind of behavior which took over her psychic life if we acknowledge Mr. K.'s refusal to corroborate her story as the cardinal event. This prevented her from granting his advances any meaning, thus precluding her from responding to them as having a clear meaning in her world (this entails not only her ability to respond to Mr. K., as Freud had in mind, but also the ability to reject him in a manner which could have enabled her to maintain a reasonably healthy relationship with everyone else involved). Throughout the entire period in which her father was seeing Mrs. K., Ida considered Mr. K. as a source of emotional support, capable of warding off the feelings of isolation and alienation engendered by her parents' behavior. This support enabled her, in spite of her difficulties at home, to encounter herself and maintain her selfhood. If we consider Ida's personality as a temporal structure, encompassing a field of self-possibilities containing the other as part of the future dimension embedded in it, Mr. K.'s refusal to verify her story is revealed as betraying his presence in her world, which he allegedly desired. Essentially, his refusal is the very moment in which the future horizon of possibility, which was created by their relationship and was letting her experience, encounter and feel herself as being-with an other, had been severed. Freud explained this in terms of an unstable Ego which caused a libidinal regression, impairing, through repression, the individual's ability to encounter objective reality. The temporal perspective construes this as a severing of the horizon of possibility through which Ida could have felt herself being-with an other and as restricting her self's ability to emerge into the present. We should keep in mind that such an attunement to the other presupposes a temporal motion through which the future continually flows toward the past and on to the present. When this temporal motion is restricted, the attunement to the other is undermined and the event of meaning is compromised.

Ida's relationship with Mr. K., as the sole alternative to her failing relationship with her family, conditioned the very existence of a horizon of self-possibilities through which the other could become present in her world.

Ida's inability to give meaning to the event at the lake is indeed the result of her being as yet unfit to experience mature sexuality and of the events that followed as well. Temporally speaking, past events can fully attain their meaning provided that these events can be integrated into the temporal unity underlying one's existential experience. This condition does not depend upon a linear sequence of events, whose intervals are causally and consciously linked, but on the individual's ability to have recourse to the event as the course of her life requires. That is, the event must still remain open to her, even after it had past. A past event's ability to remain present is a possibility inherent in the temporal unity. This possibility may or may not become actualized, depending on the unique manner in which the structure of the self is open to its temporal possibilities, transcending any reliance on the linear scheme constituting the sequence of events. Ida's present inability to give meaning to the incident at the lake stems not only from her inability to construe Mr. K.'s advances as sexual at a given moment – i.e., being unable to encounter the (sexual) self's-other Mr. K. demanded her to be. Rather, in light of the formulation of self's temporal dimension, it stemmed from the fact that the event remained closed off after its occurrence, as Mr. K.'s refusal to corroborate her story and his severing of her future horizon of self-possibilities foreclosed her existential possibility of acknowledging him as an other's-self present alongside her self's-other. In retrospect, the incident at the lake could not attain its full scope of meaning, as Ida's partner in that situation, the one who enabled her to experience being-with an other, had abandoned her, leaving her with a sense of having lost the existential field in which she had once accommodated both herself and the other. When the structure of human selfhood is understood as a manifestation of Dasein's engagement with its surrounding environment, the other is always already a part of the world in which Dasein dwells. Mr. K.'s reluctance to verify Ida's story deprived her of the possibility of trying to embrace or, if you will, actualize the self that he demanded her to be for him. It is not without reason that Ida shared this story with her family; she hoped that Mr. K.'s acknowledgment of her story might help her give meaning to what happened at the lake: she expected the person who vanished from her world as soon as he tried to seduce her to come back and stand by her. Mr. K.'s decline to affirm her story, to be part of her world, prevented her from enabling the past to go through her, from letting the contents of the situation dwell within the manner in which her self was exposed to the present.

Repression and Temporality

Ida's insistence that her father refrain from seeing Mrs. K. is not a symptom formed, as Freud asserts, due to her repressed sexuality (representations giving rise to instinctual conflict) or to the residues of unresolved Oedipal love between her and her father underlying her relationship with Mr. K. Instead, it is due to her particular Ego-formation, or, to put things in a manner more attuned to temporality, it is due to the limited capacity of her field of self-possibilities to manifest itself in the present. The changes in Ida's behavior following her inability to make sense of some of the events she experienced are not accountable solely in terms of repression. They may also be explained as resulting from a considerable decrease in the ability of the self, which is projected onto its horizon of future possibilities, to return to the past and from there emerge into the present. In Ida's case, without Mr. K.'s presence in her world (i.e., his acceptance of her world, rather than his physical proximity), certain parts of her past became sealed off to her, and, respectively, certain self-possibilities were removed from the field of self-possibilities open to her in the present. Against the background of the limited horizon of self-possibilities established in Ida's world by her relationship with her family, the horizon of possibility which was opened to her following her involvement with Mr. K. was felt, in a way, to be rescuing her from herself, from the self-possibilities she experienced in relation to her feelings of distress and alienation. Soon enough, this relationship turned out to be a disappointment, aggravating her condition even further. In light of Ida's personal history, the redeeming character of her budding relationship with Mr. K. made her cling more and more to her future self-possibilities. In retrospect, this intensified temporal motion through which the self moves toward the future (toward the realm of fantasy), proved a double-edged sword: once the presence of the other's-self was gone from her field of future possibilities, her spectrum of self-possibilities became devastatingly dwindled and diminished. As a temporal being, each moment of Ida's life already manifested a unique temporal formation comprised of past, present and future all together. The principle difference between past, present and future moments lies not in the fact that the latter are yet to manifest themselves, but in the manner in which all three modalities are organized and emerge through the ecstasis of the past. In claiming that a certain situation in Ida's past could not attain its particular significance, we are asserting that they have been precluded from emerging from the ecstasis of the past.

We may therefore redefine the mechanism Freud termed as repression as a limited form of self-organization in the present. According to this view we may argue that Ida's sexuality was not repressed, rather, that in the circumstances created by Mr. K., Ida was denied of the possibility of uncovering her sexuality as part of her self. Her subsequent phobia of conversing men, which Freud explains in terms of her fear of experiencing once more what she had felt at the store (Mr. K.'s erection and her own sexual arousal), could not have resulted from repression in its original sense. As Ida's response to Freud's attempts to verify this interpretation regarding the 'repressed scene' indicates, she had no knowledge of such qualities at the time:

> In order to show that such a supplement to the story was possible, I questioned the patient very cautiously as to whether she knew anything of the physical signs of excitement in a man's body. Her answer, as

> touching the present, was 'Yes', but, as touching the time of the episode, 'I think not' (Freud, 1953, p. 31).[65]

What is, then, the source of Ida's phobia of men? As we have seen, Ida's attempts to rescue herself from her social-familial environment through her relationship with Mr. K. proved disastrous, involving a severe sense of loss. My interpretation endeavors to link the 'loss of self' discussed throughout the previous section, and this phobia of men, demonstrating that the temporal structure manifest in Ida's Ego-formation could serve as the direct source of this behavior.

Initially, it seems that Ida is unable to walk past men in the street since something about her encounter with them terrified her. However, the specifics of this phobia do not entail a sense of terror caused by encountering men, but one caused by watching strange men speaking excitedly to a woman: "her unwillingness to walk past any man whom she saw engaged in eager or affectionate conversation with a lady" (Ibid, p. 29). What is so alarming, we might ask, about the manner in which men express their feelings in front of women? Ida had learned some harsh lessons. She recognizes this masculine behavior as expressing the man's desire to become intimately related to the woman he is addressing, i.e., as an implied proposition for being-with. In fact, noticing a couple engaged in amorous conversation and discerning the man's excitement opens, in a certain way, something from her past into her present. However, this is not the equivalent of the past which is yet to be given meaning, but a terrifying byproduct. As she observes the man, erotically engaged with his interlocutor, and the girl, tempted by his gestures and the promises they hold, she notices a very certain part of her past, of her self. She is exposed to the horizon of possibilities of the past, in which she had put her trust in Mr. K.'s conduct. But seeing that she is unable to truly comprehend what took place between them, as considerable parts of her past relationship with him were left void of meaning, she has no other choice but to rush away from any pair of lovers she encounters. While Ida can be seen as running away from any event which evokes the sense of trauma she experienced in her relation with Mr. K., her avoidance of loving couples in the street encompasses an additional aspect. Her identification with the girl facing the eager man places her once more in front of Mr. K., this time choosing not to trust him, not to introject the self-possibilities which would have allowed her to engage him. From a temporal perspective, we might say that upon seeing an amorous couple, her past which never passed becomes implicitly present in her present,

---

[65] Further on, Freud mentions his great care in employing sexual terminology in order to discover Ida's knowledge regarding sexual matters. However, it is important to note that during her analysis, Ida was already eighteen, and in possession of greater knowledge than she had had at the time of the incident. We may assume that during the four and a half years leading up to her analysis she had matured, learning quite a bit about sexuality. Freud, nevertheless, adamantly ignores this, proceeding in her analysis as if the Ida sitting in front of him is still that thirteen-and-a-half year old girl.

in a way which enables her self to return from her past, albeit with a limited field of possibility. Ida's inability to give meaning to those parts of her past involving Mr. K. and her family is manifest through a new form of Ego-organization, through the limited self that was able to return from her past possibilities (her relationship with Mr. K.) to the present. Her phobia of men allows Ida to give present meaning to a certain part of her past. By running away from the eager men on the street, she is letting a moment from the past, one in which she had chosen to trust the future opened to her by Mr. K., return to the present and gain new meaning, this time, as her refusal to cling to the future possibilities implicit in his behavior.

Reexamining Ida's phobia through our notion of the phenomenon of transference as a field in which the temporal dimension facilitates the appearance of the other through the individual's ecstasis of the future, we might argue that the field of possibility opened to her by loving couples enables her to access that part of her past which, even now, still remains open to her by means of the future. By promoting identification with girls facing eager men, her phobia engenders a reunification of the three modalities of time. Although those parts of her past which failed to fully attain their meaning create a traumatic temporal formation, she successfully handles her overwhelming sense of losing herself. She does so by allowing herself to return from the past to the present in a different fashion when facing male excitation: she leaves, thereby telling Mr. K. 'no', a word she might have been able to utter in the past had her family chosen to stand by her, had her father not traded her for a few more hours with Mrs. K., had Mrs. K. not done the same, in order to be alone with her father, had Mr. K. not used her to comfort his wounded male Ego, had her family at the very least believed her story.

The Freudian interpretation of repression accounts for Ida's behavior only in terms of defense, by means of regression and the decrease in psychic resources. That is, it considers her behavior as a reflex reaction to a repressed situation. Accounted in terms of Ego-organization, her particular form of self-organization in the present could be construed as an attempt to grant the past new meaning through the ecstasis of the future, one which nevertheless failed to fully achieve its purpose.

So far we have discussed the possibility of viewing Ego-organization as an alternative explanation for the phenomenon of repression; but what about repressed material? Claiming that Ida's behavior did not stem from repression in its traditional sense precludes us from making any reference to repressed material. It raises crucial questions regarding the status of the material whose meaning could not be attained; of those temporal formations which cannot become manifest through the individual's temporal unity; of what the temporal structure itself prevents the individual from uncovering. Must we, at this stage, having already transposed several fundamental psychoanalytic concepts onto the field of meaning provided by temporality, accept the Freudian assumption regarding the unconscious as a psychic component located outside time, functioning as a repository for any material which could not properly attain its meaning?

The Unconscious and Temporality

Acknowledging temporality as the fundamental layer in our reading of psychoanalytic concepts had brought us to focus our inquiry on the temporal status of those experiences, moments and memories which Ida was unable to endow with meaning. Freud's answer to this question is quite apparent – they are stored in the unconscious. This kind of explanation, while indeed solving the problem of the status of repressed material, comes at a high price: giving up altogether on trying to understand human experience as a constant manifestation of temporality. In temporal terms, the depiction of the status of such contents, for which the event of meaning was undermined, is two-fold. First, I will indicate several central differences between the Freudian unconscious and the manner in which the phenomenon of temporality creates an aspect which might be termed unconscious. Second, these differences will serve to guide another reading of Ida's case study, one which will aid me in formulating the temporal status of 'unconscious' material, thus offering an alternative to the Freud's articulation of the unconscious.

As discussed, Freud considers repressed experiences and the contents stored in the unconscious, accordingly, as independently significant events or representations. In essence, he believes that repressed material possesses an objective status, as representations of images or actual events which were prohibited from inhabiting the conscious domain. In contrast with this approach, viewed from the perspective of temporality, the very existence of contents whose meaning is undermined and restricted is inherent in the ability to attain meaning. As the meaning of particular material in the present may or may not be attained, the event of meaning is a contingent phenomenon. While the Freudian treatment of repressed material is tantamount to addressing the meaning of the objective event that has been repressed, the temporal understanding of this phenomenon revolves around the event of meaning, that is, around establishing the significance of the event within the temporal field. Focusing on the meaning of objective events, the Freudian analysis restricts its interpretations to the reaction-formations necessitated by repressed material. In contrast with this approach, when we view the meaning of an event as a temporal motion from the future to the past and the present, such meaning cannot be construed as the mechanical transmission of external data or as a reaction-formation pertaining to the psychic mechanism (and thus internal). It is construed, rather, as an actual mode of being in the world which one could either preserve or abandon. Temporal motion, as the particular structure underlying any meaning and the attainment thereof, is one of the unique ways in which the world is disclosed to Dasein – it is itself a mode of being.

The notion that possible events of meaning are actualized in the space between our varying modes of being in the world entails another way of distinguishing the Freudian unconscious from the unconscious formulated in light of temporality. As our possibilities for attaining meaning depend upon Dasein's mode of being in the world and as the other is an integral part of the way the world is disclosed to Dasein, the boundaries determining the field of possible events of meaning hinge on the position of the other in the individual's world and the position of the individual in the world of the other. Throughout my discussion of self-possibilities within temporality, as a field in which the self's-other and the other's-self co-exist, I have already conceptualized the field in which these dynamic boundaries take shape. In Heideggerian terms this may be formulated in the following fashion: as the Freudian notion of human existence disregards the ontological difference separating Dasein from other beings, it fails to recognize that, as human beings, our ability to provide our lives with meaning is derived from our pre-reflective, pre-thematic relation to being-there together-with other Daseins. The Freudian notion of the unconscious fails to acknowledge the other as an integral part of the event of signification in general, and of the existence of repressed material in particular; it views it as one more item in a long list of factors comprising the significance of the conscious or repressed contents of a given event.

In general, when discussing repressed material, Freud regards these contents as exempt from the influence of time. The following statement is taken from "Beyond the Pleasure Principle":

> We have learnt that unconscious mental processes are in themselves 'timeless'. This means in the first place that they are not ordered temporally, that time does not change them in any way and that the idea of time cannot be applied to them (Freud, 1955, p. 28).

Unlike the Freudian unconscious which is essentially defined as existing outside of time, the very existence of events whose meaning is undermined fundamentally belongs to the phenomenon of temporality. This last assertion requires further explanation. First, we have seen that, from the perspective of temporality, the signification of present occurrences is always contingent; second, we have seen that the possibility of any possible interpretation depends on the particular manner in which the other is present. Whenever an event, such as Mr. K.'s attempts to force himself upon Ida, fails to attain its full meaning, the Freudian view decrees that it has been repressed and stored in the unconscious, outside the course of time. From the perspective of temporality, we might argue that it constitutes no part of the possible temporal field belonging to a self that Ida can sustain. Ida, a temporal being possessing a specific self-structure, could not have maintained the kind of temporal formation which enables the threatening elements of her relationship with Mr. K. to manifest themselves in the present, thereby facilitating the remembrance of that particular past and the reflection of that particular future. Mr. K.'s conduct, together with her own personal history, deprived her of the ability to remain open to the possibilities embedded in her relationship with him and to allow them to emerge into the present from the horizon of the past.

As a temporal entity, the structure of the self is first of all ecstatic in nature, constantly self-transcending toward or beyond itself. That is, the self's existential structure entails moving in time, moving between the various modes in which it may emerge from the three ecstases into its past, present and future. That which Mr. K.'s inopportune advances robbed Ida of was her ability to move in time toward her possibilities for being-herself. While Freud considers the disappearance of these events from the individual's view of her own personal history as resulting from the removal of material from the course of time, it is in fact the unique manner in which the self, as a temporal unity, is precluded from moving through different layers of time. The personal spaces in which Ida came to know herself through her encounter with Mr. K. turned into possibilities she no longer desired; those spaces whose meaning was not fully attained maintained their impact upon her life, as evident in her phobia of men in the street.

The unconscious aspect embedded in temporality is not some psychic enclave posited outside of time, but a phenomenon related to the self's temporal boundaries. Any particular position the self occupies within the temporal unity renders other positions as unactualized possibilities and creates a potential self-field to which one may return and which may, in principle, attain new meaning. This course of events is, as it were, the normal one, by which the possibilities of the self for emerging from its past possibilities are open and sustained in the present. Our everyday life is replete with such temporal movements: in trying to remember where we had left our driver's license just before leaving the house or in contemplating a conversation in which we failed to express something. Alongside this everyday possibility, we find another possibility, one through which the self is precluded from returning to that potential past field, as certain parts of that past could not fully attain their meaning. In such cases, the self-structure is unable to transcend toward its past, and is accordingly closed off to those parts of the present whose existence depends upon that past. The self's inability to transcend toward its past and the actual and potential decrease of its present possibilities fracture its structure, manifesting this predicament through a behavioral formation which Freud would have termed symptomatic or neurotic (such as Ida's phobia of men).

The phenomenon of trauma in human experience does not stem from repressed emotions or conflict-arousing representations, nor is it the result of the immediate meaning assigned to a particular event, as trying as it may be. Rather, it is the expression of the fact that the self's temporal openness to the event is barred, together with any alternative meaning it could attain. In this sense, trauma is a latent existential predilection dwelling at the heart of temporality, which comes to the fore whenever the self is prevented from moving in time. In other words, if we truly comprehend ourselves as temporal beings, the very preclusion of the self's movement in time, as minute or comprehensive as that movement may be, is tantamount to depriving us of our ability to be ourselves.

We may detect a somewhat similar insight in the connection Freud makes between trauma and that unique temporal motion through which an event gains its significance only by means of a 'deferred action' (Nachträglichkeit). Indeed, the notion of 'deferred action' seems to embody a certain philosophical-phenomenological potential which might have paved the way for acknowledging the temporal structure of human beings. Therefore, if we should wish to develop this Freudian insight to approximate our perspective, we may assert that the phenomenon of 'deferred action' discloses itself as an integral part of the self's existence. That is, the field of the self's possibilities in time, as a motion based upon a constant transcendence between the three forms of time, already entails self-possibilities whose meaning is undermined and restricted. However, even without deciding the philosophical potential of this Freudian concept, I concur with Laplanche and Pontalis (1973), who choose to view 'deferred action' as transgressing the boundaries of Freud's theory (p. 114).[66]

THERAPY AND TEMPORALITY

In his postscript to the case study, Freud addresses the reader in order to explain why his analysis of Ida ended prematurely. The crux of his argument revolves around the phenomenon of transference:

> I must go back a little, in order to make the matter intelligible. It may be safely said that during psycho-analytic treatment the formation of new symptoms is invariably stopped. But the productive powers of the neurosis are by no means extinguished; they are occupied in the creation of a special class of mental structures, for the most part unconscious, to which the name of 'transferences' may be given (Freud, 1953, p. 116).

This link between the phenomenon of transference and the unconscious turns the clinical encounter into a setting in which the patient projects her past onto the present, i.e., a setting in which the temporal field is of crucial importance. The third section of chapter six had commented on the problematic nature of the connection Freud makes between transference and the unconscious in "The Dynamics of transference" [1912] and "Beyond the Pleasure Principle" [1920]: the connection between the present and the past is made possible seeing that the past is stored in the unconscious, which is located outside of time.

Accounting for the failure of analysis, Freud mentions Ida's first dream and stresses the particular moment in which she leaves Mr. K.'s residence. He claims that he did not notice that, due to the transference relating Mr. K. to himself, Ida was in fact warning him that she was about to terminate

[66] Unfortunately, I am unable to elaborate on 'deferred action', a notion which no doubt merits its own discussion.

analysis. He describes the cause of this transference of emotion from Mr. K. to himself in the following manner:

> [...] because of the unknown quantity in me which reminded Dora of Herr K., she took her revenge on me as she wanted to take her revenge on him, and deserted me as she believed herself to have been deceived and deserted by him. Thus she acted out an essential part of her recollections and phantasies instead of reproducing it in the treatment (Ibid, p. 119).

What is that 'unknown quantity', that part of Freud's personality which he believes made Ida perform her memories, or, to use a term Freud employs after 1914, what mysterious element of his personality caused her to 'act-out' her repressed material in analysis?

According to Freud, he had no way of recognizing the transference while it was taking place, as Ida had constructed it out of repressed materials he had no knowledge of.

> Owing to the readiness with which Dora put one part of the pathogenic material at my disposal during the treatment, I neglected the precaution of looking out for the first signs of transference, which was being prepared in connection with another part of the same material —a part of which I was in ignorance (Ibid, p. 118).

These words suggest that Freud saw that 'unknown quantity', which led to the premature termination of analysis, as shrouded in darkness, seeing that the repressed material which facilitated the transference remained hidden in Ida's unconscious. In other words, it wasn't Freud who evoked the transference, but Ida's unconscious, linking between him and Mr. K.

My analysis of the notion of the unconscious from a temporal perspective had reached the following conclusion: the same phenomena which Freud considered as the meta-psychological foundation for postulating the unconscious, although they were in no way linearly connected, may be seen as manifesting the phenomenon of temporality as traces of subjective events (thoughts, feelings, memories) or even of objective events, which failed to return from the self's field of possibility to its present field of appearance. Indeed, it is this failure which restricted and undermined their meaning. The unconscious aspect embedded in the structure of temporality is not, as Freudian theory suggests, one of the subject's internal psychic layers; it is intimately related to the temporal structure which enables the existence of the self. These statements raise several questions, such as where, exactly, is the unconscious aspect located in the clinical setting and what is its particular meaning in the patient-analyst encounter, for instance, in the one between Freud and Ida.

As I see it, the answer to these questions lies in Freud's reference to the mysterious 'unknown quantity' residing within his personality. He senses that something about him is responsible for Ida's transference but remains oblivious as to what that something is. I wish to argue that this ignorance is not accidental and that the unknown factor is not some particular element of his personality, but an existential characteristic essentially pertaining to any meaningful human encounter, and especially so regarding the clinical setting.

As I have shown in chapter five, Glenn was the first to claim that counter-transference was mainly responsible for Ida's choice to end analysis.[67] In his opinion, her choice to terminate originated not in the unconscious material she was yet to share with Freud, but in the repressed material of Dr. Freud himself (his fear that Ida will abandon him, his yearning to serve as a father-figure, Ida taking the place of his sister's maid, Dora, in his emotional landscape), which caused him to unconsciously project his own past onto Ida. While this reading indeed uncovers a hidden facet of that 'unknown quantity', it is also founded upon the Freudian notion of the unconscious, thus still relying on a linear structure of time. In the first section of the current chapter (Transference, Counter-Transference and Temporality), we learned that a temporal interpretation of transference reveals that:

a. The transference of the past onto the present is an existential phenomenon, rather than a manifestation of neurosis.
b. The self's identification with the other's-self could be accounted not only as an imaginary act by which its selfhood is only a reflection of the other, but also as opening up to the aspect of the future, which forms part of its existence.
c. The event of transference already configures the appearance of the other (a parent or any other significant figure in the individual's life) together with self-possibilities as that future which already was, or as that future which wasn't but had to be.
d. The analyst, enabling the patient to feel inseparate from her to a certain degree, is present in the world of the patient as that other's-self which appears alongside the patient's self's-other.
e. Counter-transference is a specific manner in which the patient appears in the world of the analyst as an other's-self through the horizon of future possibilities, which is, as aforementioned, an integral part of the analyst's self-structure.

In addition to being temporal, transference and counter-transference are phenomena in which the self, belonging to the field of appearance of the ecstasis of the future, responds to the encounter with the presence of an existing other's-self. In both cases, the appearance of the presence of a significant other in the world of the individual, that is, at the very heart of the temporal structure as a self's-other, loosens, even for a moment, the relentless grip of the linear-objective temporal structure on the manner in which the world is disclosed. During the occurrence of phenomena such as transference or counter-transference, the world of the individual is transformed in a sense that the ecstasis of the present has lost its sway over the manner in which her world is revealed through the temporal structure. According to this reading of these

---

[67] Glenn, 1986, p. 603.

phenomena of transference, that 'unknown quantity' in Freud's personality is simply his self's-other, which appears in Ida's world as an other's-self. Therefore, that 'unknown quantity' constitutes no part of Freud's personality but is rather a clear indication of the fact the Freud and Ida shared a meaningful encounter. It is an indication of the fact that they were being-there, where, temporally speaking, their self-transcendence into the ecstasis of the future wove together parts of their respective existences with one another. In Heidegger's terms, we may say that the encounter between Freud and Ida, the many sessions of analysis, the attempt to truly listen to what was being said, took place in light of the existential field inherent in human experience and known as being-with another Dasein (Mitdasein). Analysis was terminated prematurely as Freud failed to acknowledge that his attempt to listen to Ida's story had created an existential field through which, while his patient was projecting the images of her past onto his world, he himself was truly present in hers.

Regarding the specific whereabouts of the unconscious aspect embedded in the temporal structure within the clinical setting, we might argue that the existence of an unconscious aspect manifest in the individual's world through the temporal motion from the future to the past and the present and facilitating the signification of past events is only possible if the analyst's conduct and attention toward the patient enable her to encounter her self's-other. As a phenomenon, the unconscious is not a component of the psyche, rather, it manifests itself in the clinical setting (or, for that matter, in any significant interpersonal encounter); it is the result of the position of the analyst in the patient's world and of the ability of the self, both that of the patient and that of the analyst, to move through time. The existence of the unconscious in the clinical setting originates from the possibility of founding a therapy which is attuned to the patient's being-in-time.

In conclusion, I wish to add that while the notion of a future aspect containing both other's-selves and self's-others and grounding the conversion of concepts from psychology to ontology may seem as a narcissistic trap in which human beings see only themselves in others, nothing could be farther than the truth. While narcissistic individuals see the other as themselves or are only capable of seeing their own reflection in others, those leading their lives by letting their self's-others appear alongside their other's-selves are confined not by their own selves, but by the fact that their possibility for being-themselves appears only through the existence of others. In other words, a self-reflection arriving from the world of the other is a reflection uncovering the self as a self's-other, opening it to an existential field in which it is not a closed-off being, doomed to a life of solitude and alienation, but lives, instead, as open to the world as a whole and to its own world, whatever it may be. The self's ability to acknowledge itself and the other is derived from the fact that human beings are temporal entities, which means that their lives are first and foremost a constant motion through time.

CLOSING NOTE

This book had put forward Heidegger's ontological thinking as the foundation for rethinking the theoretical tenets of psychoanalysis. The encounter between Heidegger and Freud's psychoanalytic thinking was presented within its historical context. I have claimed that Brentano's epistemology deeply influenced the foundations of Freudian thought, proving a crucial moment in the development of the psychoanalytic method. Alongside the one between Freud and Brentano, another encounter took place, that between Brentano and Husserl, which generated a new line of thinking culminating in Heideggerian ontology. The line of thinking crossing the convergence of Freud and Brentano had formed a worldview founded on the assumption that time is a linear sequence of intervals and contained, on a much smaller scale, the very crossroads facing contemporary psychoanalysis. The line joining Brentano, Husserl and Heidegger propagated the notion that the phenomenon of temporality is the basis upon which the world is disclosed. Moving backwards in time to the historical moment in which the conceptual framework of psychoanalysis was formed and granting that moment new meaning, my interpretation is first and foremost an expression of the possibility of considering time as a manifestation of temporality.

The prism through which I proposed temporality as an alternative foundation for Freudian psychoanalysis is my reading of the narcissistic state which accompanies us throughout our lives. According to this reading, which views narcissism from the perspective of temporality as a manifestation of the self's presence through the ecstasis of the future, the existential field in which it is opened to its possibility for being a self's-other and to the possibility that the other's-self will constitute part of its existence. Properly articulated, the other's-self and the self's-other are neither independent or separates linguistic concepts, nor transcendental notions regulating our consciousness, nor are they pure psychological notions or mere cultural constructs one has to accept in order to come to terms with the estrangement life offers. Rather, they are the frontiers and the abyss of our compelled motion within the scope that temporality already unveils for us. The temporal aspect, together with its existential ramifications regarding the structure of the self, is absent from the Freudian account of narcissism. Therefore, the manner in which the individual sees herself in everything, including the other, is explained in terms of a metaphysics which is bound to the categorical distinction between subject and object. Reinstating the temporal aspect into the very heart of the psychoanalytic project enables us to acknowledge those parts of the self which exceed such dichotomous distinctions.

The temporal-ontological analysis of narcissism has in fact paved the way for understanding the Ego, repression, transference and the unconscious as concepts that are grounded in the phenomenon of temporality. By focusing on Ida's case study, I endeavored to show that we may listen to the events of her life in a manner which enables the temporal structure to function as the horizon of meaning from which her symptoms emerge. This structure is not an internal, psychic formation, nor is it the expression of power relations exclusively immersed in a social, linguistic and historical matrix; it is the particular manner in which the phenomenon of temporality articulates or unravels Ida's field of self-possibilities within the world with which she is engaged.

Following the assimilation of temporality into its theoretical foundations, the alternative formulations which I have presented for these key concepts of psychoanalysis might serve, in my opinion, as theoretical grounds for contemporary psychoanalytic concepts as well.

Epilogue

Finally, I would like to suggest, briefly, how the conclusions of this study may hopefully take the first step in extricating psychoanalysis from the crossroads it stumbled into by relying on post-modernist foundations. In particular, I wish to demonstrate how this study, by shedding the light of temporality, may provide a renewed understanding of the key concepts of Melanie Klein, Winnicott and Kohut.

a. Melanie Klein represents the clinical approach focused on 'Object-Relations'. As she mainly treated children, the central problem which occupied her in the early stages of her work was that free-association was inadequate, as a psychoanalytic tool, for uncovering the emotional world of children, whose psychic organization was not sufficiently developed. In order to overcome this difficulty, Klein developed a therapeutic method which highlighted playing as the sphere through which the child may express her emotions. The crux of Klein's conceptual array relates to two positions, which portray the child's psychic structure in early life: the paranoid-schizoid and the depressive positions.

The paranoid-schizoid position entails the infant's initial inability to perceive the mother as a whole, apprehending only parts of her, namely the breast. As long as the breast provides milk, warmth and peace, it is considered good. When it becomes empty, failing to address the infant's basic needs, it is perceived as bad, responsible for its frustrations and agonies. The infant conceives of the good and the bad breast as two distinct entities, thereby perceiving the mother as split. This conceptualization is grounded in Freud's notion of the intra-psychic power-struggle between the forces of the death and life instincts. According to Klein, the intensity of the anxiety engendered by this struggle in the infant's world leads it to try and dispose of it through the mechanism of projection. This mechanism allows it to relate the death instinct to its surrounding environment, attributing the bad breast and the mother with destructive intentions which it experiences as persecution. The inability to overcome this position will later bring about schizophrenic and paranoid states.

Observing the paranoid-schizoid position from the perspective of temporality, we find that it may be translated into the most primordial possibilities for making present in the infant's history, ones through which the infant's self-structure appears fragmented. In other words, these are the infant's very first attempts at allowing the world to emerge through the three ecstases of time. At a later stage, which Klein terms the depressive position, if the infant had experienced more good experiences than bad ones and is able to perceive its mother as a whole, it manages to understands that both good and bad experiences originate in the same mother. Anxiety recurs in this state, this time as the fear that the destructive powers dwelling within the infant might destroy the mother it so desperately needs. Accordingly, the approach which considers temporality as the most essential phenomenon to the infant's existential structure might construe this anxiety as the infant's ontological fear that it won't be able to sustain the manner in which its mother emerges from the ecstatic structure. This existential fear is especially justified as the infant is still unable to acknowledge its mother as a separate entity, seeing that its ability to allow things to emerge from temporality is, as yet, necessarily dependent upon the mother, as facilitating the appearance of its self-possibilities.

b. Winnicott, founder of 'The Middle Group', which separated itself from Anna Freud's Ego-Psychology and Klein's vision of object-relations, considers the very transition from a life which clings to the mother (i.e. departing the narcissistic stage) to a life led alongside her and eventually toward independence, as a process replete with transitional phenomena. These exist from the moment the breast appears as soon as the infant had fantasized its arrival to the stage in which the mother is perceived as existing outside the infant's omnipotent control. In discussing the field in which these phenomena occur, Winnicott refers to an 'intermediate-area', which exists between the subjective and objective fields of human experience. I believe that my formulation of the ecstasis of the future as preserving a field in which self's-others selves and other's-selves co-exist matches Winnicott's definition of an intermediate-area. According to Winnicott, one of the chief qualities of the transitional-object is that it is discovered by the infant, rather than imposed upon it. The infant must sense that the transitional object is no internal fabrication, i.e., a fantasy, and that it isn't external to it, i.e., beyond its control. In keeping with this, we may claim that in temporal terms, we could consider the presence of self's-others and other's selves as the existential infrastructure which makes such transitional phenomena possible. The self's possibilities for change and growth are dependent upon that existential field in which the other can appear. Any experience which portrays the other as excluded from forming part of the self cripples the self's ability to open up to its future possibilities.

c. Kohut, founder of the Self-Psychology school, considers empathy as the result of including the feelings of the mother in one's earliest psychic structure. Therefore, he sees empathy as the source of our ability to penetrate into the other's psychic array. From a temporal perspective, we might construe empathy as manifesting the manner in which the individual's self-structure allows the existence of the other to appear within its own world, while the other enables the continued existence of the unique presence of her partner's self-structure in time. Just as the very possibility of signification is rooted in the existence of temporality, so is the possibility for the other's-self to form part of another's world conditioned by its ability to allow another other's-self to dwell within the particular mode through which it is disclosed by temporality, that is, to maintain an empathic position toward that other. This reading illuminates temporality as the specific manner in which the other enables another to dwell in that particular field in which she appears as herself to an utmost degree, that is, in the temporal structure itself.

Bringing together Heidegger's notion of temporality, Freudian psychoanalysis and the thinking of Klein, Winnicott and Kohut, is only one example of a possible implementation of contemporary psychoanalytic insight along the lines of temporality, which reinstates the experiencing subject into the theoretical foundations of the psychoanalytic endeavor. I hope that I have been able to demonstrate, throughout this book, the importance of this attempt to restore the temporal aspect into the core of psychcanalytic theory and the new horizons opened up thereby, as the analyst listens to the patient's being-in time.

Bibliography

Aristotle (1941). Physica. In *The Basic Works of Aristotle*, Richard McKeon (ed.), 218-397. New York: Random House.

Baker, G. (1996). *Descartes' Dualism*. London: Routledge.

Blattner, W.D. (1999). *Heidegger's Temporal Idealism*. Cambridge: Cambridge University Press.

Borch- Jacobsen, M. (1988). *The Freudian Subject*. Stanford: Stanford University Press.

Brentano, F. (1973). *Psychology from an Empirical Standpoint*. London: Routledge & Kegan Paul.

Brentano, F. (1988). *Philosophical Investigation on Space, Time and Continuum*, London: Croom Helm.

Broughton, J. (2002). *Descartes' Method of Doubt*. Princeton: Princeton University Press.

Cohen, A. (1998). "The impact of Franz Brentano's Early Intentionally Thesis on the Psychoanalytic Writings of Sigmund Freud". PhD dissertation, University of Essex.

Cohen, A. (2002). Franz Brentano, Freud's philosophical mentor. In *The Pre-Psychoanalytic Writings of Sigmund Freud*, Geerardyn Filip and Gertrudis van de Vijver (Eds.), 88-100. London: Karnac Ltd.

Dalto, S. (2002). The origin of the subject from the perspective of Freudian scientific materialism. In *The Pre-Psychoanalytic Writings of Sigmund Freud*, Geerardyn Filip and Gertrudis Van de Vijver (Eds.), 215-225. London: Karnac Ltd.

Dastur, F. (1996). The ecstatiko-horizonal constitution of temporality. In *The Critical Heidegger*, Christopher Macann (Ed.), 158-170. New York: Routledge.

De Boer, K. (2000). *Thinking in the Light of Time: Heidegger's Encounter with Hegel*. Albany: State University of New York Press.

Decker, H. (1981). "Freud and Dora: constraints on medical progress". *J. Soc. Hist.*, 14, 445-464.

Descartes, R. (1970). Meditations on first philosophy. In *Descartes: Philosophical Writings*, trs. and eds. Elizabeth Anscombe and Peter T. Geach (Trs. and Eds.), 59-124. Melbourne: Nelson's University Paperbacks.

Di Givanni, G. (1992). The first twenty years of critique: The Spinoza connection. In *The Cambridge Companion to Kant*, Paul Guyer (Ed.), 418-448. Cambridge: Cambridge University Press.

Dreyfus, H.L. (1991). *Being-in-the-world : A Commentary on Heidegger's Being and Time, Division I*. Cambridge: MIT Press.

Dreyfus, H.L. (1992). *Heidegger: A Critical Reader*. Oxford: B. Blackwell.

Ellenberger, H.F. (1970). *The Discovery of the Unconscious: The History and Evolution of Dynamic Psychiatry*. New York: Basic Books.

Elliott, A. (2001). *Concepts of The Self*. Cambridge: Polity Press.

Erikson, E. (1962). Reality and actuality – an address. *Journal of the American Psychoanalytic Association*, 10, 451-474.

Findlay, J.N. (1981). *Kant and The Transcendental Object: A Hermeneutic Study*. Oxford: Clarendon Press.

Forrester, J. (1985). *Language and The Origins of Psychoanalysis*. London: Macmillan press.
Freud, S. (1953). *The Standard Edition of The Complete Psychological Works of Sigmund Freud* (1900-1901), Vol. V. James Strachey (Ed.). London: Hogarth Press and the Institute of Psycho-Analysis.
Freud, S. (1955). *The Standard Edition of The Complete Psychological Works of Sigmund Freud* (1913-1914), Vol. XIII. James Strachey (Ed.). London: Hogarth Press and the Institute of Psycho-Analysis.
Freud, S. (1955). *The Standard Edition of The Complete Psychological Works of Sigmund Freud* (1920-1922), Vol. XVIII. James Strachey (Ed.). London: Hogarth Press and the Institute of Psycho-Analysis.
Freud, S. (1957). *The Standard Edition of The Complete Psychological Works of Sigmund Freud* (1914-1916), Vol. XIV. James Strachey (Ed.). London: Hogarth Press and the Institute of Psycho-Analysis.
Freud, S. (1959). *The Standard Edition of The Complete Psychological Works of Sigmund Freud* (1925-1926), Vol. XX. James Strachey (Ed.). London: Hogarth Press and the Institute of Psycho-Analysis.
Freud, S. (1961a). *The Standard Edition of the Complete Psychological Works of Sigmund Freud* (1923-1925), Vol. XIX. James Strachey (Ed.). London: Hogarth Press and the Institute of Psycho-Analysis.
Freud, S. (1961b). *The Standard Edition of the Complete Psychological Works of Sigmund Freud* (1927-1931), Vol. XXI. James Strachey (Ed.). London: Hogarth Press and the Institute of Psycho-Analysis.
Freud, S. (1964). *The Standard Edition of The Complete Psychological Works of Sigmund Freud* (1932-1936), Vol. XXII. James Strachey (Ed.). London: Hogarth Press and the Institute of Psycho-Analysis.
Freud, S. (1966). *The Standard Edition of The Complete Psychological Works of Sigmund Freud* (1886-1899), Vol. I. James Strachey (Ed.). London: Hogarth Press and the Institute of Psycho-Analysis.
Freud, S. (1990). *The Letters of Sigmund Freud to Eduard Silberstein, 1871-1881*, Walter Boehlich (Ed.). Cambridge: Belknap Press of Harvard University Press.
Gardner, S. (1993). *Irrationality and The Philosophy of Psychoanalysis*. Cambridge: Cambridge University Press.
Gaukroger, S. (1989). *Cartesian Logic: An Essay on Descartes's Conception of Inference*. Oxford: Clarendon Press.
Gaukroger, S. (1993). Descartes: methodology. In *The Routledge History of Philosophy, Vol 4: The Renaissance and Seventeenth-Century Rationalism*. George H.R. Parkinson (Ed.),167-200. London: Routledge.
Gay, P. (1988). *Freud: A Life For Our Time*. London: J. M. Dent.
Geerardyn, F. (1997). *Freud's Project: On the Roots of Psychoanalysis*. London: Rebus Press.
Gelven, M. (1970). *A Commentary on Heidegger's Being and Time*. New-York: Harper and Row.
Glazebrook, T. (2000). *Heidegger's Philosophy of Science*. New-York: Fordham University Press.
Glenn, J. (1986). "Freud, Dora, and the Maid: A Study of Countertransference", *Journal of the American Psychoanalytic Association*, 34, 591-606.
Green, A. (2002). *Time in Psychoanalysis: Some Contradictory Aspects*. London: Free Association Books.

Grunbaum, A. (1984). *The Foundations of Psychoanalysis: A Philosophical Critique*. Berkeley: University of California Press.

Grunbaum, A. (1990). Meaning, connections and causal connections in the human sciences: The poverty of hermeneutic philosophy. *Journal of the American Psychoanalytic Association*, 38, 559-577.

Guignon, C. (1983). *Heidegger and The Problem of Knowledge*. Indianapolis: Hackett Publishing Company.

Habermas, J. (1987). *Knowledge and Human Interest*. Boston: Polity Press.

Hall, H. (1993). Intentionality and world: Division I of Being and Time. In *The Cambridge Companion to Heidegger*. Charles Guignon (Ed.), 122-140. Cambridge: Cambridge University Press.

Heidegger, M. (1968). *What is Called Thinking?* New-York: Harper and Row.

Heidegger, M. (1971). *On the Way to Language*. San Francisco: Harper San Francisco.

Heidegger, M. (1982). *The Basic Problems of Phenomenology*. Bloomington: Indiana University Press.

Heidegger, M. (1987). *Zollikon Seminars*. Medard Boss (Ed.). Evanston: Northwestern University Press.

Heidegger, M. (1993). *Basic writings*. David Farrel (Ed.). New-York: Harper and Row.

Heidegger, M. (1996). *Being and time*. Albany: State University of New York.

Hoffman, P. (1993). Death, time, history: Division II of Being and Time. In *The Cambridge Companion to Heidegger*. Charles Guignon (Ed.), 222-240. Cambridge: Cambridge University Press.

Husserl, E. (1958). *Ideas: General Introduction to Pure Phenomenology*. London: Allen & Uniwin Ltd.

Husserl, E. (1966). *The Phenomenology of Internal Time-Consciousness*. Bloomington: Indiana University Press.

Kant, I. (1996). *The critique of Pure Reason*. Indianapolis: Hackett Publishing Company.

Keller, P. (1998). *Kant and The Demands of Self-Consciousness*. Cambridge: Cambridge University Press.

Kellner, D. (1992). Authenticity and Heidegger's challenge to ethical theory. In *Martin Heidegger: Critical Assessments*. Christopher Macann (Ed.), 198-213. London: Routledge.

Kemp-Smith, N. (1962). *A Commentary to Kant's Critique of Pure Reason*. New York: Humanities Press.

Kenaan, H. (2005). *The Present Personal*. New York: Columbia University Press.

Kisiel, T. (1993). *The Genesis of Heidegger's Being and Time*. Berkeley: University of California Press.

Kierkegaard, S, (1983), *Fear and Trembling/Repetition*, Howard V. Hong and Edna H. Hong (Eds.), Princeton: Princeton University Press.

Kockelmans, J.J. (1972). *On Heidegger and Language*. Evanston: North Western Universty Press.

Kohut, H. (1966). Forms and transformations of narcissism. *Journal of the American Psychoanalytic Association*, 14, 243-272.

Lacan, J. (1985). Intervention on transference. In *Feminine Sexuality: Jacques Lacan and the école freudienne*. J. Mitchell and J. Rose (Eds.), 61-73. New York: Norton. [1952]

Lacan, J. (1988). *The Seminars of Jacques Lacan, Book II: The Ego in Freud's Theory and in the Technique of Psychoanalysis 1954-1955*. Cambridge: Cambridge University Press.

Lacan, J. (1997). *Ecrits: A Selection*. London: Routledge.
Laplanche, J. (1976). *Life and Death in Psychoanalysis*. Baltimore: Johns Hopkins University Press.
Laplanche, J. and Pontalis J.B. (1973). *The Language of Psycho-Analysis*. New York: Norton & Company.
Levine, P.M. (2000). *The Analytic Freud: Philosophy and Psychoanalysis*. London: Routledge.
Levy, D. (1996). *Freud among the Philosophers*. New Haven: Yale University.
Livingstone Smith, D. (1999). *Freud's Philosophy of the Unconscious*. Netherlands: Kluwer Academic Publishers.
Loewald, H. (1980). *Papers on Psychoanalysis*. London: Yale University Press.
Macann, C. (1992). Who is Dasein? Towards an ethics of authenticity. In *Martin Heidegger: Critical Assessments, Vol. IV: Reverberations*. M. Macann (Ed.) pp. 214-246. London: Routledge.
Macintyre, A. (2004). *The Unconscious: A Conceptual Analysis*. London: Routledge.
Marcus, S. (1976). Freud and Dora: Story, history, case history. *Psychoanalysis and Contemporary Science*, 5, 389-442.
McAlister, L.L. (1976). *The Philosophy of Brentano*. London: Duckwoth Publisher.
Mcneill, W. (1999). *The Glance of The Eye: Heidegger, Aristotle, and The Ends of Theory*. Albany: State University of New York Press
Mitchell, S. & Black, M.J. (1995). *Freud and Beyond*. New York: Harper Collins.
Neu, J. (1991). *Freud*. New York: Cambridge University Press.
Olafson, F.A. (1995). *What is a Human Being: A Heideggerian View*. Cambridge: Cambridge University Press.
Overenget, E. (1998). *Seeing the Self: Heidegger on Subjectivity*. Dordrecht: Kluwer Academic Publishers.
Ovid. (1955). *Metamorphoses*. Bloomington: Indiana University Press.
Palmer, R.E. (1969). *Hermeneutics*. Evanston: Northwestern University Press.
Popper, K. (1963). *Conjectures and Refutations: the Growth of Scientific Knowledge*. London: Routledge & Kegan Paul Ltd.
Ricoeur, P. (1970). *Freud and Philosophy: An Essay on Interpretation*. New Haven: Yale University Press.
Ricoeur, P. (1988). *Time And Narrative*, Vol 3. London: The University of Chicago Press.
Ricoeur, P. (1992). *Oneself as Another*. Chicago: University of Chicago Press.
Sagi, A. (2002). *Critique of The Jewish Identity Discourse*. Ramat-Gan: Bar-Ilan University Press. [Hebrew]
Srzednicki, J.T.J. (1983). *The Place of Space and Other Themes: Variations on Kant's First Critique*. The Hague: Martinus Nijhoff Publishers.
Taylor, C. (1987). Overcoming epistemology. In *After Philosophy: End or Transformation?* Kenneth Baynes, James Bohman and Thomas McCarthy (Eds.), 464-488. Cambridge: MIT Press.
Winnicott, D.W. (1945). Primitive emotional development. *International Journal of Psychoanalysis,* 26, 137-143.
Winnicott, D.W. (1971). *Playing and Reality*. London: Tavistock Publications.
Zimmerman, M.E. (1982). *Eclipse of the self: The Development of Heidegger's Concept of Authenticity*. London: Ohio University Press.

Index

www.ingramcontent.com/pod-product-compliance
Lightning Source LLC
Chambersburg PA
CBHW051151180926
51611CB00001B/19